PORT INFRASTRUCTURE AND ECONOMIC DEVELOPMENT

PORT INFRASTRUCTURE AND ECONOMIC DEVELOPMENT

Dr. Pradeepta Kumar Samanta
Dr. Ashok Kumar Mohanty

Publications

KALPAZ PUBLICATIONS
DELHI - 110052

Port Infrastructure and Economic Development

Rs. 750

ISBN : 81-7835-416-0

Published in 2015 in India by
Kalpaz Publication,
C-30, Satyawati Nagar
Delhi-110 052
Email : kalpaz@hotmail.com

Lasertype Setting by: Tact Computer Graphics, Delhi
Printed at: Salasar Imaging System, Delhi

Contents

List of Tables

List of Figures

Abbreviations

ADB -	Asian Development Bank
AEL -	Adani Export Limited
APDP -	Accelerated Power Development Programme
ASTA -	Average Ship Turn-Around Time
BOLT -	Build-Own-Lease-Transfer
BOO -	Build-Own-Operate
BOOST -	Build-Own-Operate-Share-Transfer
BOOT -	Build-Own-Operate-Transfer
BPCL -	Bharat Petroleum Corporation Limited
BPIP -	Bang Pakong Industrial Park
BPL -	Below Poverty Line
BSNL -	Bharat Sanchar Nigam Limited
CA -	Concession Agreement
CCB -	Central Cooperative Bank
CCI -	Communications Commission of India
C-D Ratio-	Credit-Deposit Ratio
CDC -	Commonwealth Development Corporation
CEPA -	Consolidated Electric Power Asia
CERC -	Central Electricity Regulatory Commission
CESCO -	Central Electricity Supply Company of Orissa Limited
CHPT -	Chennai Port Trust
CMIE -	Centre for Monitoring Indian Economy
Conv. -	Conventional
COPT -	Cochin Port Trust
CPT -	Calcutta Port Trust
CVR -	Classified Village Roads

CWPC	-	Central Water and Power Commission
DBFO	-	Design-Build-Finance-Operate
DIWT	-	Directorate of Inland Water Transport
DLB	-	Dock Labour Board
DLCC	-	District Level Co-ordination Committee
DMRC	-	Delhi Metro Rail Corporation
DTA	-	Domestic Tariff Area
DWT	-	Dead Weight Tonnage
EOU	-	Export Oriented Units
EPZ	-	Export Processing Zone
FDI	-	Foreign Direct Investment
FIPB	-	Foreign Investment Promotion Board
FSS	-	Farmer's Service Society
GMB	-	Gujarat State Maritime Board
GOI	-	Government of India
GRIDCO	-	Grid Corporation of Orissa
GRT	-	Gross Registered Tonnage
HDC	-	Haldia Dock Complex
HPSL	-	Hutchison Ports Shanghai Limited
HR Coil	-	Hot Rolled Coil
HSD	-	High Speed Diesel
IAY	-	Indira Awas Yojana
ICD	-	Inland Container Depot
ICRIER	-	Indian Council for Research on International Economic Relations
ICSSR	-	Indian Council of Social Science Research
IDCO	-	Industrial Development Corporation of Orissa
IDFC	-	Infrastructure Development Finance Corporation
IFC	-	International Finance Corporation
IFFCO	-	Indian Farmers and Fertiliser Cooperative
IGCC	-	Integrated Gassification Combined Cycle
IGIDR	-	Indira Gandhi Institute of Development Research
IOCL	-	Indian Oil Corporation Limited
IPP	-	Independent Power Producer
ISPL	-	International Sea Ports Limited

IWT	-	Inland Water Transport
JNPT	-	Jawaharlal Nehru Port Trust
KPCL	-	Kalinga Power Corporation Limited
KPT	-	Kandla Port Trust
MBPT	-	Mumbai Port Trust
MCL	-	Mahanadi Coal Field Limited
MDR	-	Major District Roads
Mech.	-	Mechanical
MOPT	-	Mormugao Port Trust
MOST	-	Ministry of Surface Transport
MoU	-	Memorandum of Understanding
MT	-	Million Tonnes
MTNL	-	Mahanagar Telephone Nigam Limited
MTPA	-	Million Tonnes per Annum
NALCO	-	National Aluminium Company
NASSDOC	-	National Social Science Documentation Centre
NESCO	-	North-Eastern Electricity Supply Company of Orissa Ltd.
NHAI	-	National Highway Authority of India
NINL	-	Nilachal Ispat Nigam Limited
NMPT	-	New Mangalore Port Trust
NRT	-	Net Registered Tonnage
OERC	-	Orissa Electricity Regulatory Commission
OHPC	-	Orissa Hydro Power Corporation
OPGC	-	Orissa Power Generation Corporation
ODR	-	Other District Roads
OSCB	-	Orissa State Cooperative Bank
OSEB	-	Orissa State Electricity Board
OSFC	-	Orissa State Financial Corporation
PACS	-	Primary Agricultural Cooperative Societies
PMGSY	-	Pradhan Mantri Gram Sadak Yojana
PMGY	-	Pradhan Mantri Gramodaya Yojana
POL	-	Petroleum, Oil and Lubricants
PPL	-	Paradeep Phosphates Limited
PPT	-	Paradeep Port Trust
RBI	-	Reserve Bank of India

RoRo	-	Roll On – Roll Off
RPLI	-	Rural Postal Life Insurance
RRB	-	Regional Rural Bank
SAIL	-	Steel Authority of India
SCT	-	Shanghai Container Terminals Limited
SEB	-	State Electricity Board
SEBI	-	Security and Exchange Board of India
SEZ	-	Special Economic Zone
SHG	-	Self Help Group
SKO	-	Superior Kerosene Oil
SOUTHCO	-	Southern Electricity Supply Company of Orissa Ltd.
SPCCDC	-	Shanghai Port Container Comprehensive Development Company
SPV	-	Special Purpose Vehicle
STD	-	Subscriber Trunk Dialing
TAMP	-	Tariff Authority for Major Ports
TDSAI	-	Telecom Dispute Settlement Appellate Tribunal
TISCO	-	Tata Iron & Steel Company
TNEB	-	Tamil Nadu Electricity Board
TPT	-	Tuticorin Port Trust
TRAI	-	Telecom Regulatory Authority of India
VPT	-	Visakhapatnam Port Trust
VRS	-	Voluntary Retirement Scheme
WESCO	-	Western Electricity Supply Company of Orissa Ltd.

Preface

World over, in maritime nations, ports play vital economic role in augmenting foreign trade. Maritime transportation has been the lifeblood of world trade since time immemorial. Apart from being an economic infrastructure, a port is a subsystem of the total transport network and a meeting place of other modes of transport. Though new modes of transportation have grown enormously, shipping shall continue to have the lion's share in world trade in foreseeable future because of economies inherent in sea (coastal) transportation. A port is also construed as the major cross road of traffic in ideas, peoples and goods over centuries. There is ample evidence in literature of a strong spatial relationship between transportation and economic development. Ports being an integral component of transport infrastructure have immense potentials for accelerating economic growth of nations. India with a vast coast line of nearly 6000 kms, has now 12 major ports and 160 minor ports in the country. One will be surprised to note that more than 90 per cent of India's foreign trade in volume and 75 per cent in terms of value are conducted by sea. Statistics reveal that the 12 major ports handled about 281 million tonnes (76 per cent) of cargo, whereas, the minor ports 89 million tonnes (24 per cent) of cargo in 2000–01.

On the one hand, a port grows by virtue of the trade it can attract. On the other hand, an efficient port raises the productivity of other factors of production (labour and capital) and profitability of the producing units thereby permitting higher levels of output, income and/or employment. Evidences show that for most of the underdeveloped world, the role of the port as a policy instrument for both higher mobility and lower transaction costs as well as for spreading the growth centres away from the core metropolitan locations has not been utilised so far. In India too, inspite of prevalence of immense potential for growth in the port sector, it has, so far been able to exploit only 12.5 per cent of its coastline. Further, the productivity of Indian ports is far below international standards. The freight rate of container traffic and transit times through port exceed those of even Asian competitors by large margins. While the average ship turn-around time for Singapore is only 6 to 8 hours, it is about 6 to 8 days for Indian ports. Similarly while the number of containers handled per ship hour is 35 for Colombo, 38 for Bangkok and 69 for Singapore, it is only 7–15 containers per ship hour in Indian ports. Hence, the far from satisfactory performance of ports in India seriously constrains it's export promotion goals.

During the last two decades, increased globalisation and intensified competition in world trade have resulted not only from the liberalization of trade policies, but also from significant advances in the infrastructure sector comprising mostly transport, communication, energy, banking, insurance, science and technology, education and health. The growing significance of infrastructure sector can be gauged if one goes through the World Development Report 1994, which states that one per cent increase in the stock of infrastructure is associated with one per cent increase in Gross Domestic Product (GDP) across all countries. As nations progress, infrastructure must adapt to support changing pattern of demand as shares of power; transport and telecommunication in the total stock of infrastructure increase relative to those of such basic services as water and irrigation. In conformity with resurgence of interest in the criticality of infrastructure across the world as an integral part of support mechanism, the catalytic role of infrastructure has been increasingly realised in India.

India embarked upon the policy of economic liberalization from mid-eighties and more vigorously from July 1991. Though the impacts of economic reforms have been visible in many sectors of the economy, the infrastructure sector did not receive the required impetus till the Government accepted the Rakesh Mohan Committee Report on infrastructure in 1996. One of the key recommendations of the Committee is the private sector entry into country's infrastructure sector including ports. Undeniably, the success of on-going reforms, based on the edifice of export-led growth strategy, crucially hinges on the level of development and utilisation of transport and communication facilities especially ports. Against such backdrop, Paradeep port, one of the twelve major ports, situated in the State of Orissa has been chosen as the subject of present research. The decision of the Government of India to set up Special Economic Zones (SEZ) around Paradeep port, besides a SEZ at Gopalpur is intended to bring economic transformation of this poorest State in the country. The study would encompass the performance analysis of Indian ports in general and Paradeep port in particular at the juncture when the waves of privatization and globalisation sweeping all around. The findings of the study would provide some insights into how to make Indian ports internationally competitive and epicentres of growth in the country.

The authors are grateful to the ICSSR, Western Regional Centre, Mumbai for providing study grant for enabling them to visit the various libraries of Mumbai. The authors acknowledge the support received from various organizations like, the Indira Gandhi Institute of Development Research (IGIDR), the Reserve Bank of India Central Office, the Centre for Monitoring Indian Economy (CMIE), the Tata Institute of Social Sciences (TISS), the Economic and Political Weekly (EPW) Research Foundation, the Jawaharlal Nehru Library of Mumbai University and the Mumbai Port Trust Library. The authors are also extremely grateful to the authorities of Paradeep Port Trust; Ministry of Surface Transport; Government of India and National Institute of Port Management, Chennai, for providing the relevant materials for the study.

Today, infrastructure plays a key role in the development of the economy. The existing studies are done with a limited objective as the development of infrastructure is under the control of the Government. The wave of privatization has made it necessary for the comprehensive study of infrastructure. In this context, we hope, this book will be useful for the planners and policy makers, port trust authorities, Government and the research scholars working on various fields of infrastructure in general and port infrastructure in particular.

1
Introduction

1.1. Introduction

1.1.1. Admittedly, adequate quantity, quality and reliability of infrastructure are important pre-conditions for overall economic growth and development of a country. Infrastructural development augments economic growth, initiates a process of socio-economic transformation and removes social maladies, thus helps accomplishing the task of social emancipation and economic well being of majority of deprived and under previleged people in the least developed countries (LDCs). In common parlance, infrastructure refers to physical framework of facilities, which help to generate, sustain and enhance directly or indirectly, the growth in production and income in rest of the economy besides production and income generation within infrastructure enterprises themselves because of the multiplier effects of such investments.[1] In all fairness, the adequacy of infrastructure helps to determine a country's success in diversifying production, expanding trade, coping with population growth, reducing poverty and improving environmental conditions. Research indicates that while the total infrastructure stocks increases by 1 per cent with each 1 per cent increment in per capita GDP, household access to safe water increased by 0.3 per cent, paved roads increased by 0.8 per cent, power by 1.5 per cent and telecommunication by 1.7 per cent.[2] The state of infrastructure has also positive correlation with international competitiveness and flow of foreign direct investment (FDI). According to a study, in terms of infrastructure development among the 16 Asian countries, India's position is 15th, just above Vietnam. Similarly among the 60 countries in the world, including developed countries, India ranked 58th in terms of infrastructure.[3] The government recognises the critical importance of the infrastructure sector and accords high priority to development of both economic or physical infrastructure and social infrastructure. Various reforms have been made in infrastructure sector and rules and procedure for investment have been liberalised in order to provide an enabling environment conducive for private participation. The role of government has changed from owner and sole provider to that of a facilitator and protector of the interests of the vulnerable sections of the community by legal and institutional framework.

1.1.2. Improvement in the transport infrastructure of the country is essential for the achievement of accelerated growth of GDP. Significant acceleration in GDP growth will need faster growth in all sectors of the economy viz, industries, services and agriculture. Such growth particularly in the industries sector will place heavy demands on the transport sector. In the context of an increasingly competitive international environment for manufactured goods, the cost incurred in transportation has a significant bearing on the competitiveness of Indian products. Thus, the supply of transportation services has to be improved and made more efficient in its entirety.

1.1.3. In the last decade India's economic policies have witnessed a sea change. With liberalised industrial and trade policies, India is striving to carve a niche for itself in the global economy. Exports have now become an essential plank for our policy of economic growth. Increasing foreign trade has to be supported by an efficient transport system, as a quick and reliable system of cargo movement is indispensable for export competitiveness. Adequate port infrastructure and effective inland distribution systems have become sine-qua-non for providing qualitative transportation facilities through water modes.[4]

1.2. Significance of the Study

1.2.1. Water transport is one of the most vital components of infrastructure development. Throughout the world, this mode of transport has acquired prominence and popularity as it is considered to be the cheapest mode of transport and larger capacity and flexibility to carry heavy and bulky goods thus, facilitating international trade. With large river system and long coastline of 6000 kms, India has of special significance for this mode of transport. More than 90 per cent of India's foreign trade in volume and over 75 per cent in value terms are conducted by sea through 12 major ports and 160 minor operable ports along the coastline. The 12 major ports handled about 281 MT (76 per cent) of cargo, whereas the minor ports handled about 89 MT (24 per cent) of cargo in 2000-01.[5]

1.2.2. Inspite of prevalence of immense potential for growth in this sector, India so far has been able to exploit only 12.5 per cent of its total coastline. Moreover, the productivity of Indian ports is far from satisfactory as compared to ports at other parts of the world. For example, when the average ship turn-around time for Singapore is 6-8 hours, it is about 6-8 days for Indian ports. The number of containers handled per ship hour is 35, 38 and 69 at Colombo, Bangkok and Singapore respectively, whereas this is only 7-15 containers in Indian ports. Due to inadequate capacity at the ports, they are operating at low levels. The low labour productivity at Indian ports is quite evident from the fact that against a labour requirement of one man per container in international ports the Indian system requires 59 men with all the ever-decreasing productivity in container handling. As on 31st March 2000, the overall capacity utilisation of Indian major ports was 105 per cent.[6]

1.2.3. In view of these shortcomings, the performance of Indian ports needs improvement. The process of economic liberalisation started more vigorously from July 1991 and the export led growth has become one of the prime objectives of economic policy. Since the country is fully dependent on its ports for export and import, due to inadequate infrastructural facilities at the Indian ports, the targets could not be achieved after five years of initiation of economic reform. The Government of India (GOI) constituted a committee under the chairmanship of Rakesh Mohan, to identify the bottlenecks in the infrastructure sector and to suggest measures for augmenting resources and removing constraints to make the sector a catalyst for economic growth in the country. The Committee submitted its Report on June 22, 1996 to the GOI. Keeping in view the recommendations, the GOI allowed the private sector to play a significant role in developing the infrastructure sector. As a move towards improving the efficiency of Indian ports, the Government allowed private participation through schemes like BOT (Build-operate-Transfer), BOLT (Build-operate-Lease-Transfer) and BOO (Build-own-operate) etc. So far 24 projects have been identified for private sector participation of which

17 projects have already been approved. These 24 projects will add capacity of 92.45 MT at various ports with an investment of Rs. 78.76 billion.[7]

1.2.4. Paradeep, one of the 12 major ports of the country situated in the State of Orissa. During 2000-01, 199.00 lakh tonnes of traffic handled by the port as against 45.52 lakh tonnes in 1986-87. The port has earned Rs. 111.19 crores as operating surplus in 2000-01 as against 9.73 crores in 1986-87.[8] The economic reform initiated from 1991 and infrastructure sector reform from 1996 have wide ranging impacts on the performance of Indian ports in general and Paradeep port in particular. Against this backdrop, it is thought expedient to undertake the study of role of ports in economic development of the country as well as of the State. Such a study is expected to bring to the fore the strengths and weaknesses of the port, so that appropriate measures can be taken for removing the weaknesses and consolidating the gains from the strengths to make the port the gateway for the progress of the country in the East Coast.

1.3. Objectives of the Study

1.3.1. The study broadly aims at making an analysis of the performance of Indian ports in general and Paradeep port in particular and assessing the impact of economic reform on their performance. More specifically, the objectives of the study are:

1. Analysis of the requirement of infrastructure for economic development in India.
2. Analysis of the performance of Indian ports as a whole.
3. Analysis of infrastructure development with particular relevance to port infrastructure in the State of Orissa.
4. Performance appraisal of Paradeep port in terms of productivity indicators like trends of exports and imports, utilisation of cargo handling equipment, ship turn-around time, pre-berthing detention, labour productivity, berth occupancy and berth day output etc.
5. Analysis of different modes of transport and flagwise distribution of cargo at the port.
6. Analysis of operational efficiency of Paradeep port and class wise staff strength at the port.
7. Trends of inward and outward traffic handled by railway at the port.

1.4. Sources of Data

1.4.1. The secondary data constitute the major data source for the study. The theoretical background of the study is based on an exhaustive list of research articles and books on the subject compiled by the National Social Science Documentation Centre (NASSDOC), ICSSR, New Delhi. These study materials have been collected from Jawaharlal Nehru Library, University of Bombay, Indira Gandhi Institute of Development Research (IGIDR), Mumbai, Centre for Monitoring Indian Economy (CMIE), Mumbai, Economic and Political Weekly (EPW) Research Foundation Office, Mumbai and the Reserve Bank of India Central Office, Mumbai. The quantitative information for the study were collected from Paradeep Port Trust Authorities, Ministry of Surface Transport (MOST), New Delhi, Indian Ports Association (IPA), New Delhi, Mumbai Port Trust Library, Mumbai and National Institute of Port Management (NIPM), Chennai. Economic Survey of India of the Ministry of Finance, GOI, New Delhi and Economic Survey of Orissa of Bureau of Economic and Statistics, Bhubaneswar were also collected for the study.

1.5. Study Period

1.5.1. The period of the study is confined to 15 years commencing from 1986-87 to 2000-01. The selection of this period is significant in view of the fact that, though the Paradeep Port started its operation from 1966 as the first major port in the East Coast, commissioned in independent India, its share in traffic handling was meagre till 1976. Only 25 lakh metric tonnes of traffic were handled at the port by 1985. After establishment of the public sector fertiliser plant 'Paradeep Phosphates Limited' in 1985, the volume of traffic was increased at the port during the nineties by export and import of thermal coal, coking coal and petrol, oil and lubricant (POL) products. In the meantime, the process of liberalisation in Indian economy started in mid-eighties and got intensified with the enunciation of the New Economic Policy (NEP) in 1991. Even though, due to the economic liberalization, many sectors got a boost for development, but the reforms in the infrastructure sector particularly the transport infrastructure sector did not take off till 1996. After the submission of the Rakesh Mohan Committee Report on infrastructure, the government adopted some measures in consonance with the recommendations of the Committee to remove the bottlenecks of the sector and to make it a catalyst for economic growth in the country. Thus, the period of real reform for transport infrastructure in general and port infrastructure in particular started from 1996 onwards. Therefore, the whole period of study is divided into two parts. The pre-reform period consisting of 10 years from 1986-87 to 1995-96 and the post-reform period consisting of 5 years from 1996-97 to 2000-01. Though the post-reform period of study is small for projection of the future trend but, since the port is in a higher growth trajectory, the trend may vary marginally without abnormal deviations.

1.6. Study Plan

1.6.1. The study is broadly divided into two parts. The first part comprises of the theoretical discussions on infrastructure sector in general and port infrastructure in particular. The second part constitutes the core of the study encompassing the empirical analysis of the collected data. In sum, the study is dealt in the following seven chapters. The first chapter deals with the introduction, significance, objectives, methodology, sources of data and hypotheses of the study. Second chapter covers a theoretical discussion on the role and significance of infrastructure in economic development with special reference to port infrastructure in India. The third chapter envisages the performance of Indian ports, prospects and challenges. The fourth chapter highlights the state of infrastructure including port infrastructure with the socio-economic profiles of Orissa. The fifth chapter encompasses the history, growth and achievement of Paradeep port, policy guidelines of the government and opportunities and challenges for the port. The sixth chapter seeks to make an in-depth analysis of collected data pertaining to the progress and performance of Paradeep port. The seventh, the last chapter contains the summary of the findings, testing of hypothesis, conclusions, limitations and scope for further extension of the study.

1.7. Methodology

1.7.1. The study involves the application of accounting and statistical tools like ratios, percentages, arithmetic averages, trends etc., with the help of which the performance of Paradeep Port have been critically analysed. Tables and graphs wherever necessary have been used to substantiate the inferences made in the study.

1.8. Hypothesis of the Study

1.8.1. The study aims at testing the following hypotheses on the basis of the secondary data collected exclusively for undertaking this research work. The hypotheses are:

I. Traffic handled at Paradeep port has increased over the years. The increasing trend is more pronounced in the post-reform period compared to pre-reform period.

II. Both overseas and coastal traffic at the port have increased in the post-reform period, but the increase in coastal traffic is significantly higher in the post-reform period than the rise in traffic in the pre-reform period.

III. The average ship turn-around time has declined in the study period and more particularly in the post-reform period resulting in higher operational efficiency and productivity of the port.

IV. The berthday outputs of different commodities at the port have risen during the study period. But the rise is more significant in the post-reform period than the rise in pre-reform period.

V. The port of Paradeep has witnessed higher labour productivity during the study period, but the rise is more visible in the post-reform period reflecting the positive impact of on-going infrastructure reform on the port.

VI. Paradeep port handles more export traffic as compared to import traffic.

VII. Number of ships sailed at the port increased significantly during the nineties and more particularly in the post-reform period.

VIII. Operating surplus of the port has increased during the nineties.

IX. The railways have major share of both export and import traffic by way of transportation for the port during the study period.

X. The number of accidents at the port has been reduced and more so in the post-reform period.

XI. As a sequel to on-going infrastructure reform in the country, the downsizing of employees at the port has enhanced its operational efficiency and productivity.

References

1. Sharma, M., "Infrastructure Development - Shifting Paradigms", Paper presented at Indira Gandhi Institute of Development Research (IGIDR), Mumbai in the International Symposium in Honour of Prof. K.S.Parikh, July, 2000.

2. Government of India; "The India Infrastructure Report : Policy Imperatives for Growth and Welfare" (Rakesh Mohan Committee Report), Vol. II, Main Report, 1996.

3. Shah, Y.S. and Jindal, N.K., "Western Regional Cooperation Infrastructure: Vision 2000", Background Note-Port Sector, Indian Merchant Chamber, Mumbai, 1997.

4. Datta, R. and Sundharam, K.P.M., *Indian Economy*, S.Chand & Company Ltd., 43rd Revised Edition, New Delhi, 2001.

5. Government of India, "Economic Survey 2000-01", Ministry of Finance, Economic Division, New Delhi.

6. Bongirwar, A.L., "Major Ports – Prospects and Challenges", *Journal of Indian Ports Association*, New Delhi, June 2001, p.170.

7. "Indian Infrastructure", Vol. 3, No. 12, New Delhi, July 2001, p. 24.

8. Annual Administration Report, Paradeep Port Trust, 2000-01.

2

Role and Significance of Infrastructure in Economic Development with a Special Reference to Port Infrastructure in India

2.1. Introduction

2.1.1. Today there is a common opinion shared among government, society and industry that availability of adequate infrastructure facilities is vital for the acceleration of the economic development of a country. As the wheels of the economy, good infrastructure raises productivity and lowers costs of production, ultimately leading to better standard of living. Experience worldwide indicates that the purpose of industrialisation is better served with the presence of efficient infrastructure than without it. However, the infrastructure services enjoyed by the developing countries are abysmally low compared to developed and high income countries.[1]

2.1.2. The surveys by International Development Agencies (IDA) reveal that the developing countries are investing to the tune of 4 per cent of the national output in infrastructure development. This works out to about 20 per cent (one fifth) of the total investments made for development. But the World Development Report highlights the need to augment the infrastructure in developing countries considering the fact that nearly one billion people do not have access to clean drinking water and two billions suffer from inadequate sanitation facilities. During this age of fourth technological revolution, nearly two billion of world population do not have exposure to electric power and are subjected to unreliable power supply.[2] These confirm the gigantic tasks ahead for the economic planners to bring about minimum balanced development and providing basic amenities to the world community. The study further reveals that the countries bracketed under low income appear to invest more in basic infrastructure like irrigation, railways, water and sanitation as against those with high incomes investing in infrastructure projects related to power, telecommunication, roads, etc. This clearly establishes the link between the development level of infrastructure and the state of economy, thus enabling the richer grow faster, widening the difference between the countries still further.

2.1.3. Infrastructure is an umbrella term normally referred as Social Overhead Capital (SOC) by development economists. The International Encyclopedia of Social Sciences (IESS) defines SOC, which includes transportation and communication facilities in the 'narrow sense'. On the other hand, IESS encompasses facilities such as education, health, maintenance of law and order, research, etc. in the 'broad sense' of SOC. However, in practice, infrastructure services could be classified into two broad categories namely, economic or physical infrastructure and social infrastructure.[3] Economic or physical infrastructure supports and promotes primarily the economic activities. It's components are utilities such as power, telecommunication, roads, ports, transportation, water supply, sanitation, etc. Physical infrastructure and its growth is not only indicative of the level of development and the quality of life enjoyed by the people but it is a crucial determinant directly influencing the industrial and other development in a nation. The infrastructure components like power, telecom and transportation are vital for maintaining the continuous growth of the economic system. Social infrastructure includes health and human resource development, socio-cultural, legal and administrative systems and commercial and institutional framework. However, these two segments are not only complementary to each other but interdependent too in propelling the primary sectors of agricultural and mining and secondary sectors of manufacturing.

2.1.4. Infrastructure development is of two types – demand driven and supply driven.[4] In the context of congested urban areas, there is a demand for bypasses and bridges and when bypasses and bridges are constructed it is called demand driven. On the other hand in the construction of expressways, which are meant to cater to fast moving traffic and to the requirements of the industrialists and traders who are willing to pay more for better services, this type of construction is supply driven. These facilities are made available and those who need can use it. Demand driven infrastructure is a must for development where as supply driven infrastructure is one which is desirable but not a must.

2.2. Productivity Performance of Indian Infrastructure

2.2.1. During this age of globalised business environment, infrastructure performance is a key factor in attracting foreign direct investment which has become an essential element in capital starved developing economies. A recent survey undertaken by Cooper and Lybrand to compare the infrastructure performance of six countries, e.g., Brazil, China, India, Indonesia, Hong Kong and Mexico concludes that China appears to attract larger FDI due to its infrastructure performance. India ranks top in roads, and holds second position in railways and power. In a competitive environment, one chooses the best product and best location and environment in selecting a country for investment.[5] Table 2.1 presents a comparative picture of some of productivity/performance parameters of key infrastructure elements among India and comparable economies. This explains how China has become an attractive destination inspite of both India and China having similar levels of maturity in infrastructure reforms.

Table 2.1
Productivity Performance of Indian Infrastructure

Features	*Unit*	*India*	*China*	*Indonesia*
FDI'95	4Bn.	1.75	37.50	4.50
Containarisation	%	7.7	4.9	4.0
Ship Turn-around Time	Days	3 to 12	3 to 7	1-4
Per capital generation	KWH	3900	6000	-
System losses	%	22	16	20
Rail track density	Kms/1000 sq.kms.	24	5.65	3.34
Track electrification	%	18	16.6	2
Average speed	Kmph	23	30	27
Road density	Km/1000	2309	995	1738
Cargo by road	%	65	75	90
Digitalisation of exchanges	%	66	58	77.4
Fault level	No/100 lines	218	154	32
Investment per line	$	201	291	530

Source: Khader, S.A., "Productivity in Infrastructure", *Yojana*, Vol. 42, No. 1, New Delhi, January 1998, p.14.

2.2.2. The pressing need of coping up with globalisation of economic scenario and the increasing progresses of technological innovations, coupled with paucity of much needed resources and initiatives in the country, warranted private involvement in this sector. Simultaneously, the policy of liberalisation of economy too facilitated the private internal and foreign investment in the establishment of infrastructure, starting with the more vital sectors like telecommunication, power, roads and ports etc. Thus the pace of development was accelerated and the fruits of progress reached people in all regions of the country.[6] Though not spectacular, this policy of development of efficient infrastructure through creating an enabling environment for private participation in the infrastructure sector has made noticeable impact to enlist further initiatives and higher inflow.

2.2.3. Infrastructural bottlenecks pose serious impediments in the growing path of the Indian economy. The bottlenecks, in fact, started showing up from mid-sixties. The growth in power generation capacity was slower in 1970s than in 1960s. The result was a slow-down in the power intensive manufacturing sector such as basic metals and alloys and electrical and non-electrical machinery. Due to this factor the Indian policy makers were forced to change the growth strategy in favour of consumption led growth. As government finances deteriorated, it became increasingly difficult to finance infrastructure projects. The share of investment in infrastructure in the government's total expenditure came down in the 7th Plan Period, but the government succeeded in maintaining the expenditure targets through deficit financing. This widened current account deficit which was met through external borrowings, but soon the balance of payment (BOP) crisis forced the government to launch the process of reforms and put an end to the licence and controlled *raj*. In a way, then, it is the problem of financing infrastructure development that has forced the government to open up the economy.[7]

Table 2.2

Investment in Infrastructure (Rs. Billion at Current Prices)

Year	*EGWS*	*RAIL*	*OTRANS*	*COMN*	*STORE*	*TINFRA*
1980-81	31.70	8.10	17.50	3.20	0.20	**60.80**
	(10.27)	(2.62)	(5.67)	(1.04)	(0.06)	**(19.69)**
1981-82	42.10	9.80	22.60	5.20	0.40	**80.10**
	(12.31)	(2.86)	(6.61)	(1.52)	(0.42)	**(23.41)**

(Cont...)

(Cont...)

Year	*EGWS*	*RAIL*	*OTRANS*	*COMN*	*STORE*	*TINFRA*
1982-83	48.30 (13.29)	10.70 (2.94)	26.80 (7.37)	5.80 (1.60)	0.30 (0.08)	**91.90** **(25.29)**
1983-84	50.60 (12.10)	11.90 (2.85)	25.90 (6.19)	6.80 (1.63)	0.60 (0.14)	**95.70** **(22.89)**
1984-85	55.60 (12.21)	14.00 (3.08)	34.30 (7.54)	8.30 (1.83)	0.50 (0.11)	**112.60** **(24.76)**
1985-86	72.40 (12.45)	16.90 (2.91)	37.40 (6.43)	9.20 (1.58)	0.60 (0.10)	**136.50** **(23.47)**
1986-87	96.30 (15.75)	23.10 (3.78)	45.30 (7.41)	10.70 (1.75)	0.80 (0.13)	**176.20** **(28.81)**
1987-88	103.80 (13.58)	21.50 (2.81)	44.00 (5.75)	14.30 (1.87)	0.80 (0.10)	**184.40** **(24.12)**
1988-89	113.00 (11.65)	26.40 (2.72)	57.90 (5.97)	21.40 (2.21)	0.80 (0.08)	**219.40** **(22.63)**
1989-90	123.40 (10.84)	26.40 (2.32)	73.60 (6.47)	27.30 (2.40)	0.90 (0.08)	**251.70** **(22.11)**
1990-91	144.10 (9.95)	30.80 (2.13)	83.30 (5.75)	28.60 (1.97)	0.70 (0.05)	**287.40** **(19.84)**
1991-92	189.00 (13.12)	33.20 (2.31)	95.80 (6.65)	32.10 (2.23)	0.50 (0.03)	**350.50** **(24.34)**
1992-93	189.80 (11.63)	49.20 (3.02)	97.80 (5.99)	50.00 (3.06)	0.50 (0.03)	**387.30** **(23.73)**
1993-94	213.80 (12.33)	55.80 (3.22)	124.40 (7.18)	57.50 (3.32)	0.60 (0.03)	**452.20** **(26.09)**
1994-95	233.00 (9.77)	59.60 (2.50)	128.90 (5.41)	72.10 (3.02)	0.60 (0.03)	**494.10** **(20.72)**
1995-96	241.93 (7.96)	52.10 (1.72)	161.50 (5.32)	83.74 (2.76)	0.88 (0.03)	**540.15** **(17.78)**
1996-97	241.30 (6.92)	55.50 (1.59)	201.16 (5.77)	97.81 (2.81)	1.12 (0.03)	**596.89** **(17.13)**

Note : Figures in the parentheses represent Per Cent Share to the Gross Domestic Investment (GDI)

EGWS : Electricity, gas and water supply
RAIL : Railways
OTRANS : Other transport
COMN : Communication and
STORE : Storage
TINFRA : Total Infrastructure
Source : CSO, National Accounts Statistics, New Delhi.

2.3. Investment in Infrastructure

2.3.1. Table 2.2 reflects the picture of investment in the development of various infrastructure projects such as electricity, gas and water supply, railways, other transport, communication and storage in the last 17 years from 1980-81 to 1996-97. During this period, there has been rising trends of investments in all the sectors. The investment in total infrastructure (TINFRA) rose from Rs.60.80 billion in 1980-81 to Rs.287.40 billion in 1990-91 and further it went up to Rs.596.89 billion in 1996-97. It is quite evident from the Table that the total investment in infrastructure has increased more vigorously in the post LPG (Liberalisation Privatisation and Globalisation) era than the pre-reform period. More private investors were allowed with long-term concessions made a boost for the sector during this period. Realising the importance of basic infrastructure for enhancing the overall economic development of the country, the subsequent governments adopted the liberalised policy measures which were initiated in mid-1991. The percentage of investment in infrastructure to Gross Domestic Investment moves with a fluctuating trend. It reached 28.81 per cent in 1986-87 the highest among the years and further declined to 19.84 per cent in 1990-91. The growth continued for 3 years and again declined in 1994-95 (20.72 per cent) and reached 17.13 per cent in 1996-97. Similarly, in case of electricity, gas and water supply, though the amount of investment in absolute figures increased significantly from Rs. 31.70 billion to Rs. 241.30 billion, but in terms of percentage to total GDI, the figures shows fluctuating trend and varies from the highest of 15.75 per cent in 1986-87 to the lowest of 6.92 per cent in 1996-97. The investment in Railways infrastructure also increased significantly in absolute terms from Rs. 8.10 billion in 1980-81 to Rs. 55.50 billion in 1996-97. In terms of percentage to total GDI, the share of Railway infrastructure was 1.59 per cent in 1996-97 as against 2.62 per cent in 1980-81.

2.3.2. In case of other transport infrastructure which includes road transport, water transport and civil aviation also exhibits a spectacular growth in investment during the period. In absolute terms, the amount of investment in other transport infrastructure was Rs. 17.50 billion which was increased to Rs. 201.16 billion in 1996-97. In terms of percentage to GDI, the figure varies between 5.32 per cent to 7.54 per cent during this period. The investment in communication infrastructure also reveals an upward trend from Rs. 3.20 billion in 1980-81 to Rs. 97.81 billion in 1996-97. The storage infrastructure got least investment both in absolute figures and as percentage of GDI.

Table 2.3
Public Investment in Infrastructure (Rs. In Billion at Current Prices)

Year	*GDIPUB*	*PUBINFRA*	*% of GDIPUB*	*GDI*	*% of GDI*
1980-81	117.7	47.7	40.53	308.74	15.45
1981-82	167.8	58.3	34.74	342.14	17.04
1982-83	201.0	70.3	34.98	363.31	19.35
1983-84	203.8	73.2	35.92	418.04	17.51
1984-85	249.2	86.3	34.63	454.69	18.98
1985-86	308.7	104.1	33.72	581.57	17.90
1986-87	354.2	142.2	40.15	611.61	23.25
1987-88	330.6	145.2	43.92	764.61	18.99
1988-89	393.6	167.1	42.45	969.82	17.23
1989-90	455.7	193.5	42.46	1138.23	17.00
1990-91	521.5	217.3	41.67	1448.67	15.00
1991-92	565.0	266.5	47.17	1440.54	18.50
1992-93	623.6	278.4	44.64	1631.89	17.06
1993-94	687.5	346.9	50.46	1733.63	20.01
1994-95	832.5	387.1	46.50	2383.62	16.24

Note : GDIPUB : Gross Domestic Investment in Public Sector
PUBINFRA : Public Sector Investment in Infrastructure

Source : CSO, National Accounts Statistics, New Delhi

2.3.3. Table 2.3 highlights the trends of public investment in infrastructure during the period 1980-81 to 1994-95. The trends of gross domestic investment in the economy and its share in public investment have been analysed. Also the trends of public infrastructure investment as proportion of GDI and proportion of total public investment have been projected in this table. The gross domestic investment (GDI) which was Rs. 308.74 billion in 1980-81 had been continuously increased to Rs. 2383.63 billion in 1994-95 except marginal fall in 1991-92. The public investments as proportion of GDI though have increased in absolute amount throughout the study period except a marginal decline in 1987-88, showed fluctuating trend in percentage terms during the period. Public investment in infrastructure was only Rs. 47.7 billion in 1980-81, which have risen to Rs. 387.1 billion in 1994-95 depicting an increasing trend throughout the study period. Public investment in infrastructure as percentage of gross domestic investment in public sector have fluctuated more often between the lowest of 33.72 per cent in 1985-86 to the highest of 50.46 per cent in 1993-94. It is crystal clear from the table that, though the public investment in infrastructure have increased, the degree of increase doesn't augur well when viewed against the backdrop of economic reform initiated in the country. More public investment in infrastructure is urgently called for if the Indian economy is to grow at 8 per cent of GDP in the post-reform period especially during the Tenth Five-Year Plan.

Table 2.4
Private Investment in Infrastructure (Rs. In Billion at Current Prices)

Year	*GDIPVT*	*PVTINFRA*	*% of GDIPVT*	*GDI*	*% of GDI*
1980-81	191.1	13.1	6.86	308.96	4.24
1981-82	174.3	21.8	12.51	342.23	6.37
1982-83	162.4	21.6	13.30	363.63	5.94
1983-84	214.3	22.5	10.50	418.21	5.38
1984-85	205.6	26.3	12.79	455.01	5.78
1985-86	272.9	32.4	11.87	581.68	5.57
1986-87	257.4	33.9	13.17	611.91	5.54
1987-88	434.0	39.2	9.03	764.13	5.13
1988-89	576.1	52.3	9.08	970.31	5.39
1989-90	682.5	58.2	8.53	1138.94	5.11
1990-91	927.0	70.1	7.56	1448.35	4.84
1991-92	875.2	84.0	9.60	1440.82	5.83
1992-93	1008.3	108.9	10.80	1632.68	6.67
1993-94	1045.8	105.3	10.07	1731.91	6.08
1994-95	1551.7	107.0	6.90	2383.07	4.49

Note : GDIPVT : Gross Domestic Investment in Private Sector, and PVTINFRA : Private Sector Investment in Infrastructure

Source : CSO, National Accounts Statistics, New Delhi.

2.3.4. It is evident from Table 2.4 that the private investment in infrastructure in the pre-reform era was not encouraging. The gross domestic private investment in infrastructure hovered between Rs. 191.1 billion in 1980-81 and Rs. 682.5 billion in 1989-90. But with the adoption of economic liberalisation and reforms, there has been perceptible increase in the magnitude of private investment in the infrastructure sector of the country. During the post-reform period the private sector investment in infrastructure reached the level of Rs. 107 billion in 1994-95 as against Rs. 70.1 billion in 1990-91. The gross domestic investment which was Rs. 308.96 billion in 1980-81 had been continuously increased to Rs. 2383.07 billion in 1994-95 except marginal fall in 1991-92. Private investment in infrastructure as percentage of GDI in private sector have fluctuated between the lowest of 6.90 per cent in 1994-95 to the highest of 13.30 per cent in 1982-83. Private sector investments in India's infrastructure have been encouraging in the post-reform period compared to their participation in the pre-reform period.

2.4. Transport Infrastructure

2.4.1. The demand for transport services is demand driven in India. The demand for transport services in India has been growing much faster than the rate of economic growth. The ratio being 1:1.5, i.e., for every 1 per cent rise in GDP, the demand for infrastructure goes up by 1.5 per cent. The road transport services as well as railways occupy prominent place in the economy accounting for 53.3 per cent and 31.7 per cent respectively of the total transport sector. Water transport has a share of approximately 6.5 per cent.[8]

2.4.2. Efficient transportation is indispensable to economic progress. Mining, manufacturing, trade and banking and agriculture are also necessary, but these activities like many others, depend upon transportation. It is essential for the movement of raw materials, fuel, machinery etc., to the places of production. The more extensive and continuous the production in any branch of activity, the greater will be the need for transport facilities. By linking the backward regions with the relatively more advanced regions, transport development helps in the better and fuller utilisation of resources. Finally, expansion of transport facilities itself helps industrialisation directly.[9] The demand for locomotives, motor vehicles, ships, etc., leads to the start of industries which specialise in the production of these goods. Expansion of transport is thus of fundamental importance for a developing country like India.

Development of Transport Infrastructure During the Plans

2.4.3. The programmes of transport development play a significant role in our Five Year Plans. Transport has been seen as the basic infrastructure which is crucial for the success of a developmental plan. The Second Five Year Plan was more forthright in stressing the need for transport development by stating that, "an efficient and well-developed system of transport and communication is vital to the success of a plan of economic development which lays stress on rapid industrialisation." The theme has run throughout all the Plans of development. During the first fifteen years of economic planning, about one-fourth of the total expenditure was incurred on development of transport, in the subsequent thirty years the absolute amount incurred on development programmes in the sector has been continuously increased from an annual average of about Rs. 400 crore during the Third Plan to about Rs. 2,831 crore during the Sixth Plan, Rs. 4,594 crore during the Seventh Plan and Rs. 11,185 crore during the Eighth Plan. The relative proportion of expenditure on transport, however, has fallen from 22.1 per cent during the First Plan to 12.9 per cent during the Sixth Plan and 14.43 per cent during the Eighth Plan. The Ninth Five Year Plan (1997-2002) has outlined a comprehensive transport policy with estimated cost of Rs.2,00,000 crores aiming at intensifying the measures for achieving higher level of productivity through technological upgradation.[10]

2.4.4. The reasons for the slow-down in Indian port development are many. One of the main reasons was the low plan investment in the transport sector as a whole, and only a very insignificant part of it was devoted to ports over the half century after independence. It is clear from Table 2.5 that the share of the transport sector in total plan outlay has fallen from 22.10 per cent during the First Five Year Plan (FYP) to 13.10 per cent during the Eighth Five Year Plan. Moreover, the share of ports in the transport sector has fallen from 7.31 per cent in the First Five Year Plan to 6.34 per cent in Eighth Plan. It is surprising to note that such a crucial infrastructure sub-sector like port is the worst affected area in term of both allocation and utilisation of development fund during the eight plans.

Table - 2.5

Plan Investment in Transport Sector: Allocation and Utilisation

(in Per cent)

Sl. No.	Sectors	1st FYP 1951-56	2nd FYP 1956-61	3rd FYP 1961-66	4th FYP 1969-74	5th FYP 1974-79	6th FYP 1980-85	7th FYP 1985-90	8th FYP 1992-97
1	Port Sector								
	FUR	75.68	73.33	60.78	127.69	85.46	112.06	123.01	64.72
	STTSPO	7.31	3.46	10.97	7.58	10.54	5.36	5.43	6.34
2	Road Sector								
	FUR	108.89	92.02	148.15	98.97	125.72	113.03	121.83	125.42
	STTSPO	26.68	20.25	21.29	33.88	24.96	28.47	22.96	22.88
3	Railway Sector								
	FUR	81.27	80.33	148.99	88.95	93.69	129.12	134.17	118.75
	STTSPO	52.77	69.28	63.80	40.84	40.63	42.22	54.47	48.50
4.	Civil Aviation Sector								
	FUR	79.31	113.95	89.09	87.19	87.24	111.41	256.99	177.54
	STTSPO	5.73	3.31	3.94	7.90	6.22	7.11	3.35	7.28
5.	Total Transport Sector								
	FUR	85.77	84.68	142.15	98.09	102.27	115.57	130.17	115.78
	STPO	22.10	23.50	23.10	16.00	14.10	12.80	13.50	13.10

Notes : FUR – Fund Utilisation Rate (Plan expenditures / plan outlay) STTSPO – Share in total transport sector plan outlay STPO – Share in total plan outlay

1. Plan outlay considers both central and state plan outlays 2. Road sector does not include allocation made for road transport sector 3. Port sector doesn't include allocation made for shipping, IWT, light houses and lightships

Source : Government of India, Plan Document, Vol. II Ninth Five Year Plan, Planning Commission, New Delhi.

Again in all the plans except the fourth, fund utilisation in port sector has always been marred by inefficiency. Failure to utilise the disbursed fund may have been responsible for reduced allocation in the subsequent period. And as a matter of fact, due to this low investment, adequate capacity has not been created. In fact, the government has failed to understand the crucial role the port sector can play in the liberalised regime. But this sort of reasoning cannot go beyond the proximate explanation. The more fundamental cause must be sought in the lack of export orientation of our investment policies starting from the Second Plan to the Eighth Plan. And this is a paradox for a country where ports account for more than 90 per cent of tangible trade.

2.4.5. Similarly for other sectors also the share of allocation of funds not enhanced significantly. The share of road sector was 26.68 per cent of total plan outlay in the First Five Year Plan, which reduced to 22.88 per cent during Eighth Five Year Plan. The share of railway also declined from 52.77 per cent to 48.50 per cent in the corresponding period. The share of civil aviation sector has been increased from 5.73 per cent to 7.28 per cent during the eight plans periods. Though in absolute terms, the fund allocation for transport infrastructure sector has been increased but in terms of percentage it is not satisfactory.

2.4.6. In India, we have a four-tier transport system, i.e., Roadways, Railways, Waterways and Airways. With the help of such a huge network of transport system different regions of the entire country remain well connected. Economic, administrative, social, cultural, political and all other activities of the country depend largely upon its transport system.

Road Transport

2.4.7. The road system is the main feeder to the rail system and ports and harbour thereby forming a part of an integrated transport network in India. India has more than 3 million kms of road network, making it one of the largest in the world. However, the quality of the roads is inadequate and cannot meet the needs of efficient and fast moving transportation. In terms of area and population, the total road length in the country in April 1997 worked out to be about 64 kms for every 100 sq.kms of area, i.e., a road density of 0.64 km/sq.km and 275 kms for every one lakh of population (against 2522 kms in the US and 902 kms in Japan). The surfaced length was 23 kms for every 100 sq.kms of area and 86 kms for every one lakh of population. There are wide variations in the road length in different parts of the country. National Highways which are the prime arterial routes span about 58,112 kms throughout the country and cater to about 45 per cent of the total road transport demand. The National Highway Authority of India (NHAI), which was constituted under the National Highway Authority of India Act, 1988 and was made operational in 1995. The NHAI has been entrusted with the implementation of the National Highways Development Project (NHDP) comprising 4/6 laning of 14,180 km of national highways with an investment of Rs.54,000 crore. It has three components such as:[11]

(i) The Golden Quadrilateral (GQ) connecting four metropolitan cities of Delhi, Mumbai, Chennai and Kolkata. The total length will be 5846 kms of which 1159 kms (21.13 per cent) has already been four laned and 4234 kms is under implementation. The expenditure incurred till date is Rs.6,003 cr. The project is to be completed by 2003.

(ii) North-South and East-West (NSEW) corridors connecting Srinagar to Kanyakumari and Silchar to Porbandar respectively. The total length is 7300 kms of which 773 kms (10.59 per cent) have already been fourlaned and 715 kms are under implementation. The expenditure incurred till date is Rs.1,128 crore.

(iii) Portlinks connecting all major ports with National Highways is about 1,034 kms of length. Nearly, 160 kms (15.47 per cent) have already four laned and 325 kms are under implementation. The expenditure of Rs.1,606 crores have already met for the project. The target for completion of the two projects (NSEW and Portlinks) is 2007.[12]

2.4.8. To encourage private sector participation, a model concession agreement for major projects costing more than Rs.100 crores has been finalised to be undertaken under Build-Operate-Transport (BOT) scheme. Another model concession agreement for projects less than Rs.100 crores has also been finalised. An agreement based on an annuity approach has also been finalised. To date 20 projects involving an investment of around Rs.1707 crore have already been taken under BOT scheme. This includes an agreement between NHAI and Construction Industry Development Board (CIDB). Inventure, Malasia signed in May 2001 for four-laning of NHs 5 and 9 (147 km) for Rs.740 crore. In addition 6 projects of 4-laning costing Rs.1760 crore have also been awarded by NHAI on annuity concept. In addition NHAI has set up its own Special Purpose Vehicles (SPVs) to commercialise and leverage the financial structure to the extent possible.[13]

Rail Transport

2.4.9. The Indian railway system is the largest in Asia and the fourth largest in the world, after the USA, Russia and Canada. It is also the biggest public undertaking and the principal mode of transport in the country. The Indian railways have been playing an integrating role in the socio-economic development of the country. It has an extensive network, which spreads over 63,028 route kilometer, comprising Broad Gauge (44,776 R Km.), Meter Gauge (14,897 R Km) and Narrow Gauge (3,265 R Km). Approximately, 24 per cent of the network is electrified.[14]

2.4.10. The railways have been performing the dual role of functioning as a commercial undertaking and a provider of public utility service. The railways have also taken initiatives to attract private participation. It has set up a private terminal and forgoing partnership for providing rail connectivity to upcoming ports, e.g., Special Purpose Vehicle (SPV) on Pipavav Port. Joint ventures with some State Governments, for executing projects have also been evolved. The Expert Group on Indian Railways have recommended for setting up of a tariff regulator Indian Rail Regulatory Authority (IRRA) and corporatisation of the Indian railways into Indian Railways Corporation (IRC).

Civil Aviation

2.4.11. In a vast country like India, air transport plays a vital role in meeting the development needs of fast growing economy. The civil aviation sector provides three categories of services viz., operational, infrastructure and regulatory-cum-developmental. Domestic air services are provided by Indian Airlines Ltd. and Private Airlines (Scheduled and Non-Scheduled). The international air services are handled by Air India Ltd., Indian Airlines Ltd. and other international airlines operating to India. Pawan Hans Helicopters Ltd. provides helicopter supports services to the petroleum sector including ONGC and Oil India Ltd. and connects remote and inaccessible areas of the North Eastern region of the country. It also provides air support services to several customers including States and Union Territory Governments, public sector undertakings and private sector companies. Infrastructure facilities are taken care of by the Airport Authority of India (AAI).

2.4.12. At present, two scheduled private airlines provide regular domestic air services along with Indian Airlines. In addition, there are also 37 non-scheduled operators providing air taxi/non-scheduled air transport services. Private operators presently cater to nearly 52.8 per cent of the domestic air traffic. The number of passengers availing of private sector air services (both scheduled and non-scheduled) has increased from 15,000 persons in 1990 to about 7 million persons in 2000. The terrorist attack on the World Trade Centre and Pentagon in USA on September 11, 2001 has also affected traffic growth in domestic traffic in India. This incident has not only resulted in slow down of air traffic but also increased the cost of operation through higher insurance cost.[15]

2.4.13. A proposal for restructuring the existing airports at Delhi, Mumbai, Chennai and Kolkata through long-term lease to make them world class is under consideration. This will help in attracting investments in improving the infrastructure and services at these airports. Setting up of new international airports at Bangalore, Hyderabad and Goa with private sector participation is also envisaged.

Water Transport Infrastructure in India

2.4.14. Water transport is another most vital part of infrastructure development. Throughout the world this mode of transport has acquired prominence and popularity as it is considered to be the cheapest mode of transport, larger capacity and flexibility to carry heavy and bulky goods thus, facilitating international trade. Water transport is a very ancient mode of transport found in India. In ancient time shipping was quite popular in India. Evidences from history show that water transport was very popular in trading activities among different nations. India has got about 14,500 kms of navigable waterways. Thus, this mode of transport is of special significance to our country.[16] There are two kinds of water transport – inland water transport or river transport and coastal or marine transport.

Inland Water Transport (IWT)

2.4.15. Inland Water Transport (IWT) comprises of variety of rivers, canals, back-waters, creeks etc. It is the cheapest mode of transport for certain kinds of traffic, both over long and short levels, provided the points of origin and destination are located on water front and no transshipment of goods is involved. From energy consumption point of view, IWT is one of the efficient modes of transport. Unlike in other modes of transport, there is practically no investment needed. It is also a labour intensive mode of transport and benefits weaker sections of the community.

2.4.16. Inland waterways transport played an important part in the transport system of the country. But, since the middle of the last century inland water transport suffered because of the emphasis placed on railway transport and the diversion of river water for irrigation purposes. As a result, inland water transport forms a small part of the total transport network of the country. Till the end of the Fifth Five Year Plan, inland water transport was neglected. It was only with the Sixth Plan that IWT was given high priority.[17] The Sixth Five Year Plan proposed to :

(a) Give fresh impetus and encouragement to inland water transport and the overall approach was to take up only with well-defined schemes of national and inter-state importance for development.

(b) Declare certain waterways as national waterways, replace vessels, modernise dockyards, etc.

(c) Float a scheme for grant of subsidy to IWT, entrepreneurs to acquire mechanised vessels and modernise the existing crafts including country boats.

Similarly in the Eighth Five Year Plan, the government identified some of the thrust areas and fixed the strategy to carry them out.

(i) Development of IWT in the regions where it enjoys natural advantages.

(ii) Improvement in productivity of assets, through modernisation and upgradation of technology.

(iii) Building up of trained and skilled manpower for IWT operation.

2.4.17. The Eighth Plan approved an outlay of Rs.240 crore in the central sector (Rs.155 crores in the Seventh Plan). The IWT situation in India compares very poorly with those existing in other parts of the world. The nation's navigable waterways aggregate 14,544 kms of which 5685 kms are suitable for operation of mechanised craft (5200 kms for major rivers and 485 kms of canals). The total cargo moved by IWT in the country is about 20 million tonnes, which corresponds to just over 1.5 billion tonne km or 0.15 per cent of the total inland cargo of about 1,000 billion tonnes km.[18]

2.4.18. Inland waterways, which hold out a tremendous potential for a nation's transportation sector, has been a hugely neglected sector in India. In terms of cost advantages a study by the National Council of Applied Economic Research (NCAER) has concluded that, the per tonne km cost of transportation by inland waterways is 55 paise compared to Re. 1 by road. In advanced economies such as the U.S. and Europe, which enjoy the twin advantages of a long and continued usage of inland water transport and larger movement of cargo, the advantages of IWT have been well-documented. In the U.S. for instance, the average cost of water transport was 0.73 cent per tonne-mile, compared to 2.49 cents per tonne-mile through railways, the next lowest-cost transport.[19]

2.4.19. Apart from cost advantages, IWT has proved to have strong multiplier effect on the economy. According to studies in the U.S., for every $1 spent IWT by the government, the benefit to the public is $8. The benefits range from fuel costs saved to non-economic benefits such as spin-offs from tourism. From environmental as well as safety angle, ITW systems have been placed more advantageously than roads or rails. About IWT sector, studies in the U.S. show that much of the cargo now transported in the waterways of that country are supported by capital expenditures made 25 or 50 years ago. This long-term nature of infrastructure investment as well as advantages of an inherently natural monopoly are additional economic factors for large-scale investments in the IWT sector in India.

2.4.20. The present IWT network in India consists of two categories : three systems which have been declared as national waterways and seven other for which techno-economic studies have been carried out and which have been found to have the potential to be declared as national waterways.

Table 2.6
Present State of Inland Water Transport in India

Total Navigable Waterways:		14,544 km
Waterways suitable for mechanised craft :		
Major Rivers		5,200 km
Canals		485 km
Declared National Waterways:		
NW I Ganga-Bhagirathi Hoogly		1620 km
NW II Brahmaputra		891 km
NW III West Coast Canal		205 km
Feasibility studies done for:		
• Brahmani – Mahanadi System		
• Extension of Nwill upto Kasaragod in the North and upto Kovalam in the South.		
• Integrated Canal System from Kakinada to Marakkanam (includes Buckingham Canal)		
• Narmada River		
• Mandovi, Zuari rivers and Camberjua Canal.		
• Tapti river.		
Inland Cargo Movement	:	1,000 bn tonne-km
Cargo moved by IWT	:	1.50 bn tonne-km
IWT'share of total cargo movement	:	0.15%

Source: Government of India, Ministry of Surface Transport, New Delhi.

2.4.21. Various committees and expert groups have studied the potential of the nation's waterways including the problems of the sector from the Second Plan period. These include the Estimates Committee of Parliament (1956-57), the Gokhale Committee on IWT (1959), the Committee on Transport Policy and Co-ordination (1966), the Bhagwati Committee on IWT (1970), the Committee on National Waterways (1974) and the National Transport Policy Committee (1980). Based on their recommendations, the Inland Waterways Authority of India (IWAI) was set up and three major waterways declared as National Waterways.

2.4.22. To qualify for a national waterways, the National Transport Policy Committee recommended that a system should (a) possess capability of navigation by mechanised propelled vessels of reasonable size ; (b) should have about 45 m wide channel and minimum 1.5 m depth ; (c) should be a continuous stretch of 50 kms (the only exception to be made to waterways length is for urban conglomerations and intra-port traffic) ; (d) should pass through or serve the interest of more than one State or, should connect a vast and prosperous hinterland and major ports or, should pass through a strategic region where development of navigation is considered necessary to provide logistic support for national security or, should connect places not served by any other mode of transport.[20]

2.4.23. Inland transport is highly important in Kerala, where rivers and backwaters are used for transporting goods and people. Inland river transport is important in Assam, West Bengal and Bihar. Out of the 25 lakh tonnes of traffic between Assam and Kolkata, river transport accounts for half and the railways and road transport account for the rest. It is also of some importance in Orissa, Andhra Pradesh and Tamil Nadu.

2.4.24. Realising the importance of IWT for the growing transportation problems of the country, the Government of India have decided to thrust special attention to this sector. In the Tenth Five Year Plan an outlay of Rs. 668 crore have been made as compared to Rs. 308 crore in Ninth Five Year Plan for the development of this sector. The government have also revamped the centrally sponsored schemes for development of IWT by offering 90 per cent grants to the States, instead of 50 per cent to reimbursable loan. The States would have to contribute 10 per cent for implementation of these programmes. In the case of Sikkim and the North-East, the entire money would be provided by the Centre as grant. To attract the private sector in the creation of additional IWT infrastructure and fleet operations, the government had declared several concessions. Thirty per cent subsidy on building inland vessels, floating joint ventures with the IWAI, Government participation in equity for BOT Projects, customs duty concession on equipment imports and floating of bonds by the IWAI were all part of a new policy to give a push to this sector. For the first time, proposals for assistance from the Asian Development Bank and the World Bank had been entertained. In fact, the ADB would launch a Technical Assistance Mission for the IWT sector.[21]

Marine Transport Infrastructure (Port Infrastructure)

2.4.25. The Indian ports have traversed a long distance since the country gained independence in 1947. At that time, there were only five major ports handling a little less than 19 million tonnes of cargo. Fifty-five years later, there are now 12 major ports with the volume of cargo handled by them in 2000-01 increased to 280 million tonnes. The number of minor ports also increased to 160 account for less than 15 per cent of the total port traffic. More than 90 per cent of India's foreign trade in volume and over 75 per cent in value terms are conducted by sea. About 85 per cent of the total volume of port traffic handled is in the form of dry and liquid bulk, while the remaining 15 per cent consisted of general cargo including containers.

Table 2.7

A Comparison Between Coastal and Non-Coastal States: 1996-97

Features	*Coastal States*	*Rest of India*
Area (000 sq.km.)	1388.70 (42.25)	1898.30 (57.75)
Population (000)	417598 (49.34)	428705 (50.66)
Population density (per sq.km.)	301	226
Urban population (per cent)	30	24
Literacy rate (per cent)	62.34	55.07
Share in GDP (per cent)	61.71	38.29
Average real per capita income	818.78	614.08
Share in investments made in 100 per cent EOUs (August 1991-September 1998) (per cent)**	73.71	26.21
Share in manufacturing value added (per cent)	68.05	31.95
No. of inland container depots (ICDs)	10	4

Notes : * Number of parentheses are the percentage shares of the respective features.** Total investment in this period was Rs.62,930 crores.

Source : Government of India, Central Statistical Organisation, Ministry of Planning and Programme Implementation, New Delhi

Table 2.8
Share of Coastal States in India's Gross Domestic Product (GDP)

Year	*Share in GDP (per cent)*
1960-61	57.02
1970-71	57.17
1980-81	59.12
1990-91	59.10
1996-97	61.71

Source : Government of India, Central Statistical Organisation, Ministry of Planning and Programme Implementation, New Delhi.

2.4.26. The natural advantage of having a long coastline in the economic life of a region even within a country is evident from Tables 2.7 and 2.8. First, with a perceptibly lower geographical area (42.25 per cent as against 57.75 per cent for rest of India which includes both Madhya Pradesh and Uttar Pradesh), the shares of the coastal States in total population and GDP in 1996-97 were as high as 49.34 per cent and 61.71 per cent respectively. In terms of population density, urbanisation and literacy, the coastal States stand much higher than the rest of India. Naturally, therefore, the average real per capita income of the non-coastal States (Rs. 614.08) is not only lower than the average of the coastal states (Rs. 818.78) but also lower than the all India average of Rs. 684.94. Another notable feature is that the share of the coastal States in GDP has been rising continuously since 1960-61 from 57.02 per cent in 1960-61 to 59.10 per cent in 1990-91. This disparity is strengthened in the post-reform period : 2.61 per cent increase in this share has occurred only within a span of six years. Only Delhi (Rs.1,348.96), Punjab (Rs.1,118.36), Haryana (Rs.995.35) have per capita incomes higher than the coastal States. Finally, investment in Export Oriented Units (EOUs) in the coastal States during the post-reform period has risen as high as 74 per cent. Better endowment of the coastal States is also evident from the corresponding shares of industrial value added.

2.4.27. Availability of efficient port facilities has also been an important factor influencing Indian and foreign investor's choice of greenfield project locations. Thus, new growth centres in the country have emerged, largely due to their proximity to major or minor ports. This is also the reason for the increase in the number of minor operable ports to 160 in the last few years.

2.4.28. The demand for more ports and better port facilities has also arisen because of the spurt in other areas of industry and the infrastructure sector. In the last few years, a large number of coastal power plants have come up in the country. The economic rationale for locating the power plants near the coastline, instead of near coal mines, has been that the new coal-based power projects wanted to keep open their option of importing coal with less ash content. This has created greater demand for more coal and other cargo handling capacities at the ports.

2.5. Investment Made for the Development of Ports in India during the Five Year Plans

2.5.1. From the Table 2.9 it is evident that only Rs. 26 crore was allocated for Port development during the First Five Year Plan. The reason of the low outlay may be due to the Governments Policy decision to meet the basic minimum needs of the people just after the independence of the country. But from the Second Plan onwards the Government emphasized on establishing heavy industries for reviving the economy of the country. Accordingly realising the importance of ports for industrial development and overall economic development of the country, the plan outlay for the development of ports grew significantly. Not only to import the food and other commodities to meet the growing needs of the country, but also to harness the natural resources available in the country and to export them to other countries, the ports act as an important connectivity for the country. The plan outlay for port development reached Rs. 1270 crore during the Seventh Five Year Plan. During the mid-nineties, the Indian economy has undergone a sea change in its economic policy and adopted a liberalised license free regime to save its economy. The flow of foreign investment continued to the Indian economy as a result of which like other sectors, the port sector also invited foreign investment for its development. The outlay for the Eighth Five Year Plan was Rs. 3216 crore for the development of ports, which further increased significantly to Rs. 9,428 crore during the Ninth Five Year Plan. The private sector will play a crucial role in the development of the Indian Ports in the coming years as evident from the other developing countries.

Table 2.9
Investment Made for Port Development Under Different Five Year Plans

Period	*Amount in Rs (crores)*
First Five Year Plan (1951-56)	26
Second Five Year Plan (1956-61)	46
Third Five Year Plan (1961-66)	93
Annual Plans (1966-69)	89
Fourth Five Year Plan (1969-74)	289
Fifth Five Year Plan (1974-79)	414
Annual Plans (1979-80)	101
Sixth Five Year Plan (1980-85)	544
Seventh Five Year Plan (1985-90)	1270
Annual Plan (1990-91)	195
Annual Plan (1991-92)	200
Eighth Five Year Plan (1992-97)	3216
Ninth Five Year Plan (1997-2002)	9428

Source : Indian Ports Association, New Delhi.

2.6. Projected Traffic for Indian Ports up to 2021-22

2.6.1. A study carried out by the Ministry of Surface Transport (MOST), the share of Major Ports in total traffic and the investments required f.r creating the matching port facilities including the projected total traffic by 2021-22 exhibits the following.

Table 2.10
Projected Total Traffic upto 2021-22

Type of Cargo	*2001-02*	*2006-07*	*2011-12*	*2016-17*	*2021-22*
Liquid cargo	153	236	273	368	441
Bulk cargo	129	215	275	295	330
General cargo (non-containerised)	79	110	154	201	238
Container	33	92	158	251	364
Total	**394**	**653**	**860**	**1115**	**373**

Source : Government of India, Ministry of Surface Transport, New Delhi.

Table 2.11
Share of Major Ports in Total Traffic

Traffic in million tonnes per annum (MTPA)

Year	*Total Traffic MTPA*	*Share of Major Ports In MTPA*	*in percentage*
2001-02	394	304	77
2006-07	653	384	59
2011-12	860	449	52
2016-17	1115	514	46
2021-22	1373	547	40

Source : Government of India, Ministry of Surface Transport, New Delhi.

Table 2.12
Investments Required for Creating Matching Port Facilities in the Next 20 Years

Year	*Estimated total traffic in MTPA*	*Investment required in Rs. crores*
2001-02	394	5525
2006-07	653	34955
2011-12	860	17530
2016-17	1115	25600
2021-22	1373	16965
Total		**1,00,575**

Source : Government of India, Ministry of Surface Transport, New Delhi.

2.6.2 Table 2.10 exhibits the projected total traffic up to 2021-22 in type of cargo. In 2021-22, the total cargo handled by the ports will reach to 1373 million tonnes. It will 394 MT, 653 MT, 860 MT and 1115 MT in 2001-02, 2006-07, 2011-12 and 2016-17 respectively. Among the cargoes, liquid cargo will be the highest share (441 MT) by 2012-22. Registering nearly about 3 times that of in 2001-02 (153 MT). Similarly the bulk cargo will reach to 330 MT, as compared to 129 MT in 2001-02. The General cargo traffic will be to the tune of 238 MT as to 79 MT in 2001-02. The container cargo traffic will be 364 MT registering more than 10 time growth in comparison to 2001-02 (33 MT). Table 2.11 explains the share of major ports in total traffic. It is clear from the table that the share of total traffic handled by major ports will decline significantly from 77 per cent in 2001-02 to 40 per cent in 2012-22. The expectation thus is that the minor ports in the post development period will handle about 60 per cent of the total traffic in about 20 years time. This does not imply that, the efficiency or productivity of the major ports will decrease to such an extent. There are only 12 major ports but 148 operable minor ports. In the post liberalisation era, most of the State Government are showing interest to develop their minor ports with private sector financing, and at the same time the Government of India's condusive port policy will boost the more. Table 2.12 explains the investments required for creating matching port facilities in the next 20 years. The total investment required will reach to Rs.1,00,575 crores by 2021-22 from Rs. 5525 crore in 2001-02.

2.7. Port Capacity Requirement by 2005-06

2.7.1. Port traffic consists of overseas and coastal traffic. The former is determined by the structure and pattern of international trade whereas coastal traffic depends on the structure and pattern of inter-region domestic trade. We estimate overall port traffic to reach around 390 million tonnes by 2000-01 and over 650 million tonnes by 2005-06. Overall port capacity required to handle this projected traffic is 325 million tonnes in 2000-01 and 540 million tonnes in 2005-06. Need for additional capacity has been worked out assuming an additional improvement in utilisation at the rate of 3 per cent per annum from 1996-97 onwards for a period of five years in container and general cargo-handling and coastal trade. In the year 2005-06, traffic-to-capacity ratio would be roughly 1.0207 as against around 1.147 now. Additional capacity required to be commissioned annually is estimated to be 138 million tonnes between 1996-97 and 2000-01 and 215 million tonnes from 2001-02 to 2005-06.

2.8. Development of Minor Ports

2.8.1. The picture of Indian port scenario will be incomplete without touching upon the development of minor ports. The share of minor ports traffic has increased from 10 per cent to 25 per cent of the total traffic handled at all indian ports. There is good scope of privatisation in this sector too. Future projection indicates that it should grow to 100 per cent provided the improvement are made in infrastructural facilities, berths, dredging, communications, traffic etc. Many maritime states especially Gujarat and Maharashtra have embarked upon ambitious programmes for development of their minor ports including creation of new ports in greenfield sites through private participation. States like Gujarat and Maharashtra have setup separate maritime boards for the development and management of their minor ports. Gujarat has got a number of working minor ports. They have recently commissioned private ports at Mundra, Pipavav, Dahej and Jamnagar etc.[22]

2.8.2. The experience of the Gujarat State Maritime Board (GMB) deserves special mention. The GMB adopted a proactive and flexible policy for promoting private involvement in economic development. In the last decade over six private wharfs had been constructed primarily for proprietary cargo. An equal number of proposal had been approved out of which two are intended for common user facilities. The sponsors of the projects benefited from GMB's policy to allow the entrepreneurs to set their own staffing levels and recruit personnel. Rail/Road communication which is essential for functioning of port is being coordinated by the State with entrepreneurs, MOS and Railways.

2.8.3. Similarly, Maharashtra is also taking the initiative. They had awarded a port in Wadavan for nearly 20 berths under privatisation to P & O Australia for development. The State Government of Andhra Pradesh, Tamil Nadu, Karnataka, Orissa are also making serious efforts to promote and develop existing minor ports and construction of additional ports under privatisation. Since the creation of ports are cost intensive, to optimize the development, Central Government has constituted a Maritime State Development Council to ensure co-ordinated development of minor and major ports, so that duplication of efforts does not result in. The years ahead pose for gigantic development in ports.

2.9. Development of Hub Port

2.9.1. Ports constitute an important component of a nation's infrastructure and necessary linkage to conduct, develop and promote a nation's domestic and international trade. The India ports (major and minor) on the West and East Coast have provided adequate support in the development of India's domestic as well as international trade. The ports throughout the world get affected due to changes in technology, demography, trade pattern, consumer behaviour etc. The necessity to achieve economies of scale, to cater to growing needs of demands, led to development of large sized vessels. The pre-requisite for operation of these large sized vessels was adequate aggregation of cargoes at few regional hub ports, where these vessels could call for loading as well as discharging. This led to the establishment of a Hub port.

Development of Hub Port is dependent on an interplay of 3 kinds of facilitators, which are physical, financial and procedural in nature.[23]

2.9.2. Physical Facilitator

1. A suitable geographical location is required
2. Need of a deeper draft channel and berths.
3. An adequate aggregation of cargo is required.
4. A well developed cargo feeder network required.
5. Sophisticated cargo handling equipments needed.
6. Sound labour practice needed.

2.9.3. Financial Facilitators

An economical and rational port tariff should be maintained.

2.9.4. Procedural Facilitators

Framing of appropriate but simplified customs procedure and other laws.

(a) Conservation of additional cost through cargo transhipment.
(b) Reduction in transit time and safer delivery through adequate supervision by Indian agencies.
(c) Harnessing the economic potentials of southern peninsula.

2.9.5. Feeder Network

Hub Port requires faster dissemination of cargo discharged and thus there is a need for well-developed spoke arrangement either through rail or road or water borne transport. This necessitates a well developed feeder network so as to evacuate the cargo for their ultimate destinations at a faster pace. In this context India needs to develop a more efficient feeder network through rail/road transportation for hinterland and through sea for caste based destination. India's Exim Trade has enough potential to sustain the viability of a Hub Port on the West Coast and East Coast of India. There is enough aggregation of cargo originating from and destined for the hinterland to support Hub Ports on both the coasts of India.

2.9.6. Economical and Rational Port Tariff

The vessel related costs of berth hire, pilotage and marine dues at Indian ports are very high. A recent study indicated that the vessels related costs are 3 times higher than Singapore, 4 times higher than Colombo and about 10 times higher than Dubai. So, the port tariff has not only to be economical but also provide enough compensation to offset extra steaming of 2-3 days.

2.9.7. Sophisticated and Efficient Cargo Handling Equipment

The turnaround of a vessel at any port would depend upon the loading and discharge rate, which in turn is directly dependent on the cargo handling equipment employed. The rate of loading and discharge has a direct relation to the port charges being paid, as lower rate of loading and discharge would require the vessel to stay at berth for a longer period and thus pay higher berth hire charges besides affecting the overall voyage period of the vessel and its economics. In case of productivity per hour, JNPT offers about 40 mores per hour in comparison to 65 mores at Singapore and Dubai. However, NSICT has shown the way in which productivity can be increased at Indian ports and is offering guaranteed 60 mores per hour. Thus there is a need for making a giant leap in terms of improving productivity at Indian port if at all India desires to develop an international standard Hub Port.

2.9.8. Labour Practices

The efficacy of equipment is as good as the capability of its users. The labour productivity at Indian ports is not of international standards. The Indian ports have not geared up to the fact that sound labour practices are vital for the development of a port as an international Hub.

2.9.9. Customs Procedure and Formalities and Other Laws of the Land

Facilitating customs procedures and other related laws are pre-requisites for development of a Hub Port. The quicker dissemination of cargo discharged to their ultimate destinations, simplified customs procedures and documentation, unhindered movement of containers from one port to another, etc. are some of the issues that require immediate attention before treading the path of developing a Hub Port in India.

For instance, at Colombo a discharged container takes less than half a day for loading into feeder vessels or vice-versa where as at Indian ports it may take considerably longer time due to complex customs formalities. These are the constraints in the development of a Hub Port.

2.10. Multimodal Transportation and Infrastructure Development

2.10.1. Multimodal transportation is integral to efficient port functioning. It entails integrated development of all modes of transport to bring about better linkages between rail, road, air and shipping routes. For proper coordination between the various modes, a single window service interface is necessary. Containerisation as a technology has enabled multimodal freight transportation throughout the world.[24]

2.10.2. The essential features of multimodal transportation which distinguishes it from the conventional segmented system, is that it is based on a single contract and that the multimodal transport operator, who assumes responsibility for the execution of the contract, acts as a principal. Under this system, the consignor entrusts the goods to the entity that undertakes to organise the multimodal transportation. International transportation has undergone a number of structural changes due to advances in technology. For instances, containers are increasingly being used for transportation of goods from one country to another, using more than one mode of transport and more than one carrier. Multimodal transportation has become standard practice in international trade.

2.10.3. There are several advantages to this system. These are savings in time, reduced risk of loss, pilferage and faster movement of goods. Moreover, the consignor needs to deal with only one agency. This is not only convenient but also results in cost savings. Rail-Port interface has an important role to play in providing efficient multimodal transportation in the country. The Indian Railways have the potential to become a major player in this system. As a first step, the Railways have formed a joint venture company with Gujarat Pipavav port to provide port connectivity. The Project entails gauge conversion of a 250-km section from Surendranagar to Rajula to the port. The project cost is estimated at Rs. 2.94 billion.

Regulatory Framework for Multimodal Transport

2.10.4. Based on the recommendations of a working group set up by the government, the Multimodal Transportation of Goods Act was passed in April 1993. Subsequently, the Multimodal Transportation of Goods

(Amendment) Bill, 2000 was passed. The bill provides a legal regime to govern multimodal transportation on uniform basis.[25]

Multimodal Transportation Potential in India

2.10.5. Multimodal transportation is far from being fully exploited in the country. There are several reasons for this. First, the container handling facilities at the ports are not adequate to attract mainline container vessels, which continue to rely to a large extent on feeder services entailing additional cost. Second, the cost of moving a container through an Indian port is comparatively higher than that in other South East Asian ports. Third, both road transport and rail transport has not been adequately developed for the inland movement of containers. The national highways are already overburdened with the increasing volume of container traffic. The position with regard to rail transport is not satisfactory either. The quality of rail service for catering to container traffic needs improvement. More scheduled rail services for carrying containerised cargo connecting inland container depots and gateway ports are necessary. Besides, the progress in the modernisation and technological upgradation of the railways in several areas such as electrification, track renewal, and conversion of narrow gauge into broad gauge has been slow, obviously due to resource crunch. Apart from these factors, the trade is besieged by a number of problems relating to documentation, handling and lack of co-ordination among the agencies involved such as ports, customs and the railways. As a result, most shippers, consignees and shippinglines are wary of patronising inland container depots (ICDs).[26]

2.10.6. Multimodal transport requires significant investments in ships, cargo units, port facilities, inland transport facilities, inland container depots with handling and storage facilities and container freight stations. Hence, it can be emphatically stated that development of an efficient multimodal transportation system is crucial to the smooth and effective functioning of Indian ports.

2.11. Other Infrastructures

Power Infrastructure

2.11.1. Power is an essential ingredient of economic development and it is required for commercial and non-commercial uses. Commercial uses of power refer to the use of electric power in industries, agriculture and transport. Non-commercial uses include electric power required for domestic lighting, cooking, use of mechanical gadgets like the refrigerators, airconditioners, etc. There are three main sources of generation of electric power viz. thermal power, hydel power and nuclear power. The total power generated in 2000-01 is 499.6 KWH, recording a growth of 3.9 per cent over the previous years (480.7 KWH). Thermal and nuclear generation grew by 3.5 per cent and 17.1 per cent respectively, while hydro generation decreased by 3.6 per cent. The installed capacity of power generation in the country as on March 31, 2001 was 101,630 MW of which 72 per cent was thermal power generation, 25 per cent was hydro (including wind), and 3 per cent was nuclear. The capacity addition in 2000-01 was 3776 MW against a target of 4000 MW. Thermal plants at present account for 80 per cent of the total power generation, hydro electricity plants contribute 16 per cent and the nuclear plants account for the balances 4 per cent.[27]

2.11.2. The Working Group on power constituted by Planning Commission to formulate the 10th Five Year Plan has estimated a feasible capacity addition of 47,000 MW during the 10th Plan. This is made up of 24,405 MW in Central sector, 12,033 MW in the State sector and 10,501 MW in the private sector. The fund requirements for these investment would be of the order of Rs.5,66,000 crores. The Electricity Bill 2001 has been introduced in Parliament in August 2001. The Government. has also set an objective of providing "power for all by 2012" and has launched a "Mission 2012 – Power for All" in this direction. A comprehensive blueprint for power sector development has been prepared outlining the problems and suggesting integrated solution and strategies for achieving the objective of power for all.[28]

Telecommunication Infrastructure

2.11.3. A well spread out telecommunication network provides a great impetus to the economic growth in a country. Considering the significance of its contribution and also the need to integrate with the global economy, several policy initiatives have been taken by the government. In August 2001 the government introduced the Communication Convergence Bill 2001 in the Lok Sabha. The Bill aims at promoting and facilitating the carriage and content of communications (including broadcasting, telecommunication and multimedia) in an orderly manner and develops the required infrastructure. The Bill envisages setting up of a regulatory and licensing authority known as "Communications Commission of India" (CCI).

2.11.4. The other initiatives include making the new regulatory framework Telecom Regulatory Authority of India (TRAI) and the Telecom Dispute Settlement Appellate Tribunal (TDSAT) more effective, enhancement of bandwidth availability, encouragement of Foreign Direct Investment (FDI), transparent spectrum management and restructuring of equity for fostering mergers, acquisitions and amalgamations to create globally competitive Indian entities.

2.11.5. The total telephone connections as on March 31, 2001 were 36.3 million comprising 32.4 million fixed lines provided by the Bharat Sanchar Nigam Ltd. (BSNL) and Mahanagar Telephone Nigam Ltd. (MTNL) and 0.3 million fixed lines and 3.6 million cellular connections by the private sector. During 2000-01 about 7.8 million new connections (5.9 million by BSNL and MTNL and 1.8 million by private sector) were provided. As on September 30, 2001, there were 934,726 PCOs working all over the country. The PCO population ratio as on September 30, 2001, in urban areas is 311, much better than the National Telecom Policy, 1994 target of one PCO for 500 persons. Further, according to the new Telecom Policy, every village was to be provided with one public telephone by the end of the Ninth Five Year Plan. During the period of August 1991 to August 200, 749 proposals of Foreign Direct Investment (FDI) of Rs. 53,134 crores were approved and the actual flow of FDI during the above period was Rs. 7,028 crore, i.e., 13.23 per cent of total approval. In terms of approval of FDI, the telecom sector is the second largest after energy sector.[29]

Postal Services Infrastructure

2.11.6. India possesses the largest postal network in the world with 155,000 post offices spread all over the country as on March 31, 2001, of which 89 per cent are in the rural sector. On an average, a post office serves an area of 21.21 sq.kms and a population of 5,449. During 2000-01, 52 sub-post offices and 363 branch post offices were opened. During 2001-02, a target of opening of 500 branch post offices and 50 sub-post offices has been fixed. It is also proposed to open 2,000 Panchayat Sanchar Sewa Kendras (PSKs) in 2002-03. There are about 7350 computers in more than 1660 post offices handling about 10 million transactions per month.

Postal Life Insurance (PLI) which was introduced as a welfare measure in 1984, has continued to expand and by March 31, 2001, it has procured 2.51 million PLI policies with an aggregate sum assured of Rs.10,405 crores. The Rural Postal Life Insurance (RPLI) has also gathered momentum. Approximately 820,000 RPLI policies were secured with an aggregate sum assured of Rs.2,898 crores by March 2001.[30]

Tourism Infrastructure

2.11.7. Tourism is an important sector which not only provides employment opportunities but helps to earn valuable foreign exchange. The tourism development also helps to achieve balanced and sustainable regional growth by providing employment opportunities for unskilled workers specifically from the rural areas and also developing interior and remote areas. However, the development of tourism has been constrained by poor accessibility to various places of tourist interest, due to bottlenecks in infrastructure and other facilities. There is an urgent need to remove all these constraints for development of tourism. There has been a decline of about 20 per cent in the foreign tourist arrivals and 16 per cent in the foreign exchange earnings through tourism in the two months of September and October 2001. In the aftermath of the terrorist attacks in USA on September 2001, a programme to meet the adverse conditions arising out of this incident has been drawn up and is being implemented.[31]

Urban Infrastructure

2.11.8. Urban infrastructure includes water supply and sanitation which are important basic needs for improvement of the quality of life and enhancement of the productivity efficiency of citizens. The government has taken up a number of central and centrally sponsored schemes to improve the economic and physical infrastructure and also to provide essential facilities and services in the urban areas. The India Infrastructure Report (1996) on investment requirements for infrastructure had estimated an annual requirement of funds of Rs.28,000 crore for providing infrastructure facilities. In the 9th Five Year Plans major allocation was made for Delhi Metro Rail Corporation (DMRC) where the government has been contributing towards equity of the company. The expenditure incurred on the project till November 30,2001 is Rs.1575 crores. As on December 31, 2001, HUDCO has sanctioned an amount of Rs.2153 crores for 42 urban infrastructure schemes covering areas such as water supply, sewerage and sanitation, transport area development, commercial and social infrastructure schemes. In the year 2000-01, for the water supply sector, HUDCO has financed 16 schemes amounting to 34 per cent of the total loan assistance.[32]

Rural Infrastructure

2.11.9. Rural infrastructure comprises rural roads, rural housing and rural electrification. Rural road connectivity is an extremely important aspect of rural development. A centrally sponsored scheme has been launched called the Pradhan Mantri Gram Sadak Yojana (PMGSY) which seeks to provide connectivity to all unconnected habitations in rural areas with a population of more than 500 persons through good all weather roads by the end of the Tenth Plan Period. In respect of hill States and desert areas, the objective would be to connect habitations with population of 250 persons and above. In order to achieve the objective of the programme, a requirement of Rs.60,000 crores has been estimated. For the year 2001-02, a sum of Rs.2500 crores has been earmarked for the PMGSY. According to the 1991 census, around 3.1 million households are without shelter and another 10.31 million households reside in unserviceable *kutcha* houses.

2.11.10. Considering the magnitude of the problem, a National Housing Habitat Policy was announced in 1998 which aims at providing "Housing for all" and facilitates construction of 20 lakh additional housing units (13 lakh in rural areas and 7 lakh in urban areas) annually with an emphasis on extending benefits to the poor and deprived. The government is committed to the goal of ensuring shelter for all by the end of Tenth Five Year Plan. The objective of the Indira Awas Yojna (IAY) is to provide assistance to the below poverty line households (BPL) belonging to Scheduled Caste, Scheduled Tribe, and free bonded labour categories. The central assistance under the IAY for 2001-02 is Rs.1618 crores for construction/ upgradation of 1.3 million houses. At present, there are about 80,000 villages which still remain to be electrified and which are concentrated in nine States. In order to achieve the national goal of electrification of villages by 2007, village electrification has now been included under Pradhan Mantri Gramodaya Yojana (PMGY) as basic minimum service for 2001-02. Under the scheme an allocation of Rs.418.59 crores has been made to the States for carrying out rural electrification.[33]

Banking Infrastructure

2.11.11. Commercial banking operations, after the nationalisation of banks in 1969, have become an integral part of India's economic policy. Rapid economic development pre-supposes rapid expansion of commercial banks. The number of branches has gone up from 8260 in June 1969, to 64,980 at end June, 1999 registering an increase of 800 per cent during the last three decades. Similarly the increase in rural branches was spectacular, i.e., from 1860 to 32,830 in the corresponding periods with the progress of branch expansion programmes, the national average of population per bank has progressively declined from 64,000 in 1969 to 15,000 in 1999. This indicates the greater availability of banking facilities to the public at large. Undoubtedly, the growth has been rapid, but it has not been sufficient, as compared to developed countries where the average population served per bank varies between 2,000 and 3,000. The banking sector in the country has also witnessed spectacular growth in deposits and credit. Bank deposits has increased to Rs. 8,10,070 crore in 1999-2000 as against Rs. 820 crore in 1950-50. Similarly bank credit reached at Rs. 4,43,180 crore in 1999-2000 as against Rs. 580 crore in 1950-51.[34]

2.12. Challenges for Infrastructure Development

2.12.1. Adequate quantity, quality and reliability of infrastructure are important preconditions for overall economic growth and development. The state of infrastructure has also a direct link to international competitiveness and flow of direct foreign investment. In the country, the stress on infrastructure assumed added significance only after the introduction of reform process in the economy because earlier most of the fundings for capital intensive infrastructure projects were provided by the government itself as it was following a planned economic development model. The responsibility for creating infrastructure services when it was vested with the government did not yield the requisite results to a growing economy when competitive forces assumed greater say in development schemes. The public sector was proverbially beset with severe problems like lack of accountability, low productivity, poor financial performance and over-employment. Increasingly, the old paradigm of infrastructure being a public sector monopoly has been challenged by fiscal constraints and technological innovations. Limits on budgetary allocations and public debt and the phased dismantling of the allocated system of credit have pushed private sector entry in infrastructure provision. Technological and organisational innovations have also made it possible to unbundle different segments of infrastructure services and reduce the level of public monopoly which was essential to its supply.

2.12.2. Infrastructure thus suffered from twin handicaps in India. When reforms began, it was not a matter of priority. And second, since containing fiscal deficit was the main objective, investment in infrastructure fell. Plan expenditure in the infrastructure sector during the Eighth Plan period was 14.4 per cent lower than the target as against the shortfall of 3.6 per cent in the Seventh Plan. The drop was particularly large in power (22 per cent), ports (57 per cent), railways (6.7 per cent) and roads (6.5 per cent).

2.12.3. An expert group appointed in 1994 by Dr.Manmohan Singh,the then Finance Minister of India, estimated that the total investment required for all four areas in the infrastructural sector, power, ports, next ten years beginning 1996-97. There is practically no prospect of mobilising resources of this magnitude in the public sector. Even if the share of the infrastructure in the Ninth Plan is kept at the same level as in the Eighth Plan, that is, 28 per cent, the total availability of resources would be only Rs. 2,30,000 crores. This implies that the private sector will have to play a far greater role in infrastructure development, but it is also clear that the dominant role will have to be played by the public sector. But in view of the mounting fiscal deficit, budgetary support for infrastructure can only be expected to be moderate. In other words, public investment has to be financed by a combination of internally generated surpluses and borrowings from the capital market which, in turn requires a healthy debt market.[35]

2.13. Commercialisation of Infrastructure Sector

2.13.1. A wave of privatisation and deregulation has been sweeping infrastructure sectors around the globe over the last decade. These new approaches promote improvement in efficiency and service quality whereas the specific motivations and circumstances vary by countries, and in countries by sectors. There are five basic pragmatic and non-ideology related factors that are leading economies all over the world to consider enhanced commercialisation of infrastructure provision.[36]

- The massive investment requirements arising from sharply rising economic growth rates are pushing countries to look for additional sources of financing against the backdrop of fiscal stringency in most countries.
- The rising awareness of the importance of efficiency in investment and delivery in the context of tight fiscal condition leads to rethinking on the ability of government-owned entities to supply infrastructure services in a business like manner.
- Changes in technology now make it easier to charge for marginal use of infrastructure services. Such technological changes are making possible the introduction of competition horizontally and unbundling of services vertically.
- The increasing need for countries to compete in the global market place is putting additional pressure on countries to provide efficient infrastructure services to their business in a cost-effective and competitive manner. Higher infrastructure costs in terms of both price and time delays can make the difference between firms being globally competitive or otherwise.
- The new dynamism and integration of world capital markets have vastly increased the possibility of raising large funds for infrastructure investment on a commercial basis whereas earlier, governments only had better access to resources. In many cases, it is now the private sector which has the capability of sourcing large funds internationally.

2.13.2. The present market for providing infrastructure services has two implications. One is, such services can be provided by the private sector and second, private capital would have to be accessed on competitive terms. To meet the twin objectives, regulation must primarily be viewed as a mechanism which brings about risk allocation between the service providers and various other entities in the process, making it easy to access capital. When risk allocation becomes easier, it results in reducing the cost of capital. Hence, it is necessary to have an articulate regulatory framework, which is radically different from the existing legal framework in terms of transparency, clarity of obligations and duties and responsibilities among the participants in the infrastructure projects.[37]

2.13.3. Rakesh Mohan Committee Report on Indian Infrastructure recommends a simple regulatory framework.[38]

- Existing sector-specific enactment's be unified into a single statute.
- An autonomous regulatory body be set for each infrastructure sector, on the lines of SEBI.
- The roles of the regulator and the operator must be separated in every sector.
- Mechanisms to settle disputes quickly must be setup.
- An overarching legislation be made for project formats such as Build-Operate-Transfer (BOT), Build-Own-Operate (BOO) and the like governing projects across all sectors, on the lines of the BOT law of the Philippines. Foreign Investment Promotion Board (FIPB) which will clear projects on a national level based on broad principles.
- The present restrictions in FII guidelines be removed for investment in infrastructure projects or separate guidelines similar to FII guidelines without investment limits be issued. Similar guidelines and tax regime should govern any offshore fund set up by a domestic asset management company registered with SEBI, or by a domestic institution.
- Special Purpose Vehicles (SPVs) be used for funding infrastructure projects. Such SPVs should be able to vary their capital with ease, they should be easy to wind up ; they should be tax-transparent.

2.13.4. The government has recognised that private sector participation including foreign investment is required to supplement the public sector efforts. Various reforms have been made in infrastructure sector and rules and procedures for investment have been liberalised in order to provide an enabling environment conducive for private participation. The role of government has changed from 'owner' and 'sole provider' to that of a 'facilitator' and of safeguarding the interests of the vulnerable sections of the community by legal and institutional framework.

2.14. New Delhi Action Plan

2.14.1. Under the New Delhi Action Plan (1997-2006) on infrastructure development in Asia and the Pacific, a business plan was prepared providing for establishment and launching of the Infrastructure Development Finance Corporation (IDFC) and its initial products. The business plan laid down the mission of IDFC and its role in the Indian market, products it would offer, risks associated with these products, funding of the organisation, role and functions within the organisation, competitive advantages and strategy for achieving the mission of the corporation.

2.14.2. The IDFC's short-term goal (first year of its operation) included providing value addition in the existing infrastructure finance market. Further, promoting the Indian Government efforts to improve the country's infrastructure by bringing two current pipelines projects to financial close. IDFC's medium to long-term goals included completion of the first successful securitisation and sale of an infrastructure financing within five years ; and elimination of dependence on government concessions and support after five years. The magnitude of infrastructure financing required, according to the Indian infrastructure Report is considerable. Gross Domestic Investment (GDI) in Infrastructure is expected to increase from 5.5 per cent of GDP in 1995-96 to about 7 per cent in 2000-01 and 8 per cent by 2005-06. Infrastructure investment will account for 22 to 25 per cent of the GDI, rising from about Rs.60,000 crore in 1995-96 to Rs.1,07,000 crore in 2000-01 ; Rs.1,80,000 cr in 2005-06 ; Rs.4,30,000 crore in the next five years(2006-07 to 2010-2011) and Rs.7,40,000 crore in the subsequent five years (2011-12 to 2015-16) in infrastructure.[39]

2.15. India Infrastructure Report : Sectoral Projection for Infrastructure Investment (1996-2006)

2.15.1. India infrastructure report submitted to Government of India in June 22, 1996, estimates the sectoral infrastructure investment for a period of 10 years (1996-2006). According to the report, total infrastructure investment would rise immediately to about 8 per cent of GDP in 1996-97 and further to about 11.5 per cent by the year 2005-06. The sectoral estimates are scaled down by 30 per cent to make the projections more realistic. According to this projection investment in power would range from about Rs.360 billion in 1996-97 to about Rs.500 billion in 2000-01 and Rs.690 billion in 2005-2006. Thus resources of about Rs.2000-2100 billion (US$60 billion) would be required for the power sector in the next five years and Rs.3000 to 3100 billion (about Rs.90 billion) in the following five years, making for a total of about Rs.5000 billion (US$150 billion) over the next 10 years. In telecommunications the investment required would range from about Rs.76 billion in 1997-97 to about Rs.115 billion in 2000-01 and Rs.215 billion in 2005-06. Thus total investment of about Rs.550 billion (US$16 billion) will be required in the telecommunication sector over the next five years, and about Rs.840 billion (US $ 25 billion) in the following five years.

2.15.2. In the case of roads until investment would have to be stepped up from about Rs.30 billion in 1996-97 to about Rs.75 billion in 2000-01 and Rs.100 billion in 2005-06. This amounts to about Rs.240 billion (US $ 7 billion over the next five years followed by about Rs.440 billion (US $ 12.54 billion) between 2001-2006. The investment on urban infrastructure would increase from about Rs.70 billion in 1996-97 to Rs.160 billion in 2000-01 and 420 billion in 2005-2006. Thus investment in urban infrastructure in the next five years would have to be of the order of Rs.150 billion (US $ 15 billion) and about Rs.1500 billion (US $ 40 billion) between 2000-2006. For port sector, the estimates indicates that creating 350 million tonnes of additional cargo handling capacity by 2005-06 will require about Rs.250 billion. During 1996-2001, the requirement would be about Rs.100 billion and an additional Rs.150 billion during 2001-06. The resource requirements are significantly higher when compared with actual expenditure of just under Rs.16 billion in the last four years (1992-96). Total plan allocation in 1990-1997 was also only Rs.42 billion. The resources required over the next 10 years will either have to be internally generated by the ports or will have to come from other new sources. The internal accruals of the ports are expected to be about Rs.135 billion (Rs.60 billion between 1996-97 and 2000-2001 and Rs.75 billion from 2000-02 to 2005-06). Additional requirement are estimated at Rs.40 billion from 1996-97 to 2000-2001 and Rs.80 billion between 2001-2002 and 2005-06.[40]

2.16. Tenth Five Year Plan (2002-07) and Infrastructure Development

2.16.1. With a view to achieving 8 per cent growth rate target of the GDP during the tenth plan, industry will have to grow at the rate of at least 10 per cent per annum. For achieving this rate, industrial sector will be depending heavily for support on infrastructure sector. Supply of electricity must be regular for the industries and there should be no shortages of oil. Increased cost of import of oil would affect the economy adversely. In addition, transportation, irrigation and ports have to grow rapidly and do well to support the developmental efforts of other sectors of the economy.

2.16.2. In the field of electricity generation, average annual growth of at least 8 per cent is needed during the Tenth Plan period. This can be possible only if private capital investment in huge volumes takes place in power generation sector. Further, not only the annual losses of Rs.25,000 crore being incurred by the State Electricity Board (SEBs) are to be wiped out, the tariff structure is also to be remodelled in such a manner as to attract private investment. The transmission and distribution tasks are likely to be given to the private sector during the Tenth Plan period, so that the losses and leakages could be prevented. During the Tenth Plan, restructuring and reforming of most of the SEBs would be completed and the accelerated power development programmes (APDP), introduced during the Ninth Plan is to be expanded. Optimum mix of power generation is an important issue. At present, hydroelectric power generation constitutes about 24 per cent of the total power generation in the country, whereas ideally it should be much higher. Tenth Plan aims at increasing the share of hydro power by tapping the existing potential. Nuclear power share is also as low as 2.4 per cent in India. Tenth Plan aims at expanding the nuclear power capabilities through nuclear power corporation, but investment in this field has to be made by the government only.[41]

2.16.3. In the transport sector also, several measures are proposed to be undertaken during the Plan Period. Tenth Plan aims at reducing heavy cross-subsidisation in freight and passenger fares in railways. The plan also envisages setting up of a Rail Tariff Regulatory Authority for tariff fixation for railways on technical and commercial considerations. To make the railways more efficient, it is proposed to reduce the staff strength to 12 lakh. Emphasis is also proposed to be laid on doubling the tracks, opening up of new lines, gauge conversion and increasing the high value traffic. In the field of road transportation, rationalisation of road transport taxation structure, restraining overloading promoting road safety, upgradation of national highways and encouraging private participation in road construction are some of the areas to be given more emphasis. Indian Ports are projected to handle about 800 MT of trafic by the end of the Tenth Five Year Plan. This would require 300 to 400 additional berths to handle the increased cargo. The government is targeting private investment to the tune of Rs. 24,000 crore to create additional port capacity during the Tenth Plan Period. Technologically change in telecommunication has been drastic and is constantly leading to major changes in the structure of telecommunication industry worldwide. In addition to providing telephones on demand, and opening up Internet telephony, aim should also be at tariff re-balancing at cost-based pricing and better targeting of subsidies.

2.16.4. Tenth Plan also envisages certain measures to strengthen the social infrastructure. Recognising the fact that our performance in the field of education in the past five decades has been one of the most disappointing aspects of the developmental process, the plan aims at radical transformation in this area. Education for all is one of the main objectives of the tenth plan, aiming at achieving near 100 per cent attendance at primary level, as compared to the existing 66 per cent. To improve the quality of delivery, it is aimed to provide one primary school within one kilometre of every habitation and one teacher for every 40 students. Similarly, improvement in the healthy status of the population of the country is another thrust area. Strengthening of all national programmes, reorganising and restructuring of existing health-care Infrastructure, evolving appropriate mechanisms for economic assistance to low and middle income groups in cases of severe illness, are some of the areas to be addressed properly. Properly equipping the health institutions with required manpower, medicines and equipment is another area of thrust. The development of social infrastructure is crucial for the desired expansion of economic infrastructure, which in turn leads to higher growth rate of the GDP.

2.17. Andhra Pradesh Vision Document : Vision 2020

2.17.1. Infrastructure is closely related to the overall development of the economy, and simultaneously overall growth is dependent on the quality of infrastructure. Realising the severe shortfalls in the development of infrastructure the Andhra Pradesh Government has prepared "Andhra Pradesh : Vision 2020 Swarna Andhra Pradesh", which outlines a mission to make Andhra Pradesh the foremost State in the country in terms of growth, equity and quality of life. This document is considered as a model document for infrastructure development for the Central Government as well as for other State Governments. The document enumerates the potential and resources of the State and recognises the opportunities thrown open by the liberalisation and globalisation process and the information revolution. It also identifies select growth engines to 'leverage' the strengths and advantages in various sectors and regions. Drawing upon the best practices within and outside the country, the document outlines the profile of development of the State in the first two decades of the 21st Century based on strategy of leapfrogging growth with equity and sustainable improvements in the living standards of all sections of the people. It also emphasises the need for the State Government to transform itself and quickly adopt a new role from being primarily a controller of the economy to a facilitator and catalyst of growth. Further, the document gives top priority to the development of physical or economical infrastructure which includes, development of ports, power generation, telecommunication, irrigation projects etc. The document reveals that, the state will require Rs. 4,00,000 crore till the year 2010 and Rs. 16,00,000 crore to be invested till 2020 in building infrastructure.[42]

2.17.2. Andhra Pradesh has been trying to get the private sector to build port infrastructure since 1994, on a Build-own-operate-transfer (BOOT) basis. The International Sea-Ports Ltd. (ISPL) of Singapore has submitted plans to develop the Kakinada port, which handled 1.5 MT of cargo in 1999-2000, in to a major hub building at least 10 berths and attendant infrastructure. The Vision document further forsees the state to have one mega port with capacity of 50-70 million tonnes at Visakhapatnam and four to six large ports with capacity of 30-50 million tonnes by the year 2020. The document also focuses on making the port suitable for bulk and containerised cargo handling. [43]

2.18. Export Processing Zones (EPZ)

2.18.1. Undeniably, ports throughout the world act as catalyst for boosting foreign trade. The set up of Export Processing Zone give fillip to foreign trade and today EPZs have emerged as effective instruments to boost exports of manufactured products especially in developing countries. The zones setup as enclaves separated from the Domestic Tariff Area by physical barriers, are intended to provide an internationally competitive duty free environment for export production at low cost. This enables the products to be competitive, both quality-wise and price-wise in the international market. The major objectives of setting up EPZs are:[44]

(i) expansion of the net foreign exchange earnings of the country,

(ii) attraction of foreign direct investment (FDI), and

(iii) generation of additional employment opportunities.

2.18.2. The first free trade zone was established at Kandla in 1965. The government has also permitted setting up of EPZs in private/joint sector. So far, the following eight free trade and EPZs have been established.[45]

1. Cochin Export Processing Zone, Kerala.
2. Falta Export Processing Zone (FEPZ), West Bengal.

3. Kandla Free Trade Zone (KFTZ), Gujarat.
4. Madras Export Processing Zone (MEPZ), Chennai.
5. Noida Export Processing Zone (NEPZ), U.P.
6. Santacruz Electronics Export Processing Zone (SEEPZ), Mumbai.
7. Visakhapatnam Export Processing Zone (VEPZ), Andhra Pradesh
8. Surat Export Processing Zone, Gujarat.

2.18.3. All these zones have been setup by Government of India with the support of respective State Government and these are administered by the Ministry of Commerce, Government of India. Each Zone provides basic infrastructural facilities like.[46]

- Tax holidays from corporate income tax for a period of five continuous years during the first eight years of production or operation.
- Duty free import of second hand capital goods.
- Foreign equity upto 100 per cent permitted. There is no restriction on repatriation of capital and remittance of profits and dividends.
- Decentralised single window clearance of proposals concerning units in EPZs have been provided.

Table 2.13

Achievement of EPZs in Terms of Their Main Objectives (1990-95)

Name of zone	*Net foreign exchange earnings (Rs. In crore)*	*Foreign investments including (Rs. In crores)*	*No. of additional job opportunities created*
KFTZ	1,685.61	2.41	12,000
SEEPZ	1,671.10	59.00	16,775
MEPZ	347.13	37.64	12,334
NEPZ	240.01	52.00	6,800
CEPZ	150.72	24.37	4,300
FEPZ	80.95	1.93	1,600
YEPZ	-0.09	5.47	11
Total	**4,121.43**	**182.82**	**53,820**

Source : Report of the Indian Council for Research on International Economic Relations, (ICRIER), New Delhi, 1996.

2.18.4. Table 2.13 highlights the achievements of EPZs in terms of their main objectives such as net foreign exchange earnings, foreign investments and number of additional job opportunities created. The Kandla Free Trade Zone (KFTZ) Gujarat had earned the highest amount, i.e., Rs. 1,685.61 crore of net foreign exchange during the period followed by SEEPZ. Similarly in terms of foreign investment (Rs.59.00 crore) creation of additional job opportunities (16775) the SEEPZ stood first during 1990-95. The VEPZ had experienced a poor performance among the other zones during the period. This Table also brings out the fact that, though the liberalisation of the economic policies of the country started in July 1991, the seven EPZs were found to have miserably failed in attracting foreign investment and in the creation of additional employment opportunities but were found to have marginally succeeded in earning net foreign exchange. A study by the Indian Council for Research on International Economic Relations (ICRIER) reveals the cause that international movement of capital to EPZs scattered throughout the world to be on account of (1) virtual free trade regime, availability of excellent infrastructure and cheap skilled labour ; and (2) access to the domestic markets. It is estimated that the foreign investment made in Indian EPZs are less than 0.94 per cent of the total inflow of foreign investment received by the country. Hence the achievements of EPZs were far from satisfactory.[47]

Table 2.14

Contribution of EPZs to India's Total Export during the period 1980-81 to 1999-2000

(Rs. in crores)

Year	*India's total export*	*Export of all EPZs Amount*	*Percentage of India's total expenditure*
1980-81	6,711	44.00	0.66
1984-85	11,744	333.00	2.84
1989-90	27,658	732.00	2.64
1990-91	32,527	986.00	3.03
1995-96	1,06,353	3,236.00	3.04
1996-97	1,18,817	4,338.00	3.69
1997-98	1,30,101	5,019.00	3.85
1998-99	1,39,753	6,032.00	4.32
1999-2000	1,62,925	7,653.00	4.70

Source : (i) Official records of various EPZs in India (ii) Economic Survey, Ministry of Commerce, 2000-2001.

2.18.5. Table 2.14 exhibits that even though India's exports witnessed a quantum jump during the post liberalisation period, the contribution of EPZs to India's exports remained low. After liberalisation of economic policies, the total export rose from Rs.1,06,353 crores in 1995-96 to Rs.1,62,925 crores in 1999-2000. The share of EPZs in total export rose to 4.70 per cent from 3.04 per cent in the said period respectively. During 1993-94 to 2000-01, exports grew in double digits only for five years, exceeding 20 per cent in 1995-96 and 2000-01. Other years were marked by a single digit growth or contraction as in the past. The Government of India embarked on a mid-term strategy to put exports on a sustainable growth path and mooted with the idea of setting up 10 agri export zones apart from pursuing the concept of Special Economic Zones (SEZs) to boost exports. It has already converted four export processing zones into SEZs. In the Exim Policy of 2000, the government announced the policy of converting EPZs into SEZs and establishing new SEZs. According to Chapter 9A of the Exim Policy (1997-2000), SEZs may be set up for manufacture of goods and rendering of services, production, processing, assembling, trading, repair, remaking, reconditioning, re-engineering, including of making of gold/silver jewellery and articles.

2.19. Drive Towards Setting up SEZs

2.19.1. Special Economic Zones (SEZs) have played a pivotal role in the economic growth of several countries and have been a key to paradigm shift undertaken by various countries from the planned economy to the market economy. As part of its continuing commitment to liberalisation, the Government of India, since the last decade, adopted a multipronged approach to promotion of foreign investment in India. As a result, in the 2002-03 budget as well as in the new Exim Policy (2002-07), the government has given special importance to the SEZs in the country.[48]

2.19.2. While EPZs are industrial estates, SEZs are virtually industrial townships that provide supportive infrastructure such as housing, roads, ports and telecommunication. The scope of activities that can be undertaken in the SEZs is much wider and their linkages with the domestic economy are stronger. Resultantly they have a diversified industrial base. SEZs are intended to be instruments of regional development as well as export promotion. As such SEZs can have tremendous impact on exports, inflow of foreign investment and employment generation. The factors like availability of skilled labour at reasonable costs and the availability of a large English speaking populace are likely to make SEZs successful in India.[49]

2.19.3. Since State Governments are very keen, the Central Government has approved the proposal of setting up of more than a dozen SEZs. Out of these, three are in Uttar Pradesh (Kanpur, Greater Noida and Bhadhoi) ; two are in Orissa (Paradeep, Gopalpur), two have been cleared for West Bengal (Kolkata, Kulpi), while Gujarat already has two (Surat, Kandla), with Positra waiting in the wings. While Mumbai already has a SEZ (SEEPZ), the State is planning another one at Dronagiri. Andhra Pradesh wants one at Kakinada, Madhya Pradesh has selected Indore, Karnataka has pitched for Hassan and Tamil Nadu has moved a few steps with Nangunery.[50]

Table 2.15
Progress of SEZs in India

Location	*Promoter*	*Date of approval*	*Status of implementation*
Positra (Gujarat)	Gujarat Positra Port Infrastructure Ltd. Joint Sector	3.7.2000 (in principle) 15.2.2002 (formal approval)	• Area of more than 200 kms • Commitment of about Rs.2,000 crore obtained Land acquisition in progress.
Nanguneri (Tamil Nadu)	Government of Tamil Nadu	28.9.2000 (in principle)	• 8.5 kms land in possession • Master plan • Feasibility report by Cushman & Wakefield and Ernst & Young • FIPB approval obtained for foreign equity of $89.8 million

(contd...)

(Contd...Table 2.15)

Location	*Promoter*	*Date of approval*	*Status of implementation*
Dronagiri (Maharashtra)	Government of Maharashtra	5.5.2000 (in principle) 15.2.2002 (formal approval)	• 44 kms of land in possession Business plan in preparation Land acquisition in progress.
Kakinada (Andhra Pradesh)	Government of Andhra Pradesh	26.9.2000 (in principle)	Feasibility report being prepared by KPMG
Gopalpur (Orissa)	Government of Orissa	19.3.2001 (in principle)	• 12 kms of land acquired. • Feasibility report being prepared by KPMG
Hassan (Karnakata)	Government of Karnataka	18.6.2001 (in principle)	Detail project report in preparation
Kulpi (West Bengal)	Government of West Bengal	23.5.2000 (in principle)	DPR in preparation
Salt Lake (Kolkata)	Government of West Bengal	7.11.2001 (in principle)	DPR in preparation
Bhadohi (Uttar Pradesh)	Government of Uttar Pradesh	19.9.2000 (in principle)	DPR in preparation
Kanpur (Uttar Pradesh)	Government of Uttar Pradesh	2.1.2002 (in principle)	DPR in preparation
Greater Noida (Uttar Pradesh)	Government of Uttar Pradesh	19.6.2001 (in principle)	DPR in preparation
Indore (Madhya Pradesh)	Government of Madhya Pradesh	2.1.2002 (in principle)	DPR in preparation
Paradeep (Orissa)	Government of Orissa	2000 (in principle)	DPR in preparation

Source : Government of India, Ministry of Commerce, New Delhi.

New Exim Policy (2002-07) and SEZs

2.19.4. The New Exim Policy 2002-07 contains several proposals for giving various incentives to setup Special Economic Zones (SEZs) in the country. The various incentives contained therein are enumerated as follows.[51]

- Income tax concession to exporters in SEZs is allowed.
- Exemption from CST (Central Sales Tax) for DTA (Domestic Tariff Area) sales to SEZs has been permitted.
- Duty drawback and duty entitlement passbook scheme covers supplies to SEZs.
- Overseas banking units are permitted without SLR & CRR requirement, which will enable the SEZs to access finance at a cheaper cost.
- 100 per cent prepayment of ECB (External Commercial Borrowing) from exporter earner foreign currency account is permitted for units in SEZ.
- All inputs procured by the SEZ developers as well as units located in the zones are exempted from all import duties.
- No licencing for second-hand plant and project imports is required.
- ECB norms have been simplified.
- Hedging in commodities is permitted in SEZs.
- SEZ exporters are free to make overseas investments.
- Free access to overseas funds is allowed.
- Differential rate of interest is permitted for overseas banking units in SEZs.
- Rough diamond exports have been exempted from duty and licensing.
- Special thrust for 106 items and towns of export excellence are identified.
- Tenure of export earnings retention abroad has been doubled to 360 days.
- New eight-digit classification of trade items is allowed.
- Same-day licensing in all regional centres is introduced.

2.19.5. Major Advantages of SEZ

- SEZs may export goods and services, including agro-products, partly processed jewellery, sub-assemblies and components. It may also export by-products, rejects, wastes from the production process.[52]

- SEZs may import all types of goods without payment of duty. This includes capital goods, but not prohibited items for imports. Even SEZ units can lease capital goods from a domestic / foreign leasing company.
- SEZs may procure goods required by it without payment of duty from bonded warehouses in the DTA setup under the policy.
- SEZ units may import goods for creating a central facility for use by software development units without payment of duty.
- SEZs may also import gold/silver/platinum and specified goods from DTA through the nominated agencies for setting up units without duty, but subject to various conditions laid down by the government.
- SEZ gem and jewellery units, with the Development Commissioner's permission, shall be entitled to personal carriage of gold/silver/ platinum jewellery, precious, semi-precious stones and articles. They can export jewellery, including branded jewellery, which are also permitted for display/sale in the permitted shops setup abroad.
- SEZs may bring back sold goods for repair and replacement.
- Goods may be transferred to DTA for replacement / repair / testing or calibration, quality testing and R & D purposes under intimation to the customs authorities.
- SEZ units, with the maintained records and prior intimation to customs authority, may supply or sell samples in the DTA for display / market promotion on payment of applicable duties.
- Remove samples on furnishing a suitable undertaking to customs authorities for bringing the goods back within a stipulated time without payment of duty.
- No duty shall be payable if the goods are destroyed with the permission of customs authorities.
- SEZs may subcontract a part of their production or production process through units in the DTA.
- However, the SEZ shall execute a legal undertaking with the Development Commissioner that if it fails to achieve positive foreign exchange earning, it will be liable to penalty in terms of the legal undertaking, or under any other law for the time being in force. Further, SEZ units may be debonded with the approval of Development Commissioner. Debonding shall be subjected to payment of applicable customs and excise duties and the imported and indigenous capital goods, raw materials, finished goods in stock and so on.[53]

2.20. Summary

2.20.1. Infrastructure is a basic need to create improved marketability, efficient resource utilisation and increased opportunities for the public to participate in the development process through which greater investment, employment and production can be realised. Power, telecommunication, roads, ports, transportation, water supply and sanitation, etc., are the components of physical or economic infrastructure. Social infrastructure includes health and human resource development. These two segments of infrastructure are complementary and interdependent to each other. Infrastructure developments are of two types, namely, demand driven and supply driven. Demand driven infrastructure is a must for development whereas supply driven infrastructure is desirable but not must.

2.20.2. During the age of globalised business environment, infrastructure performance is a key factor in attracting foreign direct investment which has become an essential element in capital starved developing economies. According to a study conducted recently on infrastructure development, among 16 Asian countries, India was placed 15th, just above Vietnam. And from among 60 countries in the world, including developed countries, India ranked 58th in terms of infrastructure development. Due to inadequate infrastructural facilities India is laging behind to other countries in inviting foreign direct investment. Though the investment in the infrastructure increases in absolute figures but in terms of percentage to GDI, it exhibits a declining trend. The India Infrastructure Report estimates that the GDI in infrastructure is expected to increase from 5.5 per cent of GDP in 1995-96 to about 7 per cent in 2000-01 and 8 per cent by 2005-06. Infrastructure investment will account for 22 to 25 per cent of the GDI rising from about Rs. 60, 000 crores in 1995-96 to Rs. 1, 07, 000 crores in 2000-01 ; Rs. 1, 80, 000 crores in 2005-06; Rs. 4, 30, 000 crores in 2010-11 and Rs. 7, 40, 000 crores in 2015-16.

2.20.3. Infrastructure services are often monopolistic in nature. They usually involve high upfront costs and long payback periods and investments are typically lumpy and bulky. They are also characterised by the existence of externalities which make it difficult for infrastructure entities to recoup investment costs and operational expenses through the levy of user charges. Consequently, infrastructure services have been predominantly provided by the public sector. But during the last decade, a wave of privatisation and deregulation has been sweeping infrastructure sector with the outcome of improvement in efficiency and service quality and enhanced commercialisation. The government has recognised that private sector participation including foreign investment is required to supplement the public sector efforts various reforms have been made in infrastructure sector and rules and procedure for investment have been liberalised in order to provide an enabling environment conducive for private participation. The role of government has changed from owner and sole provider to that of a facilitator.

2.20.4. Transport system is broadly considered as the artery and nerves covering the entire economy of the country. In a vast country like India, an efficient transport system is the pre-requisite for attaining a higher level of economic development. The demand for transport services in India has been growing much faster than the rate of economic growth. The road transport services as well as railways occupy prominent place in our economy accounting for 53.3 per cent and 31.7 per cent respectively of the total transport sector. Water transport has a share of approximately 6.5 per cent. The share of transport sector in total plan outlay has fallen from 22.10 per cent during the First Five Year Plan to 13.10 per cent during the Eighth Five Year Plan though in absolute figure the plan allocation has increased during the period. In India, we have a four-tier transport system, i.e., Railways, Roadways, Waterways and Airways.

2.20.5. In terms of area and population, the total road length in the country in April 1997 worked out to be about 64 kms for every 100 sq. kms of area and 275 kms for every one lakh population. The National Highways, which span about 58,112 kms throughout the country cater to about 45 per cent of the total road transport demand. The government has decided to develop 4/6 lane roads connecting four metropolitan cities and North-South, East-West corridors including connectivity for all major ports with an investment of Rs. 54,000 crore to be completed by 2007.

2.20.6. The rail mode of transport has been playing an integrating role in socio-economic development of the country being the largest in Asia and the fourth largest in the world. The railways have been performing the dual role of functioning as a commerical undertaking and a provider of public utility service. Air transport also plays a vital role in a vast country like India. Water transport is another most vital mode of transport considered to be the cheapest mode of transport. Water transport are of two types such as inland water transport and coastal or marine transport. Inland Water Transport (IWT) is the cheapest and one of the efficient modes of transport. Unlike in other modes of transport, there is practically no investment needed and is also a labour intensive mode of transport and benefiting the weaker sections of the community. At present, there are three systems declared as National Waterways. They are NW-I Ganga-Bhagirathi Hoogly (1620 km), NW-II Brahmaputra (891 km) and NW-III West Coast Canal (205 km). Realising the significance of IWT the government has declared certain scheme, for the development of IWT sector in the country. The States would be offered 90 per cent grant for implementation of these schemes. The States would have to contribute 10 per cent. For Sikkim and the North-East, the entire money would be provided by the Centre as grant.

2.20.7. The coastal or marine transport deals with the major and minor ports. With having a vast coastline of 6000 kms, India have now 12 major ports and 160 minor ports. More than 90 per cent of India's foreign trade in volume and 75 per cent in terms of value are conducted by sea. The investments made for port development during different plans have increased from Rs. 26 crore in the First Five Year Plan to Rs. 3216 crore in the Eighth Plan and Rs. 9428 crore in the Ninth Five Year Plan. The Ministry of Surface Transport has projected the total traffic to be handled at Indian ports by the year 2021-22 will be 1373 MT and the investment required will be Rs. 1,00,575 crore. The port capacity requirement will be 540 MT by 2005-06. Development of hub ports is necessary for India because of change in technology and growing demand for operation of large sized vessels. The government has decided to develop hub ports one in the East Coast at Chennai Port and one on the West Coast at Navi Mumbai for conservation of additional cost through cargo transhipment and reduction in transit time and safer delivery through adequate supervision by Indian agencies.

2.20.8. Other infrastructural facilities like power, telecommunication, postal services, tourism, urban infrastructure, rural infrastructure and banking infrastructure etc. have major roles to play for the overall development of the country. The government has paid emphasis on for the development of this basic infrastructural needs by way of more private participation which usually delivers qualitative service.

2.20.9. The development of Export Processing Zones (EPZs) and Special Economic Zones (SEZs) in the country will not only boost the export but it has tremendous impact on inflow of foreign investment and employment generation in the country. So far the government has approved 13 SEZs in the country and some of the EPZs have been converted in to SEZs for a broader venture in the country. The government in its Exim Policy (2002-07) has declared a good number of incentives for attracting the private players and encouraging the State governments to establish the SEZs in the country.

References

1. Dhingra, I.C., *The Indian Economy - Environment and Policy,* S. Chand and Sons, Fourteenth Edition, New Delhi, 2000.
2. Khader, S.A., "Productivity in Infrastructure", *Yojana,* Vol. 42, No. 1, New Delhi, January 1998, p.14.
3. Sahoo, S. "Role of Infrastructure in Economic Development : The Indian Case", An unpublished Ph.D. Thesis submitted to Department of Humanities and Social Sciences, IIT, Kanpur, July 1998.
4. Narain, Y., "New Initiatives in Infrastructure Sector", *Yojana,* Vol. 42, No. 1, New Delhi, January 1998, p.5.
5. Khader, S.A., *op.cit.,* p.17.
6. Sridharan, L., "Productivity Infrastructure – Needed A Paradigm Shift in Thinking", *Yojana,* Vol. 46, New Delhi, February 2002, p.16.
7. Dhar, P.K., *Indian Economy – Its Growing Dimensions,* Kalyani Publishers, 8th Revised Edition, New Delhi, 2000.
8. Agrawal, A.N., *Indian Economy – Problems of Development and Planning* Wishwa Prakashan, New Delhi, 27th Edition, 2001.
9. Datta, R., & Sundharam, K.P.M., *Indian Economy,* S.Chand and Company, New Delhi, 43rd Revised Edition, 2001.
10. *Ibid.*
11 Anand, M. & Jayaram, A., "The Highway Men" A Special Cover Story on National Highway Projects, *Business World,* Vol. 22, Issue 17, New Delhi, 16-22, September 2002, pp.28-36.
12. Padmapriya, J., "NHAI to Take Up Port Connectivity Projects via SPVs", *The Economic Times,* Chennai, July 19, 2001, p.12.
13. Government of India, "Economic Survey – 2001-02", Ministry of Finance, Economic Division, New Delhi, p.223.
14. *Ibid.,* p. 225.
15. *Ibid.,* p. 228.
16. Mathur, B.L., *Economics Policy and Development – Water Transport in India : Problems and Prospects* RBSA Publishers, Jaipur, 1st Edition, 2000.
17. Sambandan, V.S. "Transport Mode With Great Promise", *The Hindu (Business Special),* Visakhapatnam, March 15, 2001, p. BS-I.

18. *Ibid.*
19. Kurup, N.K., "Inland Water Transport – Untapped Potential", *The Hindu Business Line*, Chennai, September 4, 2000.
20. Sanyal, S., "Integrating Inland Waterways with Coastal Services – Ministry Forms Panel to Workout Norms", *The Hindu Business Line*, Chennai, March 9, 2001.
21. "Government Announces New Pattern of Financing For IWT", The Hindu, Vol. 125, No. 248, Visakhapatnam, October 19, 2002, p.13.
22. Sasl, A., "Major Ports Come of Age", *Business Standard*, Chennai, September 19, 2001, p.1 and 2.
23. Srivastava, P.K., "Future For Indian Ports and Development of Hub Port", *Indian Shipping*, Vol. 52, Mumbai, December 2000, p.11.
24. "Multimodal Transport : Yet To Run", *The Hindu Business Line*, Chennai, March 19, 2001.
25. Manoj, P., "New Direction For Law on Multimodal Transportation", *The Hindu Business Line*, Chennai, July 31, 2000.
26. "Multimodal Transportation – Potential Unexplored", *Indian Infrastructure*, Vol. 3, No. 12, New Delhi, July 2001, p. 37.
27. Purkayastha, P., "Power Sector Policies and New Electricity Bill – From Crisis to Disaster", *Economic and Political Weekly*, Vol. XXXVI, No. 25, Mumbai, June 23, 2001, pp. 2257-2262.
28. "Delivering on Power Reforms", *The Hindu Business Line* (Editorial), Vol. 9, No. 23, Visakhapatnam, January 24, 2002, p.8.
29. Government of India, *Economic Survey* 2001-02, *op.cit.*, p.217.
30. *Ibid.*, p. 222.
31. *Ibid.*, p. 229.
32. *Ibid.*, p. 229
33. *Ibid.*, p. 231.
34. Dutta, R & Sundaram, K.P.M. "Indian Economy", *op.cit.*, p.780.
35. Das Gupta, T., "The Infrastructure Sector", *Yojana*, Vol. 43, No. 1, New Delhi, January 1999, p. 43.
36. Kapila, U., *Indian Economy Since Independence*, Academic Foundation, New Delhi, New Revised Edition 2001-02.
37. Kapila, R., & Kapila, U., (Ed.) *India's Economy in the 21st Century*, Academic Foundation, New Delhi, 1st Edition 2001.
38. Government of India, "The India Infrastructure Report : Policy Imperatives for Growth and Welfare", Vol. II, Submitted to Ministry of Finance on June 22, 1996.
39. "Need For A New Approach" A Special Supplement on Infrastructure with the *Financial Express*, Kolkata, June 20, 2000.
40. Government of India, India Infrastructure Report, *op.cit.*, Vol. II, pp.2-19.

41. "Tenth Plan : Objectives, Targets and Strategy", *The Hindu* (Business Special), Visakhapatnam, May 17, 2001, p. BS-I.
42. Government of Andhra Pradesh, "Andhra Pradesh : Vision 2020 – Swarna Andhra Pradesh", Hyderabad.
43. Mohamad, S.H. and Rajanala, S. "Need for Focus on Infrastructure Growth", A Special Supplement on Andhra Pradesh Infrastructure, *The Economic Times*, Kolkata, August 17, 2000, p.13.
44. "Ensuring SEZs Work", *The Economic Times* (Editorial), Vol. 40, No. 86, Kolkata, June 2, 2000.
45. Dubey, S., "Export Processing Zones : An Evaluation", *Yojana*, Vol. 46, New Delhi, March 2002, p.30.
46 Gopalkrishnan, V.S., "Planning Our SEZs Properly", *The Economic Times*, Vol. 40, No. 237, Kolkata, July 24, 2000, p.8.
47. Dubey, S., "Export Processing Zones : An Evaluation", *op.cit.*, p.31.
48. Panda, J.P., "Special Economic Zones in India", *Third Concept*, Vol. 16, No. 188P, New Delhi, October 2002, p.31.
49. Kundra, A.K., "SEZs : How Well Will They Perform ?" *The Hindu (Business Special)*, Visakhapatnam, August 16, 2001, p. BS-I.
50. Subramaniam, G.G., "Trade SEZ 'AYE' " A Special Page on Infrastructure, *The Economic Times*, Kolkata, May 10, 2002, p. 5.
51. Raman, A.T., "A Dream Comes Down to Earth", A Special Article on Development of SEZs in India, *Business India*, Mumbai, April 29 – May 12, 2002, pp.68-72.
52. Sreenlvasan, N., "Exim Policy : SEZs, the Key", *The Hindu Business Line*, Vol. 9, No. 88, Visakhapatnam, March 30, 2002, p.8.
53. Prabhu, P.P., "SEZs Must Retain Distinct Character", *The Hindu Business Line*, Vol. 9, No. 143, Visakhapatnam, May 24, 2002, p.8.

3
Performance of Indian Ports, Prospects and Challenges

3.1. Introduction

3.1.1. A port is essentially an economic concept, an economic infrastructure that serves coastal and overseas traffic. Port is a sub-system of total transport network and meeting place of other modes of transport. It is a gateway for the entrance from surface water to land and vice versa. Port is also construed as the major crossroad of traffic in ideas, people and goods over the centuries. Ports play an important economic role in maritime nations by facilitating foreign trade. They are thus, catalysts for social and economic development in any maritime nation. Maritime transportation has been the life-blood of world trade since time immemorial. Though new modes of transportation have grown enormously, shipping shall continue to occupy the lion's share in world trade in the foreseeable future because of economies inherent in sea transportation.

3.1.2. India is a developing maritime nation with an extensive coastline of about 6,000 kms. There are nine coastal States namely Gujarat, Maharashtra, Karnataka, Goa, Kerala (west coast) and Tamil Nadu, Andhra Pradesh, Orissa, West Bengal (east coast). These nine States have in all 12 major and 179 minor ports.[1] Among these 12 major ports, six are located on the west coast (Kandla, Mumbai, Jawaharlal Nehru, Mormugao, Cochin and New Mangalore) and six on the east coast (Chennai, Tuticorin, Paradeep, Vizag, Calcutta and Haldia). Four of the major ports viz. Calcutta, Mumbai, Chennai and Mormugao are more than 100 years old. Cochin and

Vizag ports have recently celebrated their golden jubilee. The ports of Kandla, Tuticorin, New Mangalore and Paradeep came into existence after independence. JNPT became operational after 1989.

3.1.3. Out of total declared 179 minor ports including 13 non-working ports, 120 ports (67 per cent) belong to West Coast States, 24 ports to East Coast States and the rest (22) belong to the Island Union Territories. Maharashtra is the only State having the highest numbers of both major (Two) and minor (Fifty-three) ports in India. Next is Gujarat where one major and 40 minor ports are situated. West Bengal is the only maritime State, which, even with adequate waterfront has no declared minor port.[2] The following paragraphs explain the development of ports in the country broadly in two phases, i.e., in the pre-independence era and post-independence era.

3.2. Development of Indian Ports During Pre-independence Era

3.2.1. Realising the growing significance of ports in the Indian economy in general and transportation infrastructure in particular, the Government of India has laid adequate emphasis on the development of ports in the country. During the pre-independence era the port facilities which existed in India till about the middle of the 19th century were meagre. The ships used to lie in anchorage and cargo passengers were transhipped by small lighters. The great technological changes like advent of steam power for ship population and replacement of wooden hull by steel and also the major event of opening of Suez Canal in 1869 gave boost to world maritime commerce and triggered the first wave of port development in India.

3.2.2. A beginning was made to construct the first of the dock systems that exists today in the ports of Bombay, Chennai and Calcutta. This phase of development lasted till about the beginning of the First World War. During the period of 1915-50 there was lull in the port development activity at these ports. But the work on the development of two new major ports at Visakhapatnam and Cochin were taken up. Visakhapatnam was declared as a major port in 1933 and the new major port Cochin was born in 1936. During World War II and thereafter there was no significant port development activity in the country.

3.3. Development of Indian Ports During Post-Independence Era (Planning Era)

3.3.1. First Five Year Plan Period (1951-56)

After the attainment of independence in 1947, India adopted the strategy of planned development through various Five Year Plans. The beginning of the First Five Year Plan from 1951 onwards saw another period of hectic activity in port development. The significant development in the First Five Year Plan was the development of a major port at Kandla as a replacement to Karachi which became a part of Pakistan. A modern maritime oil terminal to receive the crude requirements of the two refineries set up at Trombay was commissioned in Bombay in 1955-56. In the other major ports, the developmental activities were mainly in the nature of making good the deficiencies which were thrown up during the war and the post war period.[3]

3.3.2. Second and Third Five Year Plan Period (1956-61 to 1961-66)

With the increased tempo of industrialisation after independence, the volume of cargo traffic handled at Indian ports almost doubled from about 19 million tonnes to about 40 million tonnes during the 10-year period from 1950-51 to 1960-61. More significantly, the composition of traffic, which is a very important parameter in planning the port facilities also, changed from break bulk to predominantly bulk cargoes. The percentage of bulk cargo increased from about 50 per cent to 68 per cent. These factors mainly governed the port development during the Second and Third Five Year Plan Period. Some of the important developments witnessed during this period are as follows:

(a) There was the creation of 4 alongside berths at Visakhapatnam with a fully mechanised berth exclusively for loading of iron-ore. This was the first installation of its kind in Indian ports for fast loading of iron ore. An oil wharf with two berths to cater to tankers bringing crude to the Caltex refineries was also constructed.

(b) Virtually the berth capacity of Madras port was doubled by construction of Jawahar Dock with three berths earmarked for handling bulk cargoes of iron-ore and coal.

(c) Four additional cargo berths and coal berth were constructed at Cochin.

(d) The port of Mormugao joined the list of Indian ports after its liberation from Portuguese control in 1961 and formal declaration as major port in 1963.

(e) Paradeep was developed as an outlet for iron-ore export with draught of 12m, which was the deepest in the country at that time.

(f) A beginning was made for the development of two all weather major harbours at Mangalore and Tuticorin with complete indigenous know-how.

In addition to the above, considerable improvement in the handling capacity at various ports was made by modernisation of handling equipments. Despite port development activities carried out during the first three Five Year Plan, port conditions remained deficient and imposed costly delays in shipping and high port costs. Draft limitations and lack of mechanised handling facilities especially for bulk cargoes proved to be a major constraint in receiving large tankers and bulk carriers. These factors alongwith pressing need to be competitive in international market influenced the port development programmes undertaken subsequent to the third Five Year Plan.

3.3.3. Fourth Five Year Plan Period (1969-74) to the beginning of Sixth Five Year Plan (1980-81)

Some of the major port development works undertaken during this period are enumerated as follows:

(a) Creation of a Satellite Port at Haldia, 56 nautical miles downstream of Calcutta was undertaken in 1966 to overcome the limitations of Calcutta port in respect of permissible drafts and lengths of vessels which could be received and to cater to modern bulk carriers and tankers. This was commissioned in 1977.

(b) An outer Harbour at Visakhapatnam port with an iron ore berth was designed to receive 1,00,000 DWT vessels initially and 2,00,000 DWT size vessels ultimately and with modern ore handling system with the rated capacity of 8000 TPH initially and capable of increasing to 16,000 TPH was commissioned in December 1976.

(c) An outer Harbour at Madras known as Bharathi Dock was created to receive 1,00,000 DWT oil tankers and ore carriers.

(d) At Mormugao, the premier ore loading port of India, modernisation of ore handling facility which was primitive and very slow was launched in 1970 to enable the port to receive 60,000 DWT ore carriers initially and 1,00,000 DWT size vessels ultimately with the rated loading capacity of the system as 8000 TPH.

(e) At Bombay, the Dock Expansion Scheme providing additional berthing facility in the Alexandra Dock (Present Indira Dock) and Ballard Pier Extension to cater to passenger traffic were completed and commissioned.

(f) At Mangalore a new lagoon type major harbour with 30 m draft was developed and a new major port called new Mangalore port was born in May, 1974.

(g) Similarly, at Tuticorin, an artificial new harbour with 30 m draft was developed and Tuticorin was declared as a major port in July, 1974.

(h) The agreement to export Kudremukh Iron Ore to Iran necessitated the creation of bulk ore handling facilities at Mangalore capable of receiving 60,000 DWT ore carriers. This project was taken up with the financial assistance of Iran and was commissioned in August, 1980. This scheme marked a technological advancement in the export of iron ore in the sense that the ore is transported in slurry form from the mines to the port where it is converted to pellet form and then were exported.

3.3.4. Sixth Five Year Plan Period (1980-85)

The notable development in the Sixth Five Year Plan was the sanctioning of construction of new port at Nhava Sheva, near Bombay which was under consideration for a long time, with the objective of decongestion and mitigation of environmental degradation of Bombay. Under this project, it was envisaged to provide the state-of-the-art handling facilities for bulk cargoes (fertilizer/food grains) and containers. POL handling berths and other facilities were added at Kandla, Bombay, Cochin and Visakhapatnam. A new fertilizer berth with fertilizer unloading equipment was completed at Cochin. The first modern container terminal was commissioned in December, 1982 at Madras port. Additional general cargo berths were commissioned at Kandla, Mormugao, New Mangalore, Tuticorin, Visakhapatnam and Paradeep.

3.3.5. Seventh Five Year Plan Period (1985-90) and Annual Plans (1990-92)

The remarkable development during the Seventh Plan period was commissioning of Nhava Sheva Port (now known as Jawaharlal Nehru Port).[4] The other important developments were:

(a) Deepening of outer harbour at Madras from 14m to 16.2m to cater to 1,30,000 DWT size ore carriers ;

(b) Commissioning of second oil berth at Madras port ;

(c) Commissioning of a captive berth for handling fertilizers at Paradeep port;

(d) Acquisition of container handling equipment at the ports of Bombay and Cochin.

The main developments during the Annual Plans 1990-92 were:

(a) Commissioning of second oil jetty at Haldia ;

(b) Completion of construction of barge unloading jetty at Mormugao for handling iron ore, and ;

(c) Completion of extension of container terminal at Madras port.

3.3.6. Eighth Five Year Plan (1992-97) and Ninth Five Year Plan (1997-2002)

In the realm of economic reform launched in mid-1991, the stress on infrastructure assumed added significance during two Five Year Plan periods. The concept of privatisation of major ports and corporatisation of some ports took its shape in this decade. The Rakesh Mohan Committee appointed by the Government of India submitted its report on present state of infrastructure and the future trend for 10 years (1996-2006).[5]

Some of the major developments in this decade are:

(a) Container terminal was commissioned at JNPT and Tuticorin port with private participation. The JNPT container terminal has been completed with the collaboration of the Pacific and Orient ports (P & O ports) of Australia at a cost of $170 million. The Tuticorin terminal, costing $21 million, was executed under a tie-up with the port of Singapore Authority.

(b) The fifth oil jetty in Kandla has been completed with an investment of $5 million with Indian Farmers and Fertilizer Cooperative (IFFCO) while the work for another facility was completed in the same port having tieing with Indian Oil Corporation at a cost of $20 million.[6]

(c) Two mega projects, namely, construction of a new port at Ennore and establishment of mechanised coal handling facility at Paradeep port costing a total of Rs. 19 billion with financial assistance from Asian Development Bank (ADB) were completed.

Admittedly, India having a vast coastline, the ports have a critical role in India's trade. But after four decades of independence India followed a policy of economic self-reliance to be achieved through import substitution. With the reform programme initiated in 1991, export-led growth was became one of the prime objectives of economic policy. With India now declaring its ambition for globalisation, international trade will play a crucial role and the role of Indian ports will be even more critical. Though economic reform was started in the mid-nineties the infrastructure sector had not got due attention till 1996.

3.4. Rakesh Mohan Committee Report and Port Infrastructure

3.4.1. Even though most of the Indian ports have completed forty years of their operation, still they are costlier than other ports in the region for handling containers. The additional cost burden due to use of second and third generation vessels has been estimated at US$250 million a year, container delays at Indian Ports cost US$70 million a year. The Government of India constituted a committee under the chairmanship of Rakesh Mohan to identify the bottlenecks in the sector and to suggest measures for augmenting resources and removing constraints to make the sector a catalyst for economic growth in the country. Rakesh Mohan Committee Report on India Infrastructure which was submitted to Government of India on June 22,1996 recommends the following for the development of ports.[7]

- Port authorities be permitted to raise resources from the primary market by way of debt and equity and from financial institutions.
- Major port trust boards be delegated powers to incur capital expenditure upto Rs. 500 million to facilitate speedy creation and operation of assets.
- The Major Port Trust Act, 1963 be amended to permit expansion of projects to be taken up on a Build-Operate-Transfer (BOT) basis.

- Options of leasing out berths or other assets, wherever it is cost effective, be considered.
- A moving away from a monolithic pay structure for workers to a piece-based wage structure.
- At least two ports, one each on the west and east coasts, be developed as mega ports, the warehouse for the Indian subcontinent.
- While commercial operations of the ports be entrusted to existing port authorities with adequate autonomy, a separate regulatory authority to be setup to consider issues relating to pricing and conditions which would govern private sector participation.
- Ports with private participation be continued to be exempted from corporate taxes to augment internal resource base and increase eligibility for raising resources from the market.

3.4.2. A scheme for joint venture formation between major port and minor foreign ports has been finalised. Also similar schemes between major port and minor ports, without tender, and between major port and company following tender route have been considered. The measure aims at facilitating port trust to :

(i) attract new technology ;
(ii) introduce better managerial practices ;
(iii) expedite implementation of schemes ;
(iv) foster strategic alliances with minor ports for creation of optimal port infrastructure.
(v) enhance confidence of private sector in funding ports.

3.4.3. In a sequel to the above recommendations of the committee, tho government has declared some liberalised measures and incentives for privatisation of the ports, such as[0]

- Port will regulate as per the major Port Trust Act.
- An independent Tariff Authority has been established to induce confidence to the investor and have a level playing field.
- Tender with the transparent conditions shall be put on BOT basis.
- Proper feasibility report shall be made at the expense of the port but subsequently recovered from the successful tender.
- Evaluation is made transparent as per the criteria indicated in the tender.
- Concession period is allowed for 30 years.

- Automatic approval of an Indian company with 74 per cent foreign equity is permitted.
- Even upto 100 per cent foreign equity shall be considered by the FIPB (Foreign Investment Promotion Board)
- Tax holiday for 5 years and tax concession for another 5 years within 12 years for infrastructure project are granted.
- Custom duties for imported equipment are drastically reduced.
- Subscription to debentures or equity of companies engaged in infrastructure would qualify for income tax relief for the investor.
- Infrastructure Development Financing Company (IDFC) has been setup for financing infrastructure project.
- HUDCO also proposed to finance such projects.
- Model tender document has been prepared.
- Bankable agreement has also been prepared so that the entrepreneurs would be able to raise funds.

3.4.4. The Special Committee for infrastructure paved the way for removing the bottlenecks and ensured smooth progress under BOT concept.[9]

- Leasing out existing assets of the port has been allowed.
- Construction and creation of additional assets, such as ;
  - (a) Construction and operation of container terminals.
  - (b) Construction and operation of bulk, break-bulk, multipurpose and specialised cargo berths.
  - (c) Warehousing container freight stations storage facilities and tank farms.
  - (d) Cranage and handling equipment
  - (e) Setting up of captive power plants.
  - (f) Dry-docking and ship repair facilities.
- Leasing of equipment for port handling and leasing of floating crafts from the private sector.
- Pilotage
- Captive facilities for port based industries including captive oil facilities.

3.5. Different Schemes of Port Privatisation

3.5.1. There are different schemes available under the privatisation concept. The Government of India has preferred the Build-Operate-Transfer

(BOT) scheme in the infrastructure facilities such as port, roads etc. This approach mitigates risks associated with infrastructure project to a level of acceptance to the private sector. It also assures that profits generated do commensurate with the risks. In BOT concept, a contractual agreement is made where a private investor finances, constructs, operates and maintains the port facility for a concession period after which the facility is transferred to the port authority at no cost.

3.5.2. Besides adding credibility to the project, the BOT Scheme can also lead to significant cost economies accruing out of a more focused private control and economic interest in design, construction, technology and operation of the project. The continued involvement of the sponsors during the life of the concession also implies a constant transfer of technology. A successful BOT project means that the government creates vital infrastructure without putting pressure on budgetary funds, and thus creates facility with better efficiency of operation. Unless all involved work in cohesion with proactive thinking, coordination, cooperation, mutual trust and in a continuous manner, the complex BOT cannot lead to success.[10]

3.5.3. Similarly another scheme is Design-Build-Finance-Operate (DBFO). Here the private operator has the flexibility to design the project to minimise the maintenance costs, which could be one per cent of the total project cost per annum. The cost is recovered by the annuity method, i.e., a fixed annual return accrues to the project operator in a pre-determined manner, irrespective of various other considerations.[11]

3.5.4. Build-Own-Operate-Transfer (BOOT) is broadly similar to BOT but ownership of project assets is more explicit and may also encompass underlying infrastructure. The project reverts to the government on completion of the stipulated period. Build-Own-Operate-Sell (BOOS) basis, where the government buys the infrastructure from the franchisee after the end of the franchisee period.

3.6. Privatisation of Indian Ports : Some Experiences

3.6.1. The first major port to increase private participation in terminal operations was the Jawaharlal Nehru Port Trust (JNPT), Mumbai. The privatisation was relatively easy. It was a comparatively new port. It had a small labour force and was established under a different Act. Private players were invited to construct and commission a container terminal at JNPT located at Nhava Sheva under a BOT agreement with a 30-year concession period. The offer was taken up by a consortium of P & O Terminals (49 per cent), Konsortium Perkepalan Berhad a Malasian logistic group (46 per cent) and DBP Port Management, a Mumbai Stevedoring Company (5 per cent). The new container terminal was commissioned in April 1999 by the Nhava Sheva International Container Terminal Limited, the SPV Company.[12]

3.6.2. With Nhava Sheva setting the pace, the government proposed private participation in other major ports as well in the form of leasing and creation of new assets. The Mumbai Port Trust has since licensed two of its berths to the shipping lines XCL / Orient and has allowed the private sector to provide all its container handling equipment, except the ship-to-shore gantry cranes. It is seeking private investment for the development of a chemical and coal berth.

3.6.3. A competitively bid container terminal concession in Tuticorin was also awarded to PSA Corporation-Sical for a period of 30 years. The terminal has been in operation for the last two years. A 30 year BOT contract for the operation of container berths at Chennai is likely to be signed soon with P & O plans for private development of bulk berths in New Mangalore are under way. Meanwhile, a BOT contract has been signed with P & O ports for a $43 million container terminal at Kandla port. And a BOOT contract has been signed with ABG for $55 million for two coal berths at Mormugao port.

Table 3.1
Private Sector Participation in Indian Port Projects

	No. of projects	*Capacity (To be created)*	*Amount (Rs. Billion)*
Already approved	17	60.05 MT	45.26
Under bidding process	4	27.40 MT	29.00
Bids yet to be invited	3	5.0 MT	4.50
Total identified projects	24	92.45 MT	78.76

Source : Indian Infrastructure, Vol. 3, No. 12, New Delhi July 2001.

3.7. Present Scenario of Private Sector Participation in Indian Ports

3.7.1. In response to governments initiatives, the private sector participation in the major ports has been quite enthusiastic. Most of the Indian ports are working beyond their capacity. So to cope with the requirement the private participation is necessary. Table 3.1 reveals that out of 24 projects identified for the private sector participation, 17 projects have already been approved, which will add capacity of 60.05 MT at various ports with an investment of Rs. 45.26 billion. Some of these projects are already operational. These projects include a capacity of 16.80 MT of containers handling at JNPT, Tuticorin, Kandla and Chennai, 28.50 MT of POL handling at JNPT and Kandla, 3.00 MT of coal handling at Tuticorin and Mumbai, 2.50 MT of fertiliser at Paradeep and Kandla and 9.25 MT of General Cargo Handling at Mormugao, Visakhapatnam and Haldia.

3.7.2. There are about 4 projects under bidding process, which will add to the capacity of 27.40 MT with an estimated investment of Rs. 29.00 billion. The capacity addition will be for the container handling by 7.4 MT at Mumbai and Cochin, coal by 5.00 MT at New Mangalore, POL and other chemicals by 15 MT at JNPT. Three more projects are ready for the private sector participation for which the bids are likely to be invited. These projects which will contribute an additional capacity of 5 million tonnes with the total investment of Rs. 450 crores includes 2 MT of multipurpose berths at Visakhapatnam, 3 MT of liquid chemical berth at Mumbai and Barge handling facilities (capacity not yet finalised) at Kandla.

3.8. Private Sector Participation in Indian Minor Ports

3.8.1. While there has been limited success in major ports, the maritime boards and minor ports have been quite successful in developing port concessions. The first State port to be concessioned to a private party was Krishnapatnam, in Andhra Pradesh, in 1997. It was intended to handle coal for a large power plant. This was followed by a concession agreement for Adewadi Port in Maharashtra.[13]

3.8.2. Gujarat has been by far the most active State in attracting private players. Two private ports – Mundra and Pipavav have already become operational. Mundra is a bulk port being developed by Gujarat Adani Port Limited. Pipvav port is under Public–Private ownership through a joint venture of Seaking Engineering and the Gujarat Maritime Board.

Andhra Pradesh, Tamil Nadu and Orissa have also invited private participation to develop minor ports by offering leases upto 50 years for developing new port projects. On the West Coast, the Government of Karnataka and Kerala have identified a number of minor ports for creating commodity-specific facilities.

3.9. Privatisation of Foreign Ports: Recent Trends

3.9.1. Privatisation, the sale or lease of the assets of public sector enterprises to private sector has gained prominence in the developed and developing world. The private sector has become increasingly involved in the operation of common-user port facilities during the 1990s, following public sector dominance of the sector since the 1940s. During the past decade the reform of port administration has gained momentum in industrial and developing countries alike. Between 1990 and 1998, 112 port projects with private participation reached financial closure in 28 developing countries, with investment commitments totalling more than $9 billion.(Table 3.2)

3.9.2. The shift towards private involvement has been driven by two main factors.[14]

(i) The strong growth in world trade has led captive port users – unable to switch to other transport modes, such as railways or airports, or to other ports – to put enormous political pressures on authorities to improve handling efficiency, reduce port user fees, and expand facilities to accommodate larger cargo flows. Yet many public port authorities have had only limited success in improving labour and other practices to increase the productivity and efficiency of existing installations.

(ii) Economies of scale in cargo shipment have led to the emergence of a few global players in shipping, able to control the allocation of transshipment business to strategically located, well-equipped and efficiently managed hub ports. To stay competitive, port authorities have to modernise and upgrade port facilities to meet the needs of the large shipping lines. But with larger ships, the advance of containerisation and the introduction of sophisticated cargo information systems, the investment required has often gone beyond the financial and managerial capacities of public port authorities.

Table 3.2
Port Projects with Private Participation in Developing Countries by Region, 1990-98

Sl. No.	*Region*	*No. of Projects*	*Total Investment (1998, $ Million)*
1.	East Asia and the Pacific	38	5,410.5
2.	Europe and Central Asia	8	23.4
3.	Latin America and the Caribbean	48	2,497.7
4.	Middle East and North Africa	5	376.5
5.	South Asia	9	942.6
6.	Sub-Saharan Africa	4	32.0
	Total	**112**	**9,282.7**

Source: Indian Infrastructure, Vol. 2, No. 7, New Delhi. February 2000.

3.9.3. Table 3.2 reveals the picture of unevenly distribution of investment in port infrastructure. This regional pattern is also largely consistent with trends in other infrastructure sectors, such as electricity and water sewerage. From the above table, Latin America and East Asia have clearly led the trend in private involvement in port operations, both in the number of projects reaching financial closure and in investment commitments.[15] Privatisation has become an instrument used by many countries mainly to improve efficiency, resource mobilisation and increase the private sector contribution to economic growth. In recent years, many industrialised countries like Italy, France, Japan and Spain have launched major privatisation programme.[16]

Experience in China

3.9.4. The Shanghai Port Authority (SPA) and Hutchigon Whampoa Ltd.(HWL) formed a joint venture between their subsidiaries Shanghai Port Container Comprehensive Development Company (SPCCDC) and Hutchison Ports Shanghai Ltd. (HPSL) to own and operate all of Shanghai's container port facilities. The contract was formalised in August 1993 when HPSL injected RMB 1 billion in cash and SPCCDC contributed RMB 1 billion in assets to the new company Shanghai Container Terminals Ltd. (SCT). The 50-50 Joint Venture Plans to invest RMB 5.6 billion during the next six years. It also has preferential rights to develop container terminals at Wai Gao Qiao in Pudong and the proposed new deep water facility at Jin Shan Zui along Hanghouw Bay. During its first year of operation, the joint venture handled 25 per cent more containers than had been channelled through Shanghai's container terminal during the preceding twelve months.

Thus the Shanghai Port Authority choose to become a joint venture partner in its own container terminals including new BOT development. This approach had several benefits. It introduced new management expertise into existing operations. It provided immediate revenue streams to the development team and it reduced the investment to be borne by the foreign partner. Finally, it ensured that the port authority would have a full (commercial) say in operations and performance.

Experience in Europe

3.9.5. Most ports in Europe other than UK operate on the landlord concept where the local municipality is the owner and custodian of infrastructure. However, they have a great amount of autonomy and utilise experts from the private sector to manage the ports. In the two main ports of Germany, i.e., Hamburg and Breman the infrastructure is owned and maintained by the local governments. In Hamburg the various terminals are leased to operators including the public company HHLA. Both Stevedoring and terminal operations are performed by various companies in the port of Bremen and Bremerhaven, the infrastructure is owned and leased to private operators. The terminal operations in container terminals include both ship and shore working and are exclusively performed by the joint venture company BLG where the municipality owns 51 per cent and private sector 49 per cent of the shares of the company. In both cases pilotage services are rendered by the governments authority and tugboat services, are provided by private operators. In Belgium and Netherlands, limited infrastructure consisting of the sea wall fairways are provided and maintained by the local municipality. The municipality also provides dredging with financial participation by the national government. All other infrastructure and services are provided by private operators.

Experience in Rotterdam

3.9.6. The world's largest port Rotterdam is a firm proponent of a public private partnership. The government provides the channel reclaims the terminal site if required and establishes bank protection. Major seaward expansion beyond the existing maasvlaket is being studied and if new breakwaters are required, these will also be publicly funded. In addition, the government ensures that the off site infrastructure (road, railway and utilities) are in place. The BOT developer is responsible for site preparation and surfacing berth construction and all equipments and structure. The port of Rotterdam identifies the type of activity it wishes to see/develop in the ports and then works closely with successful bidder to craft an agreement which bodes well for its tenant's future commercial success. Rotterdam sees nothing to be gained by an incomplete project or an abandoned enterprise.

Financial arrangements are negotiated with the developer's business plan in view. Lease payments are correspondingly agreed. Because Rotterdam is focused on increasing trade through the Netherlands and because it will itself benefit from the collection of harbour dues, it doesn't seek to capture an increasing share of the operator's income instead because the port wants to encourage the operator to pursue traffic growth. It accepts declining percentage of shared revenues as throughput increases. Finally Rotterdam imposes neither standards of performance nor controls on tariffs. Rotterdam assumes that competitive pressure within the region will suffice to enhance the one and limit the other. It also assumes that the operator/developers profit motivation will ensure maximum efficiency without the port becoming an overzealous regulator.

Experience in Singapore

3.9.7. Singapore has the reputation of not only being one of the world's business ports with one of the largest cargo tonnage but also one of the most efficient ones. The port of Singapore Authority which is a statutory body set up by government is a corporate entity that manages and operates the port of Singapore. It also has direct interactions in more than 8 subsidiary and associate companies supporting port services. The authority, which operates like a separate corporate entity, enjoys a great deal of autonomy in the management and operations of the port. The port has for a number of years been able to exclusively fund its own development plans. The port is able to not only set its tariff but also to revise individual items of tariff rather than its complete tariff at any time when costs or market conditions require the same.

Experience in Hong Kong

3.9.8. Hong Kong provides the Shipping Channel and most of the inland infrastructure links. Project developers have done the rest including reclaiming developing and equiping the terminal site. Now, that the Kwaichujng container area is fully developed, HongKong plans to direct future growth to an entirely new site on Lanta Island. Because this greenfield, location will be more costly to develop and may prove less immediately appealing to port user, the Hong Kong Government has been considering a revised approach. Accordingly the public share of development costs may increase for the initial stage of Lantau development until the new site is commercially well established

Additionally, Hongkong recognises the importance of income during construction. Onc justification given by the Hong Kong Government of frequently awarding new development rights to one or another operators already active in Hong Kong is that these parties have the ongoing revenue stream necessary to allow them to undertake the massive investments necessary for each new terminal. The Government of Hong Kong declines to involve itself in either tariffs or performance. These matters are left to the competitive market place to determine Hong Kong also receives no revenue share from port operations other than that paid through income taxation. Once the base BOT fee is agreed, the private operator is in full control aside from statutory safety and environmental regulation.

Experience in Philippines

3.9.9. The Philippines have adopted broad legislation specifically for BOT projects, ports as well as other activities fall under its purview. It has gone even further by creating a powerful department within the president's office specifically to promote BOT projects. The Manila International Container Terminal (North Harbour) is being operated by a joint venture private company (Australian / Philippines) on a long-term lease basis. When the Philippines Ports Authority sought to expand its South Harbour Container Terminal, it adopted two stage bid process. Bidders were required to bid both upgrading and operating the existing facility (Under a landlord arrangement) as well as on the expansion BOT component of the project. The successful developer was thus permitted to take over an existing operation even as he commenced investment on its expansion. He was thereby assured of a cash flow from the outset.

This also permitted the developer to commence his operational and market development programme from the first day which provided a higher level of confidence that the new berths would smoothly integrate into the terminal's operation and attract traffic from the day to doors open. An important ancillary consideration is that this shifted to the terminal operator the full responsibility and interest in ensuring that the ongoing BOT construction in no way interfered with current operation at the port. The Philippines ports authority build into the contract stringent deadlines on completion of each phase of the expansion to ensure that the successful bidder did not focus only on business in hand and postpone his committed investment.[17]

3.10. Port Financing in India: Some Issues

3.10.1. The total investment proposed in the port sector during the Ninth Five Year Plan period (1997-2002) is Rs. 135.5 billion. Of this, internal resources of the ports will account for Rs. 52.9 billion, Central Budgetary support for Rs. 12.6 billion and the balance requirement of Rs. 70 billion to be generated through private sector investment. Private investment in the port sector has become crucial. The government is increasingly reducing its subsidy to the sector. On the top of this, there has been erosion of the net surplus over the years. The total net surplus generated by the major Indian ports in 1998-99 was Rs. 11.03 billion, in 1999-2000 it came down to Rs. 8.14 billion and in 2000-01, there was a net deficit of Rs. 4.07 billion.[18]

3.10.2. Despite liberalised rules for private participation and several incentives offered by the government financing port projects remains a grey area. Uncertainties cloud such crucial issues as the rate of return and the level of comfort available to banks and financial institutions supporting private port projects. Port projects (greenfield, BOT, BOOT, etc.) are financed more conservatively, typically through a debt-equity ratio of 60:40 (as compared to the power sector's 70:30). This is because there are no traffic guarantees. Lenders can only draw comfort from the assurance of captive users promising committed usage, preferably over the medium or long term. As a result, banks and financial institutions are somewhat wary of financing this section.

3.10.3. However, multilateral agencies that have a larger developmental role have been involved in port financing, especially in greenfield projects. Among multilateral agencies, the World Bank is the biggest source of aid for the sector in India. It has provided four loans and credit amounting to $420 million to date. The World Bank's Private arm, the International Finance Corporation (IFC), has been an active participant in providing both debt and equity. The Asian Development Bank (ADB) is also a significant player.[19]

Debt Financing

3.10.4. In India, the leading domestic financial institutions (FIs) in the area of port financing are ICICI, IDBI, IFCI and IDFC. These have been more active in funding private port projects such as Dhamra (ICICI), Adani (IFCI) and Pipavav (IDBI). Domestic banks such as Canara Bank and Punjab National Bank also provide loans to port projects, mostly in conjunction with domestic FIs. ANZ, Standard Chartered and HSBC are the most prominent foreign banks involved in the sector. Among multilateral agencies, the World Bank, IFC, ADB, Commonwealth Development Corporation (CDC) and JBIC are the most active in the sector.

Equity Financing

3.10.5. The promoters of the SPV companies are usually foreign and domestic ports, shipping agents, stevedoring companies, construction companies O & M companies, shipping lines or other companies involved in the port sector. Foreign companies are allowed to hold 100 per cent equity in the SPV company. Some of the foreign companies operating in the port sector in India are P & O ports (of Australia), PSA, Stevedoring Services of the US, Maersk Shipping and Precious Shipping of Thailand. Several multilateral agencies have also contributed to the equity in SPVs. These are ADB (which is likely to pickup equity in Ennore) and CDC of the UK (in Pipavav). Globally, institutional investors, including pension funds, insurance companies and investment funds are also active equity participants. But this is not the case in India.

3.11. Regulatory Issues

3.11.1. The port sector lacks an independent, full-fledged regulatory authority. The only regulation is in the form of the Tariff Authority for Major Ports (TAMP), created in 1997. TAMP, however is only a tariff regulatory authority, that too, for only the major ports, excluding Ennore. Unlike the Central Electricity Regulatory Commission (CERC) in the power sector or the Telecom Regulatory Authority of India (TRAI) in the telecom sector, TAMP is not vested with very many powers. The new issues, such as those arising from the corporatisation and privatisation of ports, as well as the working of ports and their safety aspects, need to be under a regulator.

3.11.2. Currently, the port sector is governed by a plethora of complex laws and regulations. These include the Indian Ports Act (1908), the Major Port Trusts Act (1963), the Inland Vessels Act (1917), the Coastal Vessels Act (1838), the Merchant Shipping Act (1958), the Dock Workers (Regulation of Employment) Act (1948) and the Dock Workers (Safety, Health and Welfare) Act (1986). The financial institutions are of the view that all these acts should be consolidated into a single law.

3.12. Corporation of Indian Ports

3.12.1. Most of the ports in the country are presently run as trusts and have very little accountability. They have been showing net surpluses by ignoring prudential norms. Depreciation is either under provided or not provided at all. In an effort to make the ports more accountable, the union Government is exploring the option of corporatisation. Under this, the port trust is converted into an economically independent company run by a professional board of directors under the companies Act.[20] The idea behind corporatisation is to lower costs, increase productivity and quality of service as well as enforce greater accountability and transparency in port functioning. This, in turn, should facilitate better access to the capital markets and strategic investor's funds. It would also help in adapting to market changes.

Corporatisation of Ennore Port

3.12.2. The first port to be corporatised in the country is Ennore. A new port located 24 kms north of Chennai, Ennore Port has been designated as the twelfth major port of India. The port is being developed in two phases. Phase I consists of two captive coal handling berths for vessels upto 65,000 dwt along with the construction of break waters, harbour basin, approach channel and development of other port facilities. The port financed by the Chennai Port Trust and the Asian Development Bank (ADB), will be used by the Tamil Nadu Electricity Board (TNEB) for the transportation of coal. The first phase started commercial operation on June 22, 2001.

3.12.3. Though the port has been corporatised, its final debt-equity structure is still to be decided. Currently, the Union Government is the principal equity holder. The ADB and the Chennai Port Trust have expressed unwillingness to convert their loans into equity. Some equity will be offered to TNEB. Subsequently, fresh equity will be issued to fund the second phase of development, which is estimated to cost Rs. 5,162 million. This equity is likely to be picked up by the major port trusts, operators, captive users and others and will bc issued at a premium. Phase II will look at development through private sector participation on a BOT basis. The Union Government will provide the basic infrastructure. In this phase, there are plans to setup 12 berths, including two each for handling POL products, coal and general cargo; and one each for handling fertilizers, acids, chemicals, LNG and limestone. Ennore port has been incorporated as Ennore Port Company Limited under the Indian Companies Act and Indian Ports Act. The modalities for transferring the port assets to the corporatised entity are still being worked out.

Haldia Port

3.12.4. Haldia is another port that is looking at the corporatisation option. A model for this is currently being studied in consultation with the Calcutta Port Trust (CPT). However, CPT will continue to hold 100 per cent stake in the corporatised entity. In future, if the Government and CPT want, they can divest part of CPT's stake to one or a consortium of strategic investors. Haldia's divestment process will be different from other ports, where the Union Government is itself the promoter.

Jawaharlal Nehru Port Trust (JNPT)

3.12.5. Jawaharlal Nehru Port Trust (JNPT), one of the more recently designated major ports, is also on the list. JNPT is a profitable port. Its net surplus grew from Rs. 622 million in 1995 to Rs. 2,355 million in 1999. However, its debt burden too increased significantly. Consultants have recommended a debt-equity ratio of 1: 2.9 for the corporatised ports. The government has decided to convert the outstanding loan of Rs. 4.5 billion, taken from the World Bank for constructing the Port, into equity. Other loans taken by JNPT will be treated as the debt component. The proposed equity of Rs. 3.7 billion will be used to pay off the arrears.[21] JNPT has already appointed consultants for valuation of its assets and liabilities. The debt-equity profile will change when the debt is rapid by the company set up for operating and managing the port.[22] While the process of corporatisation has moved apace, a number of changes are called for.

First, it would entail a change in legislation establishing the major port trusts. Second, it would make the ports liable for corporate tax, something they are loath to incur. Third, it would make the management legally liable for its actions while taking away its civil service protection. Fourth, the issue of labour resistance will need to be addressed.

Other Ports

3.12.6. The port of Mormugao, New Mangalore and Tuticorin are also in the process of appointing consultants for valuation of their assets and liabilities.[23]

3.13. Problems of Major Ports

3.13.1. The Indian ports have long been plagued by many problems. The reasons for the low capacity and poor productivity of Indian major ports can be classified broadly into the following three categories viz., physical problems, institutional problems and financial problems.[24]

1. Physical Problems

3.13.2. ***Civil Port facilities:*** The lay out of many berths is outdated with low draft and insufficient space on the berths. The storage area at the port is also insufficient. The problems are further compounded by poor maintenance; high siltation necessitating increased dredging requirements, corrosion of the berth, poor conditions of road and storage areas. These factors increase the cost of transportation and affect movement of cargo.

3.13.3. ***Port Equipment*:** A port requires a wide range of equipment for its operations, e. g., quay cranes, mobile cranes, forklift trucks, trailers, reach stackers etc. For optimum efficiency, the mix of these equipment should be balanced and match the requirements of the cargo. Unfortunately, this is not so, equipment is quite outdated and of lower capacity. Moreover, the maintenance of equipment is very limited. According to a World Bank Report of 1997: "At Bombay's Indira Dock some 85 per cent of the electric Wharf Cranes are of 1955 – 65 vintage, two-thirds have a capacity of only 3 tonnes; and the 4 per cent of all cranes have a capacity of more than 6 tonnes. As a result, they are under – utilised, while they are available 85 to 90 per cent of the time, their utilization rate is only 20 per cent to 24 per cent". Most conventional cargo handling equipment would be obsolete if the criteria set by the Indian Ports Association and the Bombay and Madras Port Trusts were effectively applied.

2. Institutional Problems

3.13.4. *Organisational set-up*: The 12 major ports are under the control of Government of India (GOI) while the minor ports are under the control of the respective states. The major ports are organized as statutory corporations controlled by Trusts and act as service ports with no profit motivation. The operational freedom is greatly restricted with limited delegation of authority from the government. This invariably leads to delay in decision making in almost all areas of operation and administration.

3.13.5. *Staff and Labour*: Major Indian ports are not grossly over-staffed but also suffer from high unionisation of the work force. At the end of 1994, the establishment and work force of major ports was over 99, 000 casual workers under unregistered complementary labour force. Added to this the port labour is hostile and inefficient. It is also opposed to reforms. Consequently, labour productivity is abysmally low in Indian ports.

3.13.6. *Lack of co-ordination among outside agencies:* Broadly, there are three agencies involved in cargo handling at a port, besides the port authorities themselves viz. stevedoring companies, customs authorities and transport operators. Poor co-ordination among these organizations and different departments of the port itself, results in duplication of work, poor dissemination of information on cargo, loss of time, poor equipment, space and vehicle allocation and utilisation.

3. Financial Problems

3.13.7. *Financing of capital investment*: There are two kinds of investments required in port sector viz., for upgradation and for new facilities. While the total surplus generated by major ports is substantial and could take care of some part of investment requirements of ports in upgradation, it is subject to numerous government controls. However, recently the Government of India has delegated some authority to port trusts and now the port trusts can approve projects upto Rs. 1,000 millions. This is a welcome step and would help ports in buying equipment to improve their capacity and efficiency.

Regulated Tariffs

3.13.8. The overall level of port tariffs is modest and not cost-related. Tariff revision is also regulated by GOI, which permits such revision every three years and that too in small increments. The private sector has been demanding freedom to fix tariffs to enhance project viability. Though some State Governments have agreed to this demand, GOI has decided to set up a new regulatory authority to revise tariffs every three years. In sum the productivity of Indian ports is constrained by outdated equipment and facilities, hostile and bloated inefficient labour force and numerous government controls.

3.14. Implementation of Voluntary Retirement Scheme (VRS) in the Reform Era in Indian Ports

3.14.1. Rationalisation of manpower is one of the major aspects of increasing the efficiency as well as operating surplus of the port. The conventional old ports like Mumbai, Calcutta and Chennai have surplus manpower working at the port. The on-going economic reform in the country envisages the downsizing of the existing surplus manpower in the port sector. At present, the Mumbai port employs about 30,000 employees and handles 13 MT of cargo of which handling of more than 50 per cent is fully mechanised. In contrast, JNPT adjacent to Mumbai employs around 2000 workers to handle 14 MT of cargo. An internal study has identified that 14,000 employees of Mumbai port are redundant. As a sequel to this the Indian Ports viz. Mumbai, New Mangalore, Tuticorin and Calcutta port trusts have rolled back the age of retirement from 60 to 58 years. The Mumbai Port Trust (MbPT) announced a special VRS in January 2001, aiming at reducing the total workforce by 7000 from the existing 30,000 employees. And the MbPT succeeded in bringing down the total employees to 23,190 by an expenditure of Rs. 450 crores. However, the MbPT needs to reduce it further to 10,000 persons.[25]

3.14.2. The port trust and DLBs would finance the VRS from their own resources. The Government had categorically denied any budgetary support or in the form of loan for this purpose. According to the 1991 VRS, an employee who has completed 10 years of service at the port or completed 40 years of age can opt for VRS. Employees will be allowed two months salaries for each year of service completed. On an average every worker will be getting around Rs. 4-5 lakh. A national tribunal has been appointed by the Central Government for assessment of the manning levels in various areas of operation on all port basis and has commenced its proceedings. Rationalisation of manning levels on the basis of the award of this tribunal will give further surplus. Meanwhile, efforts are on to continue the numbers with ban on recruitment and meeting of operational requirements through retraining and deployment.[26]

3.15. Performance Analysis of Indian Ports

3.15.1. Aggregate Port Capacity and Traffic Handled at Indian Major Ports during the Five Year Plans.

Table 3.3 portrays the trend of aggregate port capacity and traffic handled at the Indian Major Ports including the percentage of during the Five Year Plans. The aggregate port capacity increased to more than ten times from 20 MT at the beginning of the First Five Year Plan to 220 MT at end of the Eighth Five Year Plan and projected to be 344 MT by the end of Ninth Five Year Plan. Similarly the traffic handled at major ports also demonstrates an upward trend during the different Five Year Plans. At the beginning of the First Five Year Plan the total traffic handled by Indian Major Ports was 23 MT which increased significantly to 227 MT at the end of Eighth Five Year Plan and 281 MT as on 31st March 2002 and further projected to handle 289 MT at the end of the Ninth Five Year Plan. The capacity utilisation during the different plans also exhibits satisfactory performances in terms of maximum percentage of utilisation of port capacity. The liberalised economic policy of the government particularly the EXIM policy during the nineties and the special emphasis for the development of the infrastructure from Mid-90's of the successive governments saw a drastic change in the development of the sea trade in the country. At the same time the government's decision to allow private sectors to play a major role in the development of infrastructure in general and port infrastructure in particular increased the operational efficiency and overall productivity of the port significantly during the period.

3.15.2. Traffic Handled at Major Ports during 1999-2000

Table 3.4 reveals the major port-wise total traffic (overseas and coastal) loaded and unloaded in 1999-2000. This has been presented in Fig. 3.1. The total traffic handled at all major ports in 1999-2000 was 271.923 tonnes, of which the total overseas traffic was 194009 tonnes (71.3 per cent) and coastal traffic 77914 tonnes (28.7 per cent). Among the ports, Kandla port handled the highest of 46303 tonnes (17 per cent) of the total 271923 tonnes and Tuticorin port has handled the lowest traffic of 9993 tonnes (4 per cent) during the same year. The cargo traffic loaded at the

Table 3.3
Aggregate Port Capacity and Traffic Handled at Indian Major Ports during the Five Year Plans

Period	*Agg. port capacity (in MT)*	*Traffic handled (in MT)*	*Capacity utilisation (in per cent)*
At the beginning of First Five Year Plan (1951-56)	20	23	115
At the end of Second Five Year Plan (1956-61)	38	33	87
At the end of Third Five Year Plan (1961-66)	54	50	93
At the end of Fourth Five Year Plan (1969-74)	71	64	90
At the end of Fifth Five Year Plan (1974-79)	101	71	70
At the end of Sixth Five Year Plan (1980-85)	132	106	80
At the end of Seventh Five Year Plan (1985-90)	163	148	91
At the end of Annual Plan (1990-92)	170	158	93
At the end of Eighth Five Year Plan (1992-97)	220	227	103
As on 31.03.2001	291	281	96
At the end of Ninth Five Year Plan (1997-2002)(P)	377	424	112

Source: Indian Ports Association, New Delhi.

ports is regarded as traffic exported and traffic unloaded as traffic imported as per the nomenclature by the Ministry of Shipping, Government of India. From the table it is evident that the share of traffic loaded (both overseas and coastal) of all major ports was 87651 tonnes (32.2 per cent), whereas traffic unloaded (both overseas and coastal) of all major ports stood at 163432 tonnes (60.1 per cent) and transhipment was 20840 tonnes (7.7 per cent) during the year 1999-2000. From the Table it is crystal clear that the cargo traffic unloaded by all major ports was double that of loaded during

Table 3.4

Traffic Handled at Major Ports in India during the Period 1999-2000 (P)

(Overseas and Coastal)

(In Tonnes)

Port	*OVERSEAS*				*COASTAL*				*OVERSEAS & COASTAL*			
	Loaded	*Unloaded*	*Tranship-ment*	*Total*	*Loaded*	*Unloaded*	*Tranship-ment*	*Total*	*Loaded*	*Unloaded*	*Tranship-ment*	*Total*
Kandla	3402	28099	6601	**38102**	266	7935	-	**8201**	3668	36034	6601	**46303**
Mumbai	3904	16637	893	**21434**	6099	2879	-	**8978**	10003	19516	893	**30412**
J.L.Nehru	5831	8068	125	**14024**	72	750	130	**952**	5903	8818	255	**14976**
Mormugao	14784	2278	-	**17062**	145	1007	12	**1164**	14929	3285	12	**18226**
New Mangalore	5911	7963	14	**13888**	3237	476	-	**3713**	9148	8439	14	**17601**
Cochin	850	6956	-	**7806**	1339	3652	-	**4991**	2189	10608	-	**12797**
Tuticorin	2029	3732	-	**5761**	30	4202	-	**4232**	2059	7934	-	**9993**
Chennai	9827	12458	491	**22776**	688	13488	491	**14667**	10515	25946	982	**37443**
Vishakha-patnam	6298	12914	3621	**22833**	8061	4409	4207	**16677**	14359	17323	7828	**39510**
Paradeep	1933	4237	-	**6170**	6927	539	-	**7466**	8860	4776	-	**13636**
Haldia	796	15445	10	**16251**	4031	431	-	**4462**	4827	15876	10	**20713**
Calcutta	935	2722	4245	**7902**	256	2155	-	**2411**	1191	4877	4245	**10313**
All Ports	**56500**	**121509**	**16000**	**194009**	**31151**	**41923**	**4840**	**77914**	**87651**	**163432**	**20840**	**271923**

Source : Government of India, Basic Port Statistics of India, Ministry of Surface Transport, New Delhi, 1999-2000, p. 6.

Fig. 3.1
Traffic Handled at Major Ports during 1999-2000

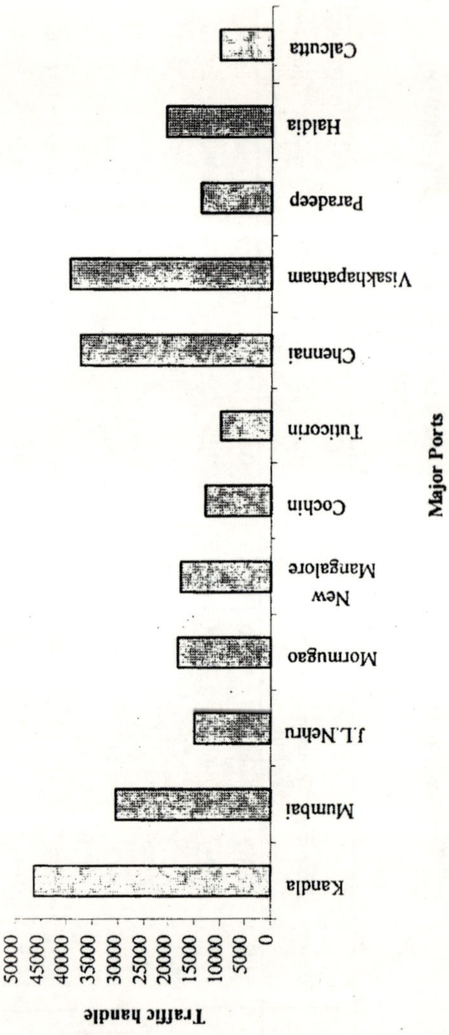

the corresponding year and also the percentage of overseas total traffic is higher than the coastal total traffic which is a good sign of satisfactory performance of the ports and for the overall development of the economy.

3.15.3. Growth of Cargo Traffic Handled at Major Ports in India during 1965-66 to 1998-99

Table 3.5 exhibits the growth of cargo traffic handled at major ports in India during the last 33 years starting from 1965-66 to 1998-99. The Table also explains the year-wise data of cargo loaded and unloaded in overseas and coastal traffic. In 1965-66 the total overseas and coastal traffic loaded and unloaded were 50.22 MT of which overseas traffic was 39.03 MT (77 per cent) and coastal traffic was 11.19 MT (23 per cent). In 1975-76 the total overseas and coastal traffic (loaded and unloaded) was 66 MT with an increase of 31 per cent in ten years. Similarly in 1985-86 and 1995-96 it reached the levels of 119.62 MT and 215.21 MT registering a growth of more than 200 and 400 per cent over the period respectively. Prior to 1990s the volume of trade was declining due to several factors including balance of payment crisis, flight in imports, loss of USSR market and higher custom duty etc. During the mid-90s, the foreign trade showed an annual increase of 10 per cent due to liberalisation and deregulation. In 1998-99 the total cargo traffic handled at major ports (overseas and coastal) reached 251.74 MT, a growth of 500 per cent in comparison to the traffic handled in 1965-66. The total overseas traffic in 1998-99 was 180.07 MT (29 per cent). In 1965-66 the total traffic unloaded (import) was 28.35 MT (56.5 per cent of total traffic) and loaded (export) was 21.87 MT (43.5 per cent of total traffic). In 1998-99 the traffic unloaded and loaded have increased significantly to 164.53 MT (65.4 per cent) and 87.21 MT (34.6 per cent) respectively. The reasons for increase in traffic during the last 33 years can be attributed to the increase in number of major ports with increasing demand for export and import. Private participation in developing the port infrastructure, mechanisation of port equipments and the overall development of the economy contributed substantially for the growth of traffic during the period.

3.15.4. Commodity-wise Cargo Traffic Handled at Major Ports of India during 1960-61 to 1998-99

Table 3.6 envisages the commodity-wise cargo traffic handled at major ports in India from 1960-61 to 1998-99. The Indian ports mainly

Table 3.5

Growth of Cargo Traffic Handled at Major Ports during 1965-66 to 1998-99

(in Million)

Year	Overseas			Coastal			Overseas & coastal		
	Unloaded	*Loaded*	*Total*	*Unloaded*	*Loaded*	*Total*	*Unloaded*	*Loaded*	*Total*
1965-66	22.41	16.62	**39.03**	5.94	5.25	**11.19**	28.35	21.87	**50.22**
1970-71	21.50	26.58	**48.08**	4.06	3.44	**7.50**	25.56	30.02	**55.58**
1975-76	29.13	29.04	**58.17**	4.20	3.63	**7.83**	33.33	32.67	**66.00**
1980-81	39.09	28.50	**67.59**	7.73	4.95	**12.68**	46.82	33.45	**80.27**
1981-82	39.78	32.23	**72.01**	8.61	7.36	**15.97**	48.39	39.59	**87.98**
1982-83	41.08	29.16	**70.24**	10.57	12.89	**23.46**	51.65	42.05	**93.70**
1983-84	38.80	29.07	**67.87**	13.41	15.10	**28.51**	52.21	44.17	**96.38**
1984-85	39.62	33.97	**73.59**	15.71	16.52	**32.23**	55.33	50.49	**105.82**
1985-86	45.82	36.73	**82.55**	22.16	14.91	**37.07**	67.98	51.64	**119.62**
1986-87	43.58	39.79	**83.37**	23.36	17.64	**41.00**	66.94	57.43	**124.37**
1987-88	49.95	40.15	**90.10**	23.39	21.11	**44.50**	73.34	61.26	**134.60**
1988-89	55.40	43.79	**99.19**	25.91	21.96	**47.87**	81.31	65.75	**147.06**
1989-90	54.13	45.26	**99.39**	26.72	21.46	**48.18**	80.85	66.72	**147.57**
1990-91	59.02	43.63	**102.65**	26.07	22.95	**49.02**	85.09	66.58	**151.67**
1991-92	59.91	44.89	**104.80**	26.66	25.18	**51.84**	86.57	70.07	**156.64**
1992-93	74.09	43.28	**117.37**	24.35	24.78	**49.13**	98.44	68.06	**166.50**
1993-94	76.02	53.48	**129.50**	24.81	24.71	**49.52**	100.83	78.19	**179.02**
1994-95	83.60	52.18	**135.78**	29.60	30.51	**60.11**	113.20	82.69	**195.89**
1995-96	94.86	57.24	**152.10**	31.79	31.32	**63.11**	126.65	88.56	**215.21**
1996-97	102.57	57.31	**159.88**	36.64	30.45	**67.09**	139.21	87.76	**226.97**
1997-98	117.36	61.64	**179.00**	38.62	34.04	**72.66**	155.98	95.68	**251.66**
1998-99	125.10	54.97	**180.07**	39.43	32.24	**71.67**	164.53	87.21	**251.74**

Source : Government of India, *Basic Port Statistics of India*, Ministry of Surface Transport, New Delhi, 1999-2000, p. 72.

Table 3.6

Cargo Traffic (Commodity-wise) Handled at Major Ports in India during the Period 1960-61 to 1998-99

(In '000 Tonnes)

Year	POL (Crude & Products)	Fertiliser	Fertiliser Raw Material	Iron Ore	Coal	Food-grains	Others	Total	of which Loaded	of which Unloaded
1960-61	12265	683	208	1333	2131	5157	11348	**33125**	22579	10546
1970-71	18893	1227	1040	19203	675	3193	11348	**55579**	25557	30022
1980-81	33578	4278	1933	22836	2110	975	14560	**80270**	46816	33454
1981-82	34154	2951	2142	25114	3148	2376	18095	**87980**	48391	39589
1982-83	45340	4023	*	22218	4875	2347	14894	**93697**	51648	42049
1983-84	49743	1893	2342	21952	4164	3417	12866	**96377**	52205	44172
1984-85	49004	4226	2915	26041	4422	1313	17902	**105823**	55334	50489
1985-86	54890	4106	2700	28841	7538	1133	20405	**119613**	67974	51639
1986-87	53070	2387	4075	30609	8551	1402	24272	**124366**	66940	57426
1987-88	58917	1417	4165	28748	12788	1672	26895	**134602**	73342	61260
1988-89	63166	1648	4738	32738	15468	3388	25915	**147061**	81310	65751
1989-90	61968	2921	5193	33186	17616	1493	25908	**148285**	80856	67429
1990-91	64004	2879	6064	31904	19659	1528	25627	**151665**	85088	66577
1991-92	67625	3153	6767	32101	22403	1539	23056	**156644**	86569	70075
1992-93	73959	3595	6318	29827	24488	2795	25515	**166497**	97922	68575
1993-94	77265	4183	5291	34096	26806	1964	29414	**179019**	100246	78773
1994-95	80753	4334	6667	34354	30798	1343	37641	**195890**	113201	82689
1995-96	90923	5727	6628	34562	33790	3852	39726	**215208**	126648	88560
1996-97	99050	3327	6588	33260	37530	4182	43032	**226969**	139207	87762
1997-98	105343	4825	7610	39611	42295	3996	47978	**251658**	155975	95683
1998-99	108231	4754	7812	32820	42869	4713	50539	**251738**	164530	87208

* Included in Fertiliser

Source : Government of India, *Basic Port Statistics of India*, Ministry of Surface Transport, New Delhi, 1999-2000, p. 74.

handle commodities like POL (crude and products), fertiliser, fertiliser raw material, iron-ore, coal, food grains and others. In 1960-61, the total cargo traffic handled at major ports was 33.1 MT of which 22.5 MT (68 per cent) unloaded i.e. imported and 10.5 MT (32 per cent) loaded i.e., exported. POL occupies the top position (37 per cent) in total commodities handled in the corresponding year. In 1970-71 and 1980-81 the total cargo handled through all major ports was increased to 55.5 MT (an increase of 68 per cent over 1960-61) and 80.27 MT (an increase of 44 per cent over 1970-71) respectively. In 1998-99 the total cargo handled at major ports was 251.74 MT of which 164.54 MT (65 per cent) unloaded and 87.2 MT (35 per cent) loaded. In 1998-99 also the POL contributes the highest cargo traffic of 108.24 (43 per cent) at all major ports, which was 41 per cent in 1997-98. Foodgrains contribute the least percentage (1.9 per cent) of total traffic handled in 1998-99. India imports huge quantity of crude oil from the oil exporting countries to meet its increasing energy demand. Thus, the POL products share at the major ports remains the highest in almost every year of the study. The traffic of other commodities also increased at different ports due to demand from the respective exporting and importing countries.

3.15.5. Trend of Cargo Traffic Handled at Indian Major and Minor Ports during 1989-90 to 1998-99

Table 3.7 envisages the trend of cargo traffic handled at Indian major and minor ports for 10 years from 1989-90 to 1998-99. The table also explains the cargo traffic of overseas and coastal with loaded and loaded parameters. In 1989-90 the total overseas traffic of major ports was 99.39 MT (67.4 per cent) and coastal traffic was 48.18 MT (32.6 per cent) of the total traffic handled by major ports. In 1998-99 the total overseas traffic reached 180.07 MT (71.6 per cent) and total coastal traffic was 71.67 MT (28.4 per cent) of the total traffic handled by major ports. Similarly the total overseas traffic (loaded and unloaded) of minor ports in 1989-90 was 8.76 MT (80.7 per cent) and total coastal traffic was 2.10 MT (19.3 per cent) of the total traffic handled by minor ports. The total overseas and coastal traffic unloaded (import) at the major ports in 1998-99 was 164.53 MT (65.3 per cent) of total cargo handled at major ports and 22.27 MT (61.3 per cent) of total cargo handled at minor ports in the corresponding year. The traffic unloaded at all ports (major and minor) stood at 186.80 MT (64.84 per cent) and loaded (export) at all ports stood at 101.25 MT (35.15 per cent) in 1998-99. Further,

Table 3.7
Trend of Cargo Traffic Handled at Indian Major Ports and Minor Ports during 1989-90 to 1998-99

(In Million Tonnes)

	Overseas			*Coastal*			*Overseas & Coastal*		
Year	*Unloaded*	*Loaded*	*Total*	*Unloaded*	*Loaded*	*Total*	*Unloaded*	*Loaded*	*Total*
MAJOR PORTS									
1989-90	54.13	45.26	**99.39**	26.72	21.46	**48.18**	80.85	66.72	**147.57**
1990-91	59.02	43.63	**102.65**	26.07	22.95	**49.02**	85.09	66.58	**151.67**
1991-92	59.91	44.89	**104.80**	26.66	25.18	**51.84**	86.57	70.07	**156.64**
1992-93	74.09	43.28	**117.37**	24.35	24.78	**49.13**	98.44	68.06	**166.50**
1993-94	76.02	53.48	**129.50**	24.81	24.71	**49.52**	100.83	78.19	**179.02**
1994-95	83.60	52.18	**135.78**	29.60	30.51	**60.11**	113.20	82.69	**195.89**
1995-96	94.86	57.24	**152.10**	31.79	31.32	**63.11**	126.65	88.56	**215.21**
1996-97	102.57	57.31	**159.88**	36.64	30.45	**67.09**	139.21	87.76	**226.97**
1997-98	117.36	61.64	**179.00**	38.62	34.04	**72.66**	155.98	95.68	**251.66**
1998-99	125.10	54.97	**180.07**	39.43	32.24	**71.67**	164.53	87.21	**251.74**
MINOR PORTS									
1989-90	4.25	4.51	**8.76**	1.14	0.96	**2.10**	5.39	5.47	**10.86**
1990-91	5.71	3.85	**9.56**	1.97	1.25	**3.22**	7.68	5.10	**12.78**
1991-92	4.77	4.10	**8.87**	3.02	1.37	**4.39**	7.79	5.47	**13.26**

(Contd...)

(Contd... Table 3.7)

Year	Overseas			Coastal			Overseas & Coastal		
	Unloaded	Loaded	Total	Unloaded	Loaded	Total	Unloaded	Loaded	Total
1992-93	6.24	4.74	**10.98**	3.09	1.34	**4.43**	9.33	6.08	**15.41**
1993-94	7.57	6.64	**14.21**	3.84	1.42	**5.26**	11.41	8.06	**19.47**
1994-95	8.62	6.43	**15.05**	5.37	1.88	**7.25**	13.99	8.31	**22.30**
1995-96	9.95	8.17	**18.12**	5.12	2.47	**7.59**	15.07	10.64	**25.71**
1996-97	10.77	7.67	**18.44**	6.11	3.28	**9.39**	16.88	10.95	**27.83**
1997-98	18.75	10.42	**29.17**	5.22	4.22	**9.44**	23.97	14.64	**38.61**
1998-99	15.93	8.42	**24.35**	6.34	5.62	**11.96**	22.27	14.04	**36.31**
ALL PORTS									
1989-90	58.38	49.77	**108.15**	27.86	22.42	**50.28**	86.24	72.19	**158.43**
1990-91	64.73	47.48	**112.21**	28.04	24.20	**52.24**	92.77	71.68	**164.45**
1991-92	64.68	48.99	**113.67**	29.68	26.55	**56.23**	94.36	75.54	**169.90**
1992-93	80.33	48.02	**128.35**	27.44	26.12	**53.56**	107.77	74.14	**181.91**
1993-94	83.59	60.12	**143.71**	28.65	26.13	**54.78**	112.24	86.25	**198.49**
1994-95	92.22	58.61	**150.83**	34.97	32.39	**67.36**	127.19	91.00	**218.19**
1995-96	104.81	65.41	**170.22**	36.91	33.79	**70.70**	141.72	99.20	**240.92**
1996-97	113.34	64.98	**178.32**	42.75	33.73	**76.48**	156.09	98.71	**254.80**
1997-98	136.11	72.06	**208.17**	43.84	38.26	**82.10**	179.95	110.32	**290.27**
1998-99	141.03	63.39	**204.42**	45.77	37.86	**83.63**	186.80	101.25	**288.05**

Source : Government of India, *Basic Port Statistics of India*, Ministry of Surface Transport, New Delhi, 1999-2000.

Table 3.8

Major Port-Wise, Commodity-Wise Capacity as on 31 March 1997, 1998, 1999 and 2000

(in Million Tonnes)

Ports Commodities	Calcutta	Haldia	Paradeep	Vizag	Chennai	Tuticorin	Cochin	New Mangalore	Marmugao	Mumbai	Kandla	J.L. Nehru	Total
POL													
as on 31.3.97	3.12	8.50	0.70	11.50	8.50	1.10	10.50	7.50	1.50	21.00	21.00	-	94.92
as on 31.3.98	3.12	8.50	0.70	11.50	8.50	1.10	10.50	7.50	1.50	21.00	23.00	-	96.92
as on 31.3.99	3.40	11.00	1.50	10.80	8.50	1.00	10.50	7.50	1.50	21.00	29.00	-	105.70
as on 31.3.2000	3.40	17.00	1.50	10.80	8.50	2.30	10.50	11.00	1.50	21.00	31.00	-	118.50
Iron Ore													
as on 31.3.97	-	-	4.00	8.00	8.00	-	-	7.50	17.00	-	-	-	44.50
as on 31.3.98	-	-	4.00	8.00	8.00	-	-	7.50	17.00	-	-	-	44.50
as on 31.3.99	-	-	3.00	8.00	8.00	-	-	7.50	16.50	-	-	-	43.00
as on 31.3.2000	-	-	3.00	8.00	8.00	-	-	7.50	16.50	-	-	-	43.00
Coal													
as on 31.3.97	-	5.00	-	-	-	4.00	-	-	-	-	-	-	9.00

(Contd...)

(Contd...Table 3.8)

Ports Commodities	*Calc-utt*	*Haldia*	*Para-dee*	*Vizag*	*Chennai*	*Tuticorin*	*Cochin*	*New Mangalo*	*Mormugao*	*Mumbai*	*Kandla*	*J.L. Nehru*	*Total*
as on 31.3.98	-	5.00	-	-	-	4.00	-	-	-	-	-	-	9.00
as on 31.3.99	-	6.80	4.80	-	-	4.00	-	-	-	-	-	-	15.60
as on 31.3.2000	-	6.80	4.80	-	-	5.20	-	-	-	-	-	-	16.80
Fertiliser													
as on 31.3.97	-	-	1.10	0.55	-	-	0.60	-	-	-	0.50	2.90	5.65
as on 31.3.98	-	-	1.10	0.55	-	-	0.60	-	-	-	0.50	2.90	5.65
as on 31.3.99	-	-	0.85	0.50	-	-	0.60	-	-	-	-	2.90	4.85
as on 31.3.2000	-	-	0.85	0.50	-	-	0.60	-	-	-	-	1.50	3.45
Break-Bulk cargo													
as on 31.3.97	2.60	3.90	5.10	11.40	6.90	2.50	1.40	1.45	0.68	5.30	2.50	3.50	47.23

(Contd...)

(Contd...Table 3.8)

Ports Commodities	Calcutt	Haldia	Paradee	Vizag	Chennai	Tuticorin	Cochin	New Mangalo	Mormugao	Mumbai	Kandla	J.L. Nehru	Total
As on 31.3.98	2.60	3.90	5.10	11.40	6.90	2.95	1.40	1.45	0.63	5.30	2.50	3.50	47.68
as on 31.3.99	1.90	4.60	1.10	11.00	7.62	2.95	1.35	1.75	0.63	4.00	8.00	2.50	47.45
as on 31.3.2000	1.90	4.60	2.70	11.50	8.62	3.20	1.35	1.75	1.43	4.00	8.00	2.50	51.60
Container													
as on 31.3.97	2.15	0.30	-	-	2.50	-	0.96	-	-	4.50	-	3.50	13.91
as on 31.3.98	2.15	0.30	-	-	2.50	-	0.96	-	-	4.50	-	3.50	13.91
as on 31.3.99	3.00	0.30	-	-	2.50	-	1.00	-	-	5.50	-	10.60	22.90
as on 31.3.2000	3.00	0.30	-	-	2.50	1.80	1.00	-	-	5.50	-	10.60	24.70
TOTAL													
as on 31.3.97	7.87	17.70	10.90	31.45	25.90	7.60	13.46	16.45	19.18	30.80	24.00	9.90	215.21
as on 31.3.98	7.87	17.70	10.90	31.45	25.90	8.05	13.46	16.45	19.18	30.80	26.00	9.90	217.66
as on 31.3.99	8.30	22.70	11.25	30.30	26.62	7.95	13.45	16.75	18.68	30.50	37.00	16.00	239.50
as on 31.3.2000	8.30	28.70	12.85	30.80	27.62	12.50	13.45	20.25	19.48	30.50	39.00	14.60	258.05

Source : Government of India, *Basic Port Statistics of India*, Ministry of Surface Transport, New Delhi, 1999-2000.

Table-3.9

Traffic Handled at Major Ports of Selected Commodities during - 1999-2000 (P)

(in '000 Tonnes)

Major Port	*POL (Crude & Products)*	*Iron Ore*	*Fertiliser*	*FRM*	*Food-grains*	*Coal*	*Container Cargo*		*Others*	*Total*
							'000 Tonnes	*'000 TEUs*		
Kandla	34612	-	1020	496	1050	829	1134	79	7162	**46303**
Mumbai	16785	-	140	749	141	-	6157	429	6440	**30412**
J L Nehru	1414	132	627	164	555	-	1067	889	1405	**14976**
Mormu-gao	1143	14831	112	-	-	683	50	6	1407	**18226**
New Manga-lore	8318	6387	172	18	315	117	-	-	2274	**17601**
Cochin	9947	-	52	359	99	156	1247	130	937	**12797**
Tuticorin	461	7	423	446	196	3580	1633	137	3247	**9993**
Chennai	10054	6188	686	472	95	9646	3977	322	6325	**37443**
Visakha-patnam	15288	7520	2172	805	208	8115	262	20	5140	**39510**
Paradeep	2219	1025	-	643	-	7451	-	-	2298	**13636**
Calcutta	5622	-	14	61	48	-	2117	147	2451	**10313**
Haldia	10851	-	122	351	12	6508	434	28	2435	**20713**
All Ports	**116714**	**36090**	**5540**	**4564**	**2719**	**37085**	**27690**	**2187**	**41521**	**271923**

Source : Government of India, *Basic Port Statistics of India,* Ministry of Surface Transport, New Delhi, 1999-2000. p.5.

the total overseas and coastal traffic loaded (export) at major ports in 1998-99 was 87.21 MT (34.6 per cent) of total cargo handled at major ports and 14.04 MT (38.6 per cent) of total cargo handled at minor ports.

3.15.6. Commodity-wise Capacity at Major Ports as on 31st March 1997, 1998, 1999 and 2000

Table 3.8 reveals the commodity-wise capacity of measure ports as on 31st March 1997, 1998, 1999 and 2000. The total capacity of all ports in terms of commodity has increased except iron ore and fertilizer. The capacity of POL at all major ports which was 94.92 MT in 31st March 1997 reached 118.50 MT as on 31st March 2000 registering a 24 per cent increase. Similarly the coal capacity has also increased to 16.80 MT from 9.00 MT (86 per cent) in the said period. The capacity of container and break bulk cargo registered an increase of 77 per cent and 9 per cent respectively. On the other hand the capacities of iron ore and fertilizer have reduced after 31st March 1998. The capacity of iron ore was 44.50 MT as on 31st March 1997, which was reduced to 43.00 MT as on 31st March 1999. Similarly the fertilizer capacity also got reduced to 3.45 MT from 5.65 MT during the same period. The capacity reduction for fertiliser is due to self-sufficiency of the country in producing fertilisers, resulting less import from other countries. The Tuticorin port registered an increase in capacity of 64 per cent in the said four years whereas the ports like Mumbai, Cochin and Visakhapatnam have shown the same or negative increase in capacity. Similarly Calcutta, Haldia, Paradeep, Chennai, New Mangalore, Mormugao, JNPT have shown an increase in capacity during the period. The overall port capacity has increased to 258.05 MT as on 31st March 2000 which was 215.21 in 1997 registering a 20 per cent growth during the period.

3.15.7. Traffic Handled at Major Ports of Selected Commodities 1999-2000.

Table 3.9 exhibits the traffic handled at major ports of selected commodities during 1999-2000. The total traffic handled at 12 major ports in 1999-2000 was 271.9 MT of which POL (Crude and products) occupies highest share of 116.7 MT (43 per cent) followed by other commodities (15.27 per cent) coal (13.63 per cent), iron ore, (13.27 per cent) container cargo (10.98 per cent) fertilizer (2.03 per cent), fertilizer raw material (1.67 per cent) and food grains (1 per cent). Among the ports Kandla stood first in handling POL, (nearly 29 per cent) of total POL handled by all ports in

1999-2000. Similarly the Mormugao port handled more than 41 per cent of iron are the highest among all ports in the corresponding year. Paradeep port handled a total 13.6 MT of cargo traffic in the said year, of which 2.21 MT (16 per cent) POL, 1.02 MT (7.5 per cent) iron ore and 7.4 MT (54.4 per cent) coal handled during the year. The share of Paradeep port to all Indian ports concerning the commodities such as POL 1.9 per cent, iron ore 2.8 per cent, coal 20 per cent and other commodities 5.5 per cent.

Over the years, the cargo profile has been changing, reflecting the increase in imports of petroleum, oil and lubricants (POL). The changing cargo profile calls for a corresponding change in cargo handling facilities and creation of cargo-specific berths. For example, container handling facilities at many ports would be insufficient to handle the increase in container cargo of 64 per cent by 2006-07.

3.15.8. Output Per Ship Berth-day of Vessels at Major Ports during 1997-98 and 1998-99

Table 3.10 highlights the output per ship berth-day by type of vessels and major ports. Output per ship berth-day describes the total tonnage handled distributed over the total number of berth-days per ship. The output per ship berth-day depends on the number of ships entering into the berth and the efficiency of the berths to handle the tonnage during a year. So increase in output per ship berth-day reveals a positive growth and productivity of the port. Here in this table the comparative figures are given for two years, i.e., 1997-98 and 1998-99 on various types of vessels such as container, break-bulk, dry bulk (mechanised and conventional) and liquid bulk at major ports. In the case of all types of vessels, at all major ports except liquid bulk have shown an increasing trend in output per ship berth-day. This has been shown in Fig. 3.2. In liquid bulk, there is a fall of 1153 tonnes in 1998-1999 in comparison to 1997-98. The output per ship berth-day at Mormugao port have increased to 11076 tonnes (an increase of 6 per cent) as against the previous year's figure of 10446 tonnes. Similarly the berth day output of all ports was 5167 tonnes in 1998-99 registering a growth of 5 per cent over the previous years berth-day output of 4912 tonnes. Among the vessels, the dry bulk (mechanical) occupies the highest figure of 13346 tonnes (8 per cent increase over the previous year) output per ship berth-day at all major ports followed by

Table 3.10

Output Per Ship Berthday – By Type of Vessels and Major Ports during 1997-98 and 1998-99

(in tonnes)

Major Ports	Container		Break-Bulk		Dry Bulk (Mech.)		Dry Bulk (Conv.)		Liquid Bulk		All Types	
	97-98	98-99	97-98	98-99	97-98	98-99	97-98	98-99	97-98	98-99	97-98	98-99
Calcutta	2316	2089	385	395	-	-	555	592	3992	4949	1325	1697
Haldia	1499	1631	659	510	8579	9169	2496	2678	15451	16583	5590	5282
Paradeep	-	1878	239	335	9578	9730	5143	6612	7512	6937	6252	7012
Visakhapatnam	1464	1439	1697	1688	12035	13025	4741	5269	13419	14103	6383	7057
Chennai	2899	3066	911	930	32634	36135	4541	5461	15632	12093	5694	5762
Tuticorin	2045	2367	897	965	8374	8303	2053	2437	4732	4698	2970	2984
Cochin	2026	2650	564	628	1374	2016	1017	1451	14831	15085	5253	5651
New Mangalore	-	-	816	747	29400	27411	1311	1522	15432	14421	7248	7507
Mormugao	1517	1727	1292	2977	18295	21344	2174	2869	5806	6351	10446	11076
J.L.Nehru	8587	10907	1384	1341	3068	3500	5415	4257	5840	4283	3737	6957
Mumbai	2731	2983	864	894	-	-	759	852	10557	9431	2746	2940
Kandla	3714	3366	1616	2090	3068	3030	1954	3085	17642	18129	7346	8778
All Ports	**3156**	**3612**	**919**	**949**	**12275**	**13346**	**3245**	**3798**	**12772**	**11619**	**4912**	**5167**

Source : Government of India, *Basic Port Statistics of India*, Ministry of Surface Transport, New Delhi, 1999-2000, p.182.3.15.9. Commodity-wise Output Per Ship Berth-day at Major Ports during 1999-2000.

Fig. 3.2
Output per Ship Berth-day at Major Ports during 1997 and 1998

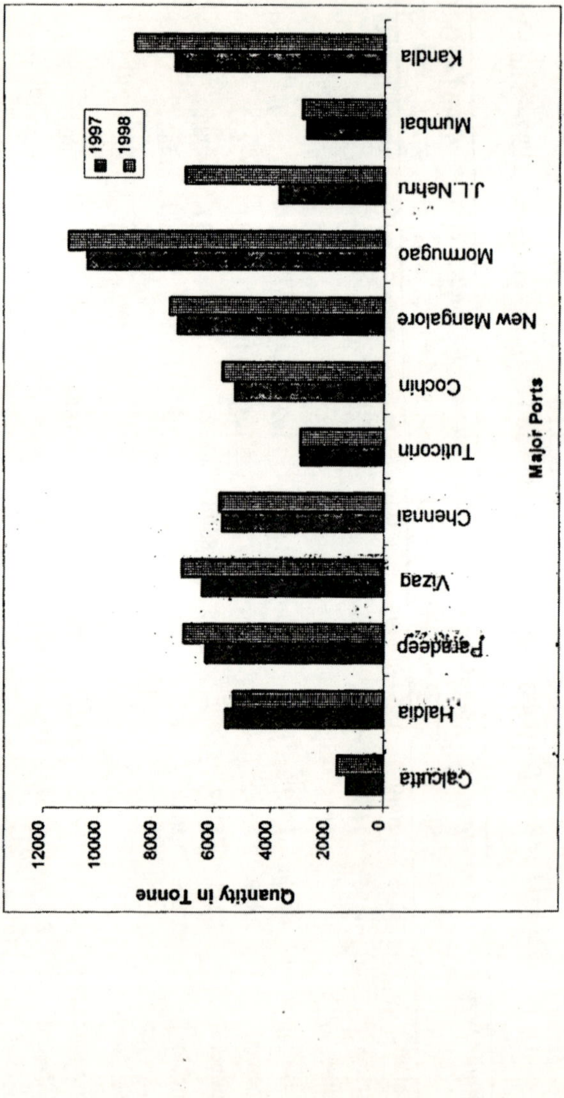

Table 3.11

Commodity-Wise Output Per Ship Berth-Day at Major Ports during 1999-2000 (P)

(in tonnes)

Major Port Commodity	*Calcutta*	*Hal-dia*	*Para-deep*	*Vizag*	*Chen-nai*	*Tuti-corin*	*Co-chin*	*New Manga-lore*	*Mor-mugao*	*Mum-bai*	*Kan-dla*	*J.L. Nehru*
P.O.L.	24239	19067	7272	16420	17493	4906	16511	25362	6376	16786	29339	5784
Iron Ore	-	-	15444	32325	30265	-	-	32443	23091	-	-	-
Coking Coal	-	4644	6883	7736	7774	-	4235	3257	4186	-	10510	-
Thermal Coal	-	15816	10156	9154	-	8256	-	-	8657	-	-	-
Fertilisers	332	843	-	2979	1629	2439	1346	1505	1825	1172	3202	-
Raw Materials	750	1186	5345	3476	1870	1787	2209	1095	-	986	4255	-
Other Dry Bulk	-	1757	3336	4983	2701	2476	1440	1761	3405	850	2430	3772
Other Liquid Bulk	1852	4971	1424	5637	3494	4638	5959	5416	5176	2454	5203	-
General Cargo	440	912	2647	1583	1018	1040	668	984	2207	1154	1978	1525
Containers	2533	1895	-	1579	4217	3410	2489	447	1199	3435	3120	8387
Total	**2157**	**5599**	**7106**	**7579**	**5883**	**2891**	**5952**	**9000**	**11162**	**3876**	**8740**	**5905**

Source : Indian Ports Association, New Delhi.

liquid bulk. The break bulks have the least figure of 949 tonnes output per ship berth-day.

3.15.9. Commodity-wise output per ship Berth-day at Major Port during 1999-2000

Table 3.11 highlights the commodity wise output per ship berth-day at 12 major ports during 1999-2000. The Mormugao port has the highest output per ship berth-day (11162 tonnes) followed by New Mangalore (9000 tonnes), Vizag (7579 tonnes), and Paradeep (7106 tonnes), whereas Calcutta port has the least output of 2157 tonnes per ship berth-day. Similarly in commodity wise berth-day output, POL occupies the first position in creating maximum output per ship berth-day at almost all the major ports. The Kandla port has the highest output per ship berth-day (29339 tonnes) in POL products followed by New Mangalore (25362 tonnes) and Calcutta (24239 tonnes).The port of New Mangalore leads in iron ore (32443 tonnes), and Haldia port in thermal coal (15816 tonnes) registering the highest output per ship berth-day among all major ports. The share of general cargo has the least contribution towards the output per ship berth-day at all major ports.

3.15.10. Share of Foreign Trade by Sea Mode and Other Modes of Transport in Total Foreign Trade of India during 1981-82 to 1999-2000

The Table 3.12 reveals the estimated share of foreign trade by sea in total and foreign trade by all modes of transport during 1981-82 to 1999-2000. From the table it is crystal clear that the total export and import have increased to Rs. 162925 crore and Rs. 204583 crore in 1999-2000 from Rs. 7806 crore and Rs. 13606 crore respectively in 1981-82 respectively. But the share of trade by sea in both export and import have declined to 58.9 per cent and 67.9 per cent in 1999-2000 from 79.2 per cent and 91.9 per cent in 1981-82 respectively. Similarly the percentage of trade by sea in total foreign trade (export and import) have also declined to 63.9 per cent in 1999-2000 from 87.2 per cent in 1981-82. Despite the fact that the Government of India have provided various sops and incentives through the announcement of policies from time to time, foreign trade by sea mode has declined. The reasons attributed to such fall are global economic slowdown, availability of other cheaper modes of transport etc.

Table 3.12
Estimated Share of Foreign Trade by Sea in Total Foreign Trade of India by All Modes of Transport During 1981-82 to 1999-2000

(Value in Rs.Crore)

Year	*Total exports including Re-exports*	*Share in exports (in Percentage)*	*Total Imports*	*Share in Imports (in Percentage)*	*Share of sea borne trade to total foreign trade (in percentage)*
1981-82	7806	79.2	13606	91.9	87.2
1982-83	8803	79.0	14293	86.5	83.7
1983-84	9771	74.4	15831	85.4	81.2
1984-85	11744	77.3	17134	87.7	83.6
1985-86	10895	71.7	19658	87.9	82.2
1986-87	12569	65.8	20201	82.7	76.1
1987-88	15674	62.1	22244	77.2	71.0
1988-89	20232	59.7	28235	72.9	67.4
1989-90	27681	59.5	35416	69.6	65.2
1990-91	32553	67.3	43193	81.1	75.1
1991-92	44042	66.6	47851	80.8	74.0
1992-93	53688	64.9	53375	78.0	72.0
1993-94	69751	66.1	73101	96.0	81.4
1994-95	82673	64.3	89971	79.8	72.4
1995-96	106353	63.7	122678	80.7	72.8
1996-97	118817	67.4	138920	82.4	75.5
1997-98	130101	64.4	154176	74.7	70.0
1998-99(P)	139752	62.2	178332	67.9	65.4
1999-00(P)	152925	58.9	204583	67.9	63.9

Note : P : Provisional

Source : (i) Ministry of Commerce (DGCI & S) New Delhi, March 2000 Issue

(ii) Reserve Bank of India, *Report on Currency and Finance*, Mumbai.

Table 3.13

Selected Performance Indicators of Major Ports during 1997-98 and 1998-99

Ports / Item	Kan-dla	Mum-bai	Mormu-gao	New Mang-alore	Cochin	Tutico-rin	Chen-nai	Vizag	Para-deep	Hal-dia	Calcu-tta	J.L. Neh-ru	All ports
1. No. of vessels sailed													
1997-98	1685	2385	561	729	872	984	1771	1529	643	1275	1009	634	**14077**
1998-99	1708	2375	483	724	969	1073	1761	1482	678	1291	1041	955	**14540**
2. Av. Pre- berthing waiting time (days)													
1997-98	5.2	3.0	1.9	1.1	1.1	1.7	2.9	2.0	1.7	2.0	1.1	1.7	**2.3**
1998-99	4.5	2.1	1.4	0.9	0.9	1.6	3.4	1.6	1.2	1.3	1.0	1.4	**2.0**
3. Average Turn around time (days)													
1997-98	8.4	8.5	5.6	4.1	3.9	5.2	6.5	6.0	5.1	5.3	7.4	5.6	**6.3**
1998-99	8.3	7.0	4.8	3.7	3.4	4.9	7.0	5.3	4.1	4.7	6.7	3.8	**5.7**
4. % of Idle time at berth to time at working berth													
1997-98	17	35	24	48	42	40	37	24	30	46	48	10	**35**
1998-99	22	32	23	46	36	41	38	29	25	44	44	9	**34**
5. Output per ship berth day (tonnes)													
1997-98	7346	2746	10445	7248	5253	2970	5694	6383	6252	5590	1325	3737	**4912**
1998-99	8778	2940	11075	7507	5651	2984	5762	7057	701[illegible]	5282	1697	6957	**5167**

Source : Government of India, *Basic Port Statistics of India*, Ministry of Surface Transport, New Delhi, 1999-2000, p.173.

3.15.11. Performance Indicators of Major Ports during the Year 1997-98 and 1998-99.

Table 3.13 highlights the port-wise major performance indicators in 1997-98 and 1998-99. From the Table, it is crystal clear that at all major ports, the indicators like number of vessels sailed, average pre-berthing waiting time, average turn-around time, percentage of idle time at working berth and output per ship berth-day depict favourable performance. The total number of vessels sailed in 1997-98 was 14077, which has gone up to 14540 in 1998-99. Similarly, the output per ship berth-day has increased to 5167 tonnes in 1998-99 from 4912 tonnes in 1997-98. At the same time, the average pre-berthing waiting time has declined to 2 days in 1998-99 from 2.3 days in 1997-98. The average turn-around time has also came down to 5.7 days in 1998-99 as against 6.3 days in 1997-98. The percentage of idle time at berth to time at working berth have also reduced to 34 per cent in 1998-99 from 35 per cent in 1997-98. In the realm of liberalised economic policy, the government has allowed private participation in the developmental activities of Indian ports. All the major ports and some of the minor ports are in the pipeline for using private fund for improving their services. Some of the ports like JNPT, Ennore, Paradeep, etc., have been following standards of international ports.

3.15.12. Average Berth Occupancy at Indian Major Ports during 1989-90 to 1998-99

Table 3.14 reveals the average berth occupancy at major Indian ports from 1989-90 to 1998-99. Berth occupancy indicates the time for which a berth is occupied by a ship in a year. So, higher the percentage of berth occupancy, higher the productivity performance of the port. All the 12 major ports have shown fluctuating trends of their berth occupancy during the last 10 years, i.e., 1989-90 to 1998-99. The port of Kandla has the highest percentage of berth occupancy (93.1 per cent) in 1998-99 against 97.7 per cent in 1997-98 followed by Tuticorin (85.27 per cent) and Chennai port (81.2 per cent). At the same time Calcutta port has the least percentage of berth occupancy of 48.4 per cent in 1998-99. In 1989-90 Chennai port has the highest percentage of (86.2 per cent) berth occupancy and Cochin has the least (52.3 per cent) percentage of berth occupancy during the same year. There are many reasons for this fluctuation. Most of the ports are affected by natural calamities like cyclones, tornados etc. which affect the berths and creates disturbances in smooth running of the ports.

Table 3.14

Average Berth Occupancy at Major Ports during the Period 1989-90 to 1998-99

(Percentage)

Major Ports	*1989-90*	*1990-91*	*1991-92*	*1992-93*	*1993-94*	*1994-95*	*1995-96*	*1996-97*	*1997-98*	*1998-99*
Kandla	86.0	88.5	89.8	89.1	90.5	93.8	92.8	93.6	97.7	93.1
Mumbai	81.6	77.0	62.6	71.2	72.4	78.4	81.6	77.7	78.7	68.1
J.L.Nehru	-	-	-	65.8	71.7	80.5	78.8	70.0	53.6	59.8
Mormugao	69.0	66.0	67.0	83.8	80.7	70.6	55.7	59.6	74.3	78.3
New Mangalore	69.0	55.9	57.3	64.9	49.6	52.9	49.3	45.5	59.4	56.2
Cochin	52.3	49.7	45.3	53.2	49.7	50.8	51.7	48.0	55.5	58.4
Tuticorin	73.3	72.6	76.1	84.5	85.1	84.9	86.2	83.0	85.5	85.2
Chennai	86.2	86.6	79.0	78.8	80.4	81.0	84.2	83.3	83.8	81.2
Vizag	63.3	77.9	81.9	91.0	87.5	92.7	81.3	77.5	85.1	79.2
Paradeep	70.2	68.5	60.6	68.6	69.9	78.6	85.0	65.0	65.5	66.8
Haldia	67.4	69.1	63.2	73.5	63.7	77.1	77.0	75.8	82.6	81.1
Calcutta	59.9	56.9	53.8	52.3	48.5	53.9	52.5	53.8	57.8	48.4

Source: Government of India, *Basic Port Statistics of India*, Ministry of Surface Transport, New Delhi, 1999-2000, p.183.

Sometimes, the strikes and lockouts by the labour unions also delay the handling of cargo in a berth. The factors like international demand for export and import, purchasing power of people, state of global economy and above all the taste and preference of people for imported items are equally responsible for declining percentage of berth occupancy.

3.15.13. Average Pre-berthing Time and Average Turn-around Time of Major Ports during 1996-97 to 1999-2000

Table 3.15 envisages the comparative analysis of average pre-berthing time and average turn-around period of all major ports during 1996-97, 1997-98, 1998-99 and 1999-2000. The average pre-berthing time of all ports has come down significantly from 3.6 days in 1996-97 to 1.5 days in 1999-2000. Similarly, the average turn-around time of all ports have also declined considerably from 8.4 days in 1996-97 to 4.55 days in 1999-2000. Pre-berthing time means the time for which a ship waits before getting entry into a berth. Similarly, turn-around time means the total time spent by a ship since its entry till its departure. So the lower the pre-berthing time and turn-around time the higher is the productivity of a port. The Table exhibits a favourable trend in both the cases. Mumbai port has the lowest pre-berthing time (0.29 days) and Kandla port has the longest time of 3.04 days during 1999-2000. Similarly JNPT being the modest port has the least average turn-around time (1.72 days) and Chennai has the longest average turn-around time (6.80 days) during 1999-2000. The Paradeep port has an average pre-berthing time of 1.14 days and average turn-around time of 3.89 days in 1999-2000, which were 1.6 days and 5.6 days in 1996-97 respectively. The decline of pre-berthing and average turn-around time during the period under study indicates satisfactory performance of the concerned ports.

3.15.14. Average Turn-around Time by Type of Vessels at Major Ports during 1997-98 and 1998-99.

Table 3.16 reveals the average turn-around time by type of vessels at major ports in 1997-98 and 1998-99. This has also been exhibited in Fig. 3.3. In almost all the major ports the average turn-around time has declined considerably in all type of vessels. In case of container vessels, the turn round time has come down to 3.4 days in 1998-99 from 3.9 days in 1997-98. Similarly in the case of break bulk it was reduced to 9.2 days from 10.5 days. In the case of dry bulk (mech.) and dry bulk (conv.) the average turn-

Table 3.15

Average Pre-berthing and Turn-around Time of Major Ports during 1996-97, 1997-98, 1998-99 and 1999-00

(in days)

Major Ports	*Average Pre-berthing Time*				*Average Turn-around Time*			
	1996-97	*1997-98*	*1998-99*	*1999-00(P)*	*1996-97*	*1997-98*	*1998-99*	*1999-00(P)*
Calcutta	1.1	1.0	1.10	1.03	8.5	8.3	7.12	6.59
Haldia	2.3	2.6	1.30	1.61	6.3	6.3	4.84	5.21
Paradeep	1.6	2.1	1.22	1.14	5.2	5.3	4.16	3.89
Visakhapatnam	1.5	2.1	1.65	1.37	5.7	6.1	5.51	4.75
Chennai	4.4	3.1	3.56	2.80	8.7	7.2	7.58	6.80
Tuticorin	1.7	1.7	1.61	2.98	5.5	5.0	4.91	6.39
Cochin	1.0	1.2	0.87	0.87	4.2	4.4	3.61	3.23
New Mangalore	1.6	1.2	0.94	1.07	4.8	4.4	3.75	3.80
Mormugao	0.7	0.5	1.38	1.09	7.0	7.6	5.44	4.30
JNPT	1.9	3.3	1.38	0.64	5.4	7.2	3.38	1.72
Mumbai	5.4	3.2	1.91	0.29	11.8	8.8	6.84	3.95
Kandla	8.9	6.3	4.63	3.04	13.6	11.1	8.30	4.00
All major ports	**3.6**	**2.9**	**2.07**	**1.5**	**8.4**	**7.4**	**5.89**	**4.55**

Source : Government of India, *Basic Port Statistics of India*, Ministry of Surface Transport, New Delhi, 1999-2000, p.183.

Table 3.16

Average Turn-around Time – by Type of Vessels and Major Ports

(In days)

Major Ports	*Container*		*Break*	*Bulk*	*Dry Bulk (Mech.)*		*Dry Bulk (Conv.)*		*Liquid Bulk*		*All Types*	
	1997-98	*1998-99*	*1997-98*	*1998-99*	*1997-98*	*1998-99*	*1997-98*	*1998-99*	*1997-98*	*1998-99*	*1997-98*	*1998-99*
Calcutta	4.5	4.8	14.4	11.8	-	-	17.2	14.8	4.7	4.5	**7.4**	**6.7**
Haldia	1.8	1.5	13.1	14.4	4.7	4.2	11.3	10.5	4.0	3.1	**5.3**	**4.7**
Paradeep	-	0.6	1.4	18.7	5.6	4.6	5.6	4.4	4.3	3.5	**5.1**	**4.1**
Visakha-patnam	2.3	2.1	8.3	6.6	7.6	7.5	9.8	7.4	2.3	3.1	**6.0**	**5.3**
Chennai	3.8	6.1	6.8	6.6	5.2	5.1	9.7	9.2	5.9	6.3	**6.5**	**7.0**
Tuticorin	3.1	2.6	7.2	5.9	4.2	5.1	9.2	8.2	2.6	3.0	**5.2**	**4.9**
Cochin	2.3	2.2	4.1	4.1	13.2	10.0	14.2	13.4	3.8	3.1	**3.9**	**3.4**
New Mangalore	-	-	5.8	5.9	3.0	2.8	17.2	15.1	2.5	2.4	**4.1**	**3.7**
Mormugao	0.8	0.9	7.2	5.0	7.6	6.2	8.6	7.7	2.0	2.2	**5.6**	**4.8**
J.L.Nehru	2.6	1.5	1.10	1.40	18.5	9.2	6.9	6.1	2.3	3.2	**5.6**	**3.8**
Mumbai	5.9	4.8	12.4	10.4	-	-	24.2	23.6	5.3	4.4	**8.5**	**7.0**
Kandla	5.3	5.6	17.5	16.3	14.9	9.7	13.2	13.6	4.5	5.4	**8.4**	**8.3**
All ports	**3.9**	**3.4**	**10.5**	**9.2**	**6.1**	**5.3**	**10.5**	**9.3**	**4.1**	**4.1**	**6.3**	**5.7**

Source : Government of India, *Basic Port Statistics of India*, Ministry of Surface Transport, New Delhi, 1999-2000, p.183.3.15.15. Commodity-Wise Average Turn-around Time at Major Ports during 1999-2000.

Fig. 3.3
Average Turn-around Time at Major Ports during 1997 and 1998

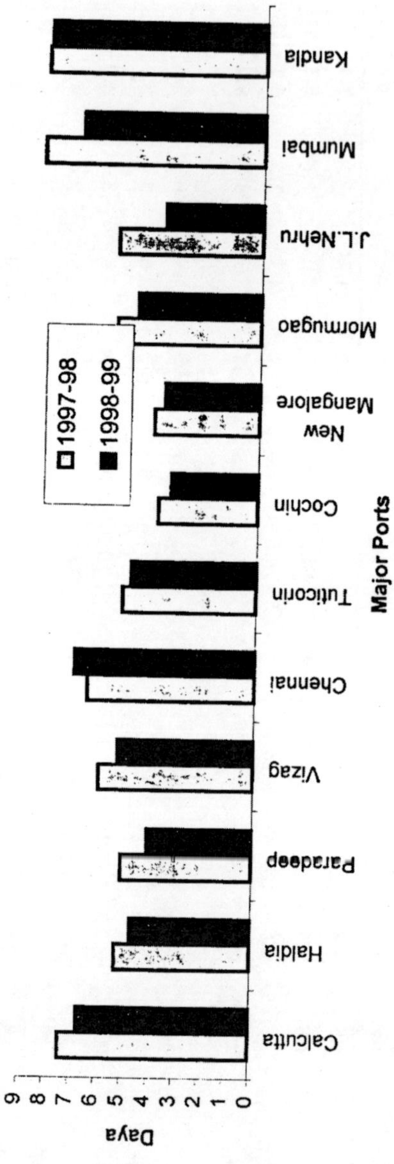

around time declined to 5.3 days and 9.3 days in 1998-99 as against 6.1 days and 10.5 days in 1997-98 respectively. At the same time the liquid bulk has the same average turn-around time in both the years. The average turn-around time for all vessels also reduced to 5.7 days in 1998-99 as against 6.3 days in 1997-98. But it is significantly higher than the average ship turn-around time for Singapore ports which are 6 to 8 hours only. Cochin port has the lowest turn-around time of 3.4 days whereas Kandla port has the highest turn-around time of 8.3 days during 1998-99. From the Table it is also clear that container vessels have the least turn-around time of 3.4 days in 1998-99 as against 3.9 days in 1997-98 and both break bulk and dry bulk (conv.) vessels have the highest average turn-around time of 10.5 days in 1997-98 which got reduced to 9.2 days and 9.3 days in 1998-99 respectively. Decline in average turn-around time at Indian major ports is due to addition of more specialised berths and availability of mechanised handling process at most of the ports.

3.15.15. Commodity-wise Average Turn-around time at the Major Ports during 1999-2000

Table 3.17 highlights the commodity-wise average turn-around time at all major ports during 1999-2000. JNPT port occupies the first position for the lowest average turn-around time (1.61 days) in handling POL commodity. Similarly New Mangalore port in handling iron ore (3.73 days), Paradeep in coking coal, (4.33days), Haldia in thermal coal (2.75 days), Mormugao in fertilizers (9.72 days), again Paradeep for raw matrials (4.62 days), other dry bulk (5 days) and other liquid bulk (1.20 days). JNPT for general cargo (0.47 days) and also for containers (1.17 days) exhibits the lowest average turn-around time in 1999-2000. In addition, some new mechanised projects are under progress with private sector participation at various major ports. After completion of those projects, the Indian ports will handle more traffic with efficiency and can compete with the international ports in the coming years.

3.15.16. Commodity-Wise Average Pre-Berthing Time at Major Ports during 1999-2000

Pre-berthing time is the time for which a ship waits before getting entry into a berth. So lesser the pre-berthing time, higher will be the efficiency and productivity of the port. Due to capacity addition into major ports with commissioning of new mechanised berths and opening

Table 3.17

Commodity-Wise Average Turn-around Time at Major Ports during 1999-2000 (P)

Port / *Commodity*	*Calcutta*	*Haldia*	*Paradeep*	*Vizag*	*Chennai*	*Tuticorin*	*Cochin*	*New Mangalore*	*Mormugao*	*Mumbai**	*Kandla**	*J.L. Nehru*
P.O.L.	8.17	2.87	3.32	2.94	5.40	2.46	3.27	2.49	1.80	2.39	1.86	1.61
Iron Ore	-	-	4.79	4.07	6.10	-	-	3.73	4.67	-	-	-
Coking Coal	-	8.58	4.33	5.39	-	-	7.03	6.41	13.48	-	6.98	-
Thermal Coal	-	2.75	3.44	4.23	7.40	5.16	-	-	5.48	-	-	-
Fertilizers	17.60	24.72	-	14.06	29.10	18.82	19.93	16.77	9.72	13.46	12.94	-
Raw Materials	14.96	18.92	4.62	7.76	11.20	15.15	0.41	6.57	-	11.76	7.14	-
Other Dry Bulk	-	16.42	5.00	7.07	8.00	11.22	12.10	9.30	5.14	11.84	7.59	5.96
Other Lqd. Bulk	5.56	3.17	1.20	2.45	4.50	2.37	1.51	2.46	1.82	2.67	3.65	-
General Cargo	10.81	15.48	5.43	5.74	7.10	8.74	5.36	5.22	8.41	5.58	7.43	0.47
Containers	4.77	1.62	-	1.89	5.80	2.67	2.08	0.30	0.97	3.09	2.13	1.17
Total	**6.59**	**5.21**	**3.89**	**4.75**	**6.80**	**6.39**	**3.23**	**3.80**	**4.30**	**3.95**	**4.00**	**1.72**

* : Excluding pré berthing time due to non port A/C.

Source : Indian Ports Association, New Delhi

Table 3.18

Commodity-Wise Average Pre-berthing Time at Major Ports during 1999-2000 (P)

(in days)

Port Commodity	Calcutta	Haldia	Paradeep	Vizag	Chennai	Tuticorin	Cochin	New Mangalore	Mormugao	Mumbai*	Kandl	J.L. Nehru
P.O.L.	1.67	1.32	1.85	1.09	3.00	0.51	1.40	1.05	0.33	0.36	1.52	0.96
Iron Ore	-	-	1.57	1.37	3.80	-	-	2.24	1.23	-	-	-
Coking Coal	-	2.38	0.64	1.49	-	-	0.71	0.15	1.04	-	1.05	-
Thermal Coal	-	0.34	0.56	0.27	2.70	1.22	-	-	1.10	-	-	-
Fertilizers	2.62	9.27	-	4.36	9.30	9.04	0.27	0.12	1.75	0.48	3.32	-
Raw Materials	1.80	4.60	1.16	2.32	3.80	7.88	0.54	0.92	-	0.37	3.81	-
Other Dry Bulk	-	4.26	1.06	1.79	2.00	6.14	0.74	0.72	0.10	0.40	4.40	2.01
Other Lqd. Bulk	1.83	1.19	0.49	0.94	2.30	1.04	0.53	0.89	0.53	0.42	3.89	-
General Cargo	0.91	4.43	1.52	1.61	1.90	4.49	0.62	0.28	2.39	0.24	5.05	0.47
Containers	0.56	0.05	-	0.41	2.20	0.96	0.55	-	0.10	0.19	1.47	0.41
Total	**1.03**	**1.61**	**1.14**	**1.37**	**2.80**	**2.98**	**0.87**	**1.07**	**1.09**	**0.29**	**3.04**	**0.64**

* : Excluding pre berthing time due to non port A/C.

Source : Indian Ports Association, New Delhi.

of new minor ports by the State Governments with private participation enhanced the efficiency of the ports in general and decline in pre-berthing time in particular during the last decade. Table 3.18 highlights the commodity-wise pre-berthing time of major ports in 1999-2000. Mormugao port has the lowest pre-berthing time (0.33 days) in handling POL, Vizag in iron ore (1.37 days), New Mangalore in Coking coal (0.15 days), Vizag in thermal coal (0.27), New Mangalore in fertilizer (0.12 days), Mumbai in raw material (0.37 day) and other dry bulk (0.40 days) and also in other liquid bulk (0.42) and general cargo (0.24 days). In case of containers, Haldia has the lowest (0.05 day) average pre berthing time during 1999-2000.

3.15.17. Average Pre-Berthing Detention by Type of Vessels and Major Ports during 1997-98 and 1998-99

Table 3.19 reveals the average pre-berthing detention by types and major port during the year 1997-98 and 1998-99. Pre-berthing detention means the time for which a ship waits before getting entry into a berth. So lesser the pre-berthing detention time more will be the productivity of the port and vice-versa. The average pre-berthing detention time declined considerably in all the 12 major ports in 1998-99 as compared to 1997-98, which is a healthy sign of improved port performance. Cochin and New Mangalore port have recorded the least average pre-berthing detention of 0.9 each in comparison to 1.1-day average each in the previous year. Similarly Kandla port recorded the highest average pre-berthing detention of 4.5 days during 1998-99 as against 5.2 days during the previous year. In the case of type vessels the pre-berthing time increased to 1.3 days in 1998-99 from 1.2 days during 1997-98. However, the other vessels such as break bulk, dry-bulk (Mech. and Conv.) and liquid bulks depict a declining trend of pre-berthing time in 1998-99 as against the previous year. The pre-berthing time of all vessels at all major ports also come down to 2 days in 1998-99 from 2.3 days in 1997-98.

3.15.18. Commodity-Wise Average Non-Working Time at Major Ports during 1999-2000

Table 3.20 reveals commodity-wise average non-working time (idle time) at berths of major ports in 1999-2000. It is of the general view that the lesser the non-working time at berth, higher will be efficiency of ports and vice-versa. From the figure, it is clear that out of 12 major ports, 6 have less

Table 3.19

Average Pre-berthing Detention by Type and Major Ports during 1997-98 and 1998-99

(in days)

	Container		*Break*	*Bulk*	*Dry Bulk (Mech.)*		*Dry Bulk (Conv.)*		*Liquid Bulk*		*All Types*	
	97-98	*1998-99*	*1997-98*	*1998-99*	*1997-98*	*1998-99*	*1997-98*	*1998-99*	*1997-98*	*1998-99*	*1997-98*	*1998-99*
Calcutta	0.6	0.8	1.2	1.1	-	-	1.6	1.1	1.5	1.2	**1.1**	**1.0**
Haldia	0.1	0.1	3.1	2.9	1.1	0.7	3.1	2.2	2.4	1.5	**2.0**	**1.3**
Paradeep	-	0.1	0.1	3.5	1.3	0.6	1.0	0.6	2.8	2.0	**1.7**	**1.2**
Visaskha-patnam	1.4	0.7	2.9	2.0	2.4	2.2	3.3	1.8	0.7	1.3	**2.0**	**1.6**
Chennai	1.4	3.8	2.0	1.7	2.6	2.8	3.7	3.7	4.2	4.2	**2.9**	**3.4**
Tuticorin	0.7	0.6	3.0	2.4	1.2	1.7	2.3	2.0	1.0	1.1	**1.7**	**1.6**
Cochin	0.5	0.7	0.4	0.4	0.7	0.5	0.6	0.4	1.8	1.3	**1.1**	**0.9**
New Mangalore	-	-	0.6	0.7	1.4	1.1	1.1	1.2	1.2	0.9	**1.1**	**0.9**
Mormugao	0.1	0.1	1.7	0.6	3.4	2.4	0.7	0.8	0.7	0.8	**1.9**	**1.4**
J.L.Nehru	1.0	1.0	0.6	0.8	6.3	3.3	0.8	-	0.6	2.5	**1.7**	**1.4**
Mumbai	1.9	1.3	3.8	2.6	-	-	8.0	4.5	2.7	2.1	**3.0**	**2.1**
Kandla	2.5	2.6	10.0	8.4	2.0	1.8	6.5	5.3	3.2	3.3	**5.2**	**4.5**
All ports	**1.2**	**1.3**	**3.4**	**2.7**	**2.0**	**1.6**	**3.3**	**2.5**	**2.2**	**2.0**	**2.3**	**2.0**

Source : Government of India, *Basic Port Statistics of India*, Ministry of Surface Transport, New Delhi, 1999-2000, p.175.

Table 3.20

Commodity-Wise Average Non-Working Time at Berth (Major Ports) during 1999-2000 (P)

(in days)

Port / *Commodity*	*Calcutta*	*Haldia*	*Para-deep*	*Vizag*	*Chennai*	*Tuticorin*	*Co-chin*	*New Manga-lore*	*Mor-mugao*	*Mum-bai**	*Kandla*	*J.L. Nehru*
P.O.L.	1.73	0.43	-	0.66	0.60	0.69	0.48	0.32	0.41	0.58	0.43	0.10
Iron Ore	-	-	1.61	1.26	1.10	-	-	0.51	0.71	-	-	-
Coking Coal	-	2.06	0.72	0.96	-	-	1.74	2.83	2.75	-	0.44	-
Thermal Coal	-	1.07	0.78	0.83	1.20	0.76	-	-	0.39	-	-	-
Fertilizers	7.94	4.66	-	2.70	6.60	2.93	4.21	7.47	1.22	3.69	0.83	-
Raw Materials	3.92	6.65	1.40	1.59	2.60	2.96	2.06	3.03	-	3.60	0.42	-
Other Dry Bulk	-	4.52	0.78	1.29	1.90	1.78	5.31	4.06	1.19	5.86	0.47	0.39
Other Lqd. Bulk	0.98	0.49	-	0.47	0.40	0.37	0.24	0.27	0.30	0.76	0.51	-
Break Bulk	4.31	4.22	0.81	1.18	2.50	1.77	2.24	2.44	0.90	1.93	0.57	0.08
Containers	0.85	0.39	-	0.52	1.10	0.58	0.42	0.04	0.18	0.58	0.28	0.21
Total	**1.88**	**1.24**	**0.99**	**0.98**	**1.40**	**1.23**	**0.81**	**1.05**	**0.61**	**1.11**	**0.46**	**0.13**

Source : Indian Ports Association, New Delhi.

than one-day average non-working time at their berths. These are Paradeep, Vizag, Cochin, Mormugao, Kandla and J.L. Nehru port. The rest of the Ports are also in just above average of a day but less than 2 days. Calcutta port has the highest average non-working time of 1.88 days and JNPT has the least average non-working time of 0.13 day in the corresponding year. It is also evident from the table that in almost all ports, fertilizer berths have the highest and other liquid bulk berths have the lowest non-working days as compared to other commodities.

3.15.19. Capacity Utilisation (Productivity) of Major Ports during 1999-2000

During the last five decades, there has been a phenomenal growth of traffic at the country's major ports. In 1950-51, the major ports handled traffic of 19.38 million tonnes (MT). This rose to 33.12 MT during 1960-61, 55.58 MT in 1970-71 and 80.37 MT in 1980-81. The next decade witnessed a rise in traffic to a record level of 281.1 MT during 2000-01. Almost all the terminals dedicated bulk terminals and general cargo berths have been providing cargo-handling services beyond their capacity levels. As per the norms fixed by Government of India, normally the berth occupancy should be 75 per cent. Handling of traffic beyond the normal capacity of berths at Indian ports indicates the absence of adequate matching facilities. A survey on port-wise capacity vis-à-vis the traffic handled at major ports during 1999-2000 reveals capacity constraints that are choking the system. Indian ports are today operating at near saturation levels of capacity, resulting in high pre-berthing detention and turn around time of vessels.

Table 3.21 exhibits the capacity utilisation of major ports in 1999-2000. The overall capacity utilisation for all major ports was 105 per cent, with 271.92 MT of traffic handled against the capacity of 258.05 MT. Capacity utilisation was as high as 135 per cent in Chennai, 128 per cent in Visakhapatnam, 124 per cent in Calcutta, 119 per cent in Kandla and 106 per cent in Paradeep. The Kandla port has handled the highest (46.56 MT) amount of traffic in the corresponding year, whereas the port of Tuticorin handled the least (9.99 MT) amount of traffic. The Haldia port have the least percentage of capacity utilisation (72 per cent) during the year 1999-2000.

Table 3.21

Capacity Utilisation of Major Ports during the period 1999-2000

(in million tonnes)

Name of the ports	*Capacity as on 31.3.2000*	*Traffic handled 1999-00 (P)*	*Capacity utilisation 1999-00 (in percent)*
Calcutta	8.30	10.31	124
Haldia	28.70	20.71	72
Paradeep	12.85	13.64	106
Visakhapatnam	30.80	39.51	128
Chennai	27.62	37.44	135
Tuticorin	12.50	9.99	80
Cochin	13.45	12.80	95
New Mangalore	20.25	17.60	87
Mormugao	19.48	18.23	94
Mumbai	30.50	30.41	100
JNPT	14.60	14.98	103
Kandla	39.00	46.36	119
Total	**258.05**	**271.92**	-
Average for all ports			**105**

Capacity utilisation	*Name of the ports*
Above 100%	Calcutta, Paradeep, Visakhapatnam, Chennai, Mumbai, JNPT, Kandla
Below 100%	Haldia, Tuticorin, New Mangalore, Mormugao

Source : Government of India, *Basic Port Statistics of India*, Ministry of Surface Transport, New Delhi, 1999-2000.

3.15.20. Growth of Cargo Traffic Handled at Minor/Intermediate Ports during 1988-89 to 1999-2000

Table 3.22 exhibits the growth of cargo traffic handled at minor/intermediate ports during 1988-89 to 1999-2000. The Table also highlights the overseas and coastal traffic of minor ports with unloaded, loaded and trans-shipment parameters. This has been shown in Fig. 3.4. In 1988-89, the total overseas, coastal and trans-shipment traffic was 9.07 MT, of

Table 3.22

Growth of Cargo Traffic Handled at Minor/Intermediate Ports during the period 1988-89 to 1999-2000

('000 tonnes)

Year	Overseas				Coastal			Overseas & Coastal		Tranship-ment total	Overseas Coastal & Tranship-ment Total
	Unloaded	Loaded	Tranship-ment	Total	Unloaded	Loaded	Total	Unloaded	Loaded		
1988-89	4263	2890	-	7153	967	955	1922	5230	3845	-	**9075**
1989-90	4244	4513	-	8757	1144	955	2099	5388	5468	-	**10856**
1990-91	5713	3854	-	9567	1964	1251	3215	7677	5105	-	**12782**
1991-92	4765	4104	-	8869	3016	1373	4389	7781	5477	-	**13258**
1992-93	3908	4737	2325	10970	3094	1339	4433	7002	6076	2325	**15403**
1993-94	3637	6625	3948	14210	3839	1421	5260	7476	8046	3948	**19470**
1994-95	5397	6424	3209	15030	5367	1885	7252	10764	8309	3209	**22282**
1995-96	7064	8172	2887	18123	5116	2471	7587	12180	10643	2887	**25710**
1996-97	7376	7671	3393	18440	6115	3277	9392	13491	10948	3393	**27832**
1997-98	14246	10419	4498	29163	5221	4223	9444	19467	14642	4498	**38607**
1998-99	15017	8423	907	24347	6343	5616	11959	21360	14039	907	**36306**
1999-00	29445	7968	653	38066	10564	13890	24454	40009	21858	653	**62520**

Source : Government of India, *Basic Port Statistics of India*, Ministry of S■rface Transport, New Delhi, 1999-2000, p.209.

Fig. 3.4
Growth of Cargo Traffic Handled at Minor/Intermediate Ports during 1997 and 1998

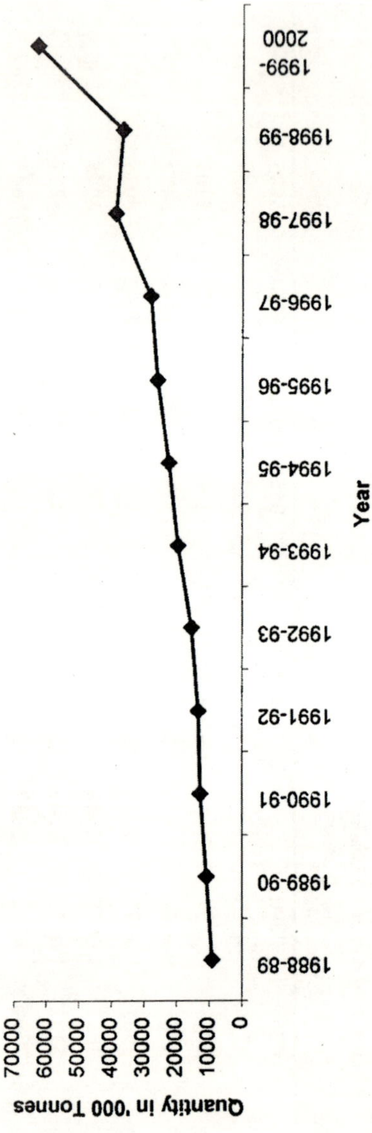

which 7.1 MT overseas traffic and 1.9 MT coastal traffic. In 1999-2000 the total cargo traffic reached 62.5 MT and the total overseas and coastal traffic were 38.06MT (60 per cent) and 24.45MT (39.1 per cent) respectively. Similarly, the share of unloaded and loaded traffic to total traffic were 40 MT (64 per cent) and 21.8 MT (35 per cent) respectively in 1999-2000. The share of trans-shipment was negligible 0.65 MT (1 per cent). In the last 12 years (1988-89 to 1999-2000) the cargo traffic handled by minor/intermediate ports shows a steady growth registering a 400 per cent increase in 1998-99 and further it jumped to more than 600 per cent rise in 1999-2000.

3.15.21. Share of Major Ports in Total Indian Port Traffic during 1970-71, 1980-81, 1985-86, 1990-91 and 1998-99

Table 3.23 portrays the share of major ports in total traffic of Indian ports in 1970-71, 1980-81, 1985-86, 1990-91 and 1998-99. During 1970-71 the share of Paradeep port was highest among the ports for handling 27.9 per

Table 3.23
Share of Major Ports in Total Indian Port Traffic during the period 1970 71, 1985-86, 1990-91, and 1998-99

(In percent)

Major Ports	*1970-71*	*1980-81*	*1985-86*	*1990-91*	*1998-99*
Kandla	2.08	10.88	13.79	12.96	16.16
Mumbai	18.56	21.10	20.32	19.02	12.30
JNPT	*	*	*	1.34	4.66
Mormugao	14.22	17.10	13.48	9.81	7.17
New Mangalore	**	1.19	3.08	5.28	5.65
Cochin	6.21	6.50	4.41	4.79	5.04
Tuticorin	**	3.18	3.53	3.34	4.04
Chennai	8.95	12.90	15.17	16.14	14.00
Vizag	11.27	12.57	13.30	12.78	14.18
Paradeep	27.90	2.78	2.78	4.53	5.21
Calcutta	7.98	5.04	3.48	2.71	3.63
Haldia	2.80	6.76	6.65	7.31	7.96

Notes : * not in operation, ** Insignificant share

Source : Government of India, ***Basic Port Statistics of India***, Ministry of Surface Transport, New Delhi, 1999-2000.

Fig. 3.5
Share of Major Ports in Total Indian Port Traffic during 1990-91 and 1998-99

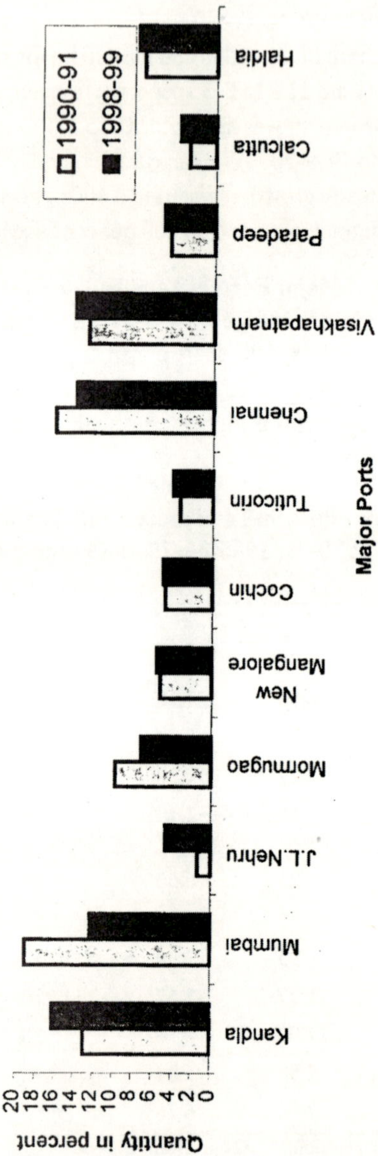

cent of total cargo. Similarly Mumbai port stood first in 1980-81, 1985-86 and 1990-91, for handling traffic of 21.10 per cent, 20.32 per cent and 19.02 per cent in the respective years. In 1998-99 Kandla port handled the highest share of traffic (16.16 per cent) among all the ports. This has been exhibited in Fig. 3.5. Jawaharlal Port came into operation in 1989 and thus have no figures of share in 1970-71, 1980-81 and 1985-86. Similarly Tuticorin and New Mangalore were newly established ports in 1970-71, so they have negligible share of cargo handled in that year. In 1998-99, the share of Calcutta port was least, i.e., 3.63 per cent among the major ports. In 1990-91, JNPT handled the least percentage of traffic, i.e., 1.34 per cent. In 1985-86 Paradeep's share was lowest of 2.78 per cent among the ports.

3.15.22. Share of Minor/Intermediate Ports in Total Cargo Handled by Indian Ports

The role of minor ports in the development of a nation's economy cannot be ignored. The minor and intermediate ports play an important role with the major ports in handling the export and import traffics. In the post-reform period the minor ports got boost for development by the State Governments with the private sector participation. Table 3.24 succinctly reveals the share of minor/intermediate ports in the handling of cargo by Indian ports. Cargo handled by minor ports exhibits a rising trend with marginal fluctuations in 1987-88 and 1998-99. The minor ports handle cargo of 8.37 million tonnes (6.31 per cent) in 1986-87 increased to 38.60 million tonnes (13.30 per cent) in 1997-98 and further grew up significantly to 62.50 MT (18.7 per cent) and 87.9 MT (23.9 per cent) in 1999-2000 and 2000-01 respectively. On an average the cargo handled by minor ports stood at 26.413 MT (10.48 per cent) per annum during the whole study period.. During the pre-reform period the average annual cargo handled by the minor ports was 14.30 MT (7.79 per cent) which was increased to 50.62 MT (15.88 per cent) representing more than three-fold rise during the period. Similarly the cargo handled by the 12 major ports also shows an increasing trend of 124.37 MT in 1986-87 to 281.1 MT in 2000-01. During the post-reform period the average traffic of major ports was 256.66 MT as against 161.81 MT in the pre-reform period. The total cargo handled by both major and minor ports also increased significantly during the study period from 132.74 MT in 1986-87 to 369.13 MT in 2000-01. On an average, the total cargo traffic handled by both major and minor ports was 176.12 MT in the

Table 3.24

Cargo Handled by Indian Ports and Share of Minor/Intermediate Ports during the period 1986-87 to 2000-01

(Traffic in Million Tonnes)

	Study period	*Cargo Handled by minor ports*	*Cargo Handled by major ports*	*Total cargo Handled by Indian Ports*	*Share of Minor Ports (Per cent)*
Pre-reform Period	1986-87	8.37	124.37	132.74	6.31
	1987-88	5.89	134.60	140.49	4.19
	1988-89	9.07	146.71	155.78	5.82
	1989-90	10.85	147.57	158.42	6.85
	1990-91	12.78	151.66	164.44	7.77
	1991-92	13.25	156.64	169.89	7.80
	1992-93	15.40	166.49	181.89	8.47
	1993-94	19.47	179.01	198.48	9.81
	1994-95	22.28	195.89	218.17	10.21
	1995-96	25.71	215.20	240.91	10.67
	Average	**14.30**	**161.81**	**176.12**	**7.79**
Post-reform Period	1996-97	27.83	226.96	254.79	10.92
	1997-98	38.60	251.65	290.25	13.30
	1998-99	36.30	251.73	288.03	12.60
	1999-00	62.50	271.9	334.4	18.7
	2000-01	87.9	281.1	369.13	23.9
	Average	**50.62**	**256.66**	**307.29**	**15.88**
	Whole period average	**26.41**	**193.43**	**219.84**	**10.48**

Source: Government of India, *Basic Port Statistics of India*, Ministry of Surface Transport, New Delhi.

pre-reform period which was increased considerably to 307.29 MT in the post-reform period as against 219.84 MT during the whole study period. The performance of the minor ports have increased, more significantly during the post-reform period because, more number of minor ports came into operation with private participation and active supports from the State Government during this period.

3.16. Summary

3.16.1. India has a vast coastline of nearly 6000 kms stretching from east to west coast. There are 12 major ports and 179 minor ports situated in the nine coastal States. Of the 12 major ports, six are located on the west coast and six on the east coast. Out of the total declared 179 minor ports, 13 are non-working ports, 120 ports belong to West Coast States, 24 ports belong to East Coast States and the rest 22 belong to the Union Territories. The primary responsibility for development and management of major ports rests with the Central Government. The major ports are governed by the Major Port Trust Act, 1963, which enables these ports to conduct regulatory as well as commercial functions. The State Governments administer the minor and intermediate ports. The ports handle 90 per cent of the country's foreign trade by volume and 70 per cent by value. Before independence, there was no such significant development in the establishment and development of ports except the two major ports at Visakhapatnam and Cochin including the ports of Bombay, Chennai and Calcutta.

3.16.2. After independence, the Government put emphasis on planned development through various Five Year Plans. During the First Five Year Plan, Kandla Major Port was developed as a replacement to Karachi, which became a part of Pakistan. With the increased emphasis on industrialisation after independence, the volume of cargo handled by the Indian ports almost doubled from about 19 MT to about 40 MT during the decade of 1950-51 to 1960-61. During the Second and Third Five Year Plan period, some new berths were added to Visakhapatnam port, Madras port and Cochin port. The port of Mormugao was enlisted in the major port list in 1963. The ports of Paradeep, Mangalore and Tuticorin were developed during this plan. From the Fourth Five Year Plan to the beginning of Sixth Five Year Plan (1969 to 1980-81) developmental works of some major ports were undertaken such as creation of Satellite Port at Haldia and berth capacity addition at all major ports.

3.16.3. During the Sixth Five Year Plan period, a new port was sanctioned for construction at Nhava Sheva, near Bombay. During the Seventh Plan, the Nhava Sheva port was commissioned (now known as Jawaharlal Nehru Port) and some new berths were added to the existing major ports. The Eighth and Ninth Five Year Plans are important from the overall port development point of view because the Indian economy had undergone a sea change in its economic policy and in 1996, the Government adopted the recommendations of the Rakesh Mohan Committee Report on infrastructure development. A new port at Ennore was constructed and a mechanised coal handling plant was inaugurated at Paradeep port with financial assistance from Asian Development Bank. To meet the emerging challenges of growing port sector at par with international standards and also to cope-up with the huge investments needs for such developments, the Government had adopted policy measures aimed at opening of the port sector to private investment. Besides the objective of mobilising substantial resources, the other objectives are the improvement in productivity, efficiency and quality of services, reduction in gestation period for setting up new facilities and to bring in new technology and improved management techniques for enhancing international competitiveness.

3.16.4. Under the private sector participation in major ports the government has already identified broad areas for investment and the guidelines in respect of procedures to be followed for inviting private investors into the port sector. The government has also announced the guidelines for joint sector participation between major port and minor port, between major port and foreign port and between a major port and company. To enable the implementation of joint venture scheme and facilitate equity participation by major ports in any other port including a minor port, the Major Port Trust Act, 1963 has been amended. Since the formulation of the private sector participation guidelines by the Government of India, the response from the private sector has been encouraging. There are in 24 projects identified, which will add a capacity of 60.05 MT at various ports with an investment of Rs. 78.76 billion in the next five years.

3.16.5. During the last five decades the major ports have witnessed a lot of ups and downs but the thirst for upsurge in achieving the new heights in traffic handling is still continuing. The traffic handled was 19.38 MT during 1950-51, 33.12 MT during 1960-61, 55.58 MT during 1970-71 whereas it was 80.37 MT during 1980-81. Out of the total traffic handled at major ports, POL maintains the largest share of 43 per cent, coal 13 per cent, iron ore 21 per cent and fertiliser 5 per cent. Out of the total traffic of 369 MT during 2000-01, 76 per cent was handled by the major ports and 24 per cent by the minor ports. Ports like Kandla, Visakhapatnam, Chennai and Mumbai together handled around 57 per cent of the total traffic of all major ports.

3.16.6. The output per ship berth-day depicts an increasing quantity of 5167 tonnes during 1998-99, against 4912 tonnes in 1997-98. The Mormugao port has the highest output per ship berth-day in all types of vessels of 11076 tonnes in 1998-99 as against 10446 tonnes during 1997-98 followed by Kandla and New Mangalore ports of 8778 tonnes and 7507 tonnes respectively. Calcutta port has the lowest output per ship berth-day of 1697 tonnes in 1998-99. Due to increase in number of ships entering into the port and also the increasing efficiency of the berths with the use of mechanised instruments resulted higher output per ship berth-day at all major ports.

3.16.7. The average berth occupancy at all major ports exhibit a fluctuating trend during the ten years of study from 1989-90 to 1998-99. During 1998-99, the Kandla port has the highest berth occupancy of 93 per cent followed by Tuticorin and Chennai of 85.2 per cent and 81.2 per cent respectively. Calcutta port has the least percentage of berth occupancy of 48.4 per cent during the year. The reasons of fluctuating trend may be due to individual port problems such as labour unrest at the port, breakdown of machinery, natural calamities like cyclones, higher tonnage tariffs and non-availability of mechanised berths.

3.16.8. The average turn-around time at almost all-major ports have come down significantly to 5.7 days during 1998-99 as against 6.3 days during 1997-98. But at the same time the average turn-around time for the ports at Singapore was only 6 to 8 hours. The decline in the ASTA is due to addition of more number of mechanised berths and efficient labour management at all major ports. The analysis reveals that during 1998-99, Kandla port had the longest turn-around time of 8.3 days where as Cochin port had the least turn-around time of 3.4 days. The break bulk and dry bulk (conv.) vessels have the longest turn-around time during 1997-98 and 1998-99 at all the major ports whereas container vessels and liquid bulk vessels have the least turn-around time during the years. Similarly commodity-wise fertilisers have the longest average turn-around time at all major ports followed by dry bulks.

3.16.9. Average pre-berthing time has also declined significantly during the last four years from 1996-97 to 1999-2000. The average pre-berthing time of all major ports was 3.6 days in 1996-97, which reduced more than half to 1.5 days in 1999-2000. The average pre-berthing is the time for which a ship waits before getting entry into a berth. Due to capacity addition into the ports by expansion and mechanisation of berths and operation of new minor ports, the average pre-berthing time have reduced significantly at the Indian major ports. The container type vessels have the least pre-berthing time whereas break bulks have the longest pre-berthing time in overall at major ports during 1998-99. Similarly, during 1999-2000 the Kandla port has the longest pre-berthing time of 3.04 days whereas J.L.Nehru Port has the least pre-berthing time of 0.64 day. The commodity-wise average non-working time at major ports also declined considerably during 1999-2000. During the year, Calcutta port has the longest average non-working time of 1.88 days and JNPT has the least average non-working time of 0.13 day. The fertiliser berths have the longest and liquid bulk berths have the least non-working time at major ports during 1999-2000. The traffic handled by minor/intermediate ports has increased in absolute terms from 8.37 MT in 1986-87 to 87.9 MT in 2000-01. The post-reform period average traffic was 50.62 MT per annum which is significantly higher than the pre-reform period average of 14.30 MT. Similarly the percentage share of minor ports to all ports also rose to 24 per cent from 6 per cent during the study period. In the post-reform period the different State Governments showed interest in developing their minor ports including creation of new ports through private participation.

3.16.10. The capacity utilisation at Indian major ports was satisfactory during the Five Year Plans. With the increase in aggregate port capacity from 20 MT in First Five Year Plan to 377 MT in the Ninth Five Year Plan, the traffic handled at major ports also increased from 23 MT in First Five Year Plan to 424 MT in Ninth Five Year Plan. Out of the nine plans the port capacity were utilised above 100 per cent during 3 plans and above 90 per cent during 5 plan periods. The overall capacity utilisation of major ports was 105 per cent during 1999-2000, with 271.92 MT of traffic handled against a capacity of 258.05 MT. The ports with above 100 per cent capacity utilisation during the same year were Chennai (135 per cent), Visakhapatnam (128 per cent), Calcutta (124 per cent), Kandla (119 per cent) and Paradeep (106 per cent) and the rest have above 70 per cent of capacity utilisation.

3.16.11. The structural re-organisation of major port trust is made to provide the necessary independence of authority and decision making, to coagulate investment, execute projects and manage operations with professional expertise, through corporatisation of major ports. A beginning in this direction has been made by declaring Ennore port as a company. It has also been decided to corporatise JNPT and Haldia port. It is expected that corporatisation would facilitate speedier decision making, more autonomy and better accountability leading to efficiency and commercial functioning. The new set up of major ports functioning as a company would create conducive environment to function on commercial lines.

3.16.12. The on-going economic reforms in the country envisage the downsizing of existing surplus manpower in the port sector to increase the efficiency and enhance productivity of the ports. As a sequel to this, the Indian ports viz. Mumbai, New Mangalore, Tuticorin, Calcutta and Paradeep port trusts have rolled back the age of retirement from 60 to 58 years. The Mumbai Port Trust also reduced its workforce from 30,000 to 23,000 with an expenditure of Rs.450 crore by announcing a special VRS in January 2001 and it has the plan of further reducing the workforce to 10,000. On the other hand fresh recruitment are banned and operational requirements are met through retraining of the existing staff.

3.16.13. Today, the existing Indian Port infrastructure is insufficient to meet the growing demands of the country. The port sector suffers due to many problems, such as, operational constraints like break-down of port equipment and use of obsolete cargo handling equipment, inadequate facilities for dredging of berths and channels, inefficient and non-optimal deployment of port equipment, excessive reliance on labour-intensive methods of bulk handling of cargo, and poor interdepartmental co-ordination between the customs department and the port authorities. The poor productivity, over-stretching of capacity and congestion of the ports are reflected in higher throughport cost and high sea transport cost to India. The throughport cost of containerised cargo in India is around 50 per cent higher than the cost incurred at Bangkok, Colombo and Singapore. The sea transport cost to India is also high due to higher ship waiting time at Ports and slower loading/unloading of cargo. As per the World Bank Study, a moderate reduction of ship time at berth in line with international output standards would allow potential savings to the tune of Rs. 3,000 million per year based on 1990-91 traffic volumes. It is obvious that these inadequate port infrastructural facilities are to the detriment of Indian exporters/importers which results in costlier inputs for industries and makes the Indian exports relatively un-competitive.

References

1. Ramakrishnan, R., "Potentials, Problems and Strategies for Port Development in India", *Indian Shipping*, Vol. 50, No. 5, Mumbai 1998, pp.17-26.
2. De, P. and Ghosh, B., : "Indian Ports and Globalisation Grounding Economics in Geography" *Economic and Political Weekly*, Vol.XXXVI, No. 34, Mumbai, August 25, 2001, p. 3273.
3. Gopalan, S. and Motiwani, S.C., "Modernisation of Ports" *Indian Shipping*, Vol. 45, No. 425, Mumbai,1993, pp. 23-25.
4. Gopalan, S., "Port Development Scenario in India" *Indian Shipping*, Vol.49, No.5, Mumbai,1997, pp. 11-13.
5. Sampath, R., "Port Management - Privatisation Holds the Key" *The Hindu Survey of Indian Industry*,Chennai, 2001, pp. 123-126.
6. Satya Sundaram, I. "Ports - Productivity Holds the Key" *Facts for You*, Vol. 22, No. 4, New Delhi, January 2002, p. 17.
7. "Need and Approach to Commercialisation of Infrastructure Projects". *The India Infrastructure Report* (Rakesh Mohan Committee Report), Vol. II, submitted to Government of India on June 22, 1996.
8. Ganesh, G. "Privatisation in India" A Series on Concept and Applications in Management, Mittal Publication, New Delhi, 2001, pp. 178-181.
9. Ramakrishna, R., "Privatisation of Port Development – Indian and Foreign Ports", *Indian Shipping*, Vol. 53, Mumbai, Sept-Oct, 2001, p. 19.
10. Sharma M, "Infrastructure Development Shifing Paradigms" A paper presented in International Symposium on Development Policies for the New Millennium at Indira Gandhi Institute of Development Research (IGIDR), Mumbai on 12-14 July, 2000.
11. "Private Sector Role in Port Privatisation Finalised", *Business Standard*, No. 173, Vol. XXV, Kolkata, February 24, 2002, p. 9.
12. "Private Participation in Ports – Picking up at Last" *Indian Infrastructure*, Vol. 3, No. 12, New Delhi, July 2001, p. 24.
13. "Do Privately Run Ports Have the Edge?" *The Hindu Business Line*, No. 354, Vol. 8, Visakhapatnam, December 24, 2001.
14. "Private Participation in Ports Facilities – Recent Trends" *Indian Infrastructure*, Vol. 2, No. 7, New Delhi, February 2000, pp. 36-39.

15. "Privatisation in Developing Countries – A Global Perspective on Recent Divestitures" A Global Development Finance Report 2000 of World Bank published in *Indian infrastructure*, Vol. 2, No. 10, New Delhi, May 2000, pp.14-18.
16. Ramakrishna, R. "Certain Experiences on Privatisation of Port Development–Foreign Ports and Indian Ports" *Indian Ports*, Vol. XXXIII, No. 2, Mumbai, October 2002,
17. The World Bank, "Private Infrastructure in East Asia", Technical Paper No.501, Washington D.C. 2001.
18. "Port Financing – Still a Trickle", *Indian Infrastructure*, Vol. 3, No. 12, New Delhi, July 2001, p. 28.
19. *Ibid.*
20. "Corporatisation of Ports" *Indian Infrastructure*, Vol. 3, No. 12, New Delhi, July 2001, p. 30.
21. "J N Port Corporatisation Likely by Fiscal-End" *The Hindu Business Line*, New Delhi. May 8, 2001,
22. Kurup. N. K., "Corporatisation of Ports–Time-Bound Plan Called For" *The Hindu Business Line*, Vol. 7, No. 342, Visakhapatnam, December 11, 2000, p. 4.
23. "Mormugao Appoints PwC for Corporatisation", *The Hindu Business Line*, New Delhi, January 6, 2001.
24. Shah. Y. S., and Jindal. N. K. "Western Regional Cooperation Infrastructure – Vision 2000 – Port Sector" Indian Merchants Chamber, Mumbai 1997, pp. 94-95.
25. Rajwadkar, K., "Mumbai Port Trust Gets 6,000 Applications for VRS" *The Financial Express*, Chennai, March 13, 2001.
26. Sanyal, S., "Centre May Unveil Modified VRS for Port Workers" *The Hindu Business Line*, New Delhi, October 19, 2001, p. 2.

4

State of Infrastructure Including Ports in Orissa

4.1. Introduction

4.1.1. Orissa, comprising the geographical area of 1.56 lakh square kilometres which account for about 4.74 per cent of India's landmass. It lies between 17.31 degree and 22.27 degree north latitude and 81.27 degree and 87.30 degree east latitude. The population of the State according to 2001 census was 36.71 million, which is for 3.57 per cent of the total population of the Country.[1] Nearly 85 per cent of its population live in the rural areas and depend mostly on agriculture for their livelihood. The State is surrounded by West Bengal, Bihar and Jharkhand in the north, Chattisgarh in the west, Andhra Pradesh in the south and the Bay of Bengal in the east. The length of its coastline is nearly 480 kms. As per the All India Minerals Resources Estimates made for 2000-01, the reserve of coal was the highest at 51,571 million tonne followed by iron ore (3567 million tonnes), bauxite (1733 million tonnes) and limestone (1032 million tonnes) in Orissa.[2] The mineral deposits of Orissa in respect of chromite, bauxite, iron ore, limestone were about 98.39 per cent, 59.53 per cent, 27.99 per cent and 1.35 per cent respectively of the total deposits of India. Though Orissa is rich in mineral resources, the rate of exploitation of mineral in the State is less than one per cent in all cases except graphite (2 per cent) lead ore (9 per cent) and manganese (1.1 per cent). The availability of adequate and developed physical or economic infrastructure could definitely show the way for rapid economic development of the State.

4.1.2. Infrastructure is generally defined as the physical framework of facilities through which goods and services are provided to the public.

Infrastructure is considered as the wheels of the economy, because it has multiple and complex linkages among various productive activities of the economy. It affects production and consumption directly, creating positive and negative spillover effects and involves large flows of expenditure.[3] The place of infrastructure sector as well as of its soundness, are crucial to the stability of nation's total development. The all-pervading importance of infrastructure sector would be clear from the fact that it encompasses the whole spectrum of vital services such as transportation (railways, roads and road transport, civil aviation, port and shipping), power generation, transmission and distribution, telecommunications, postal facilities and urban development.[4]

4.1.3. Infrastructural facilities could be classified into two broad categories namely economic or physical infrastructure and social infrastructure. The economic or physical infrastructure includes services from major dams, sanitation and sewerage, canal works for irrigation, drainage, storage, transport services including urban and inter-urban railways, ports and water-ways and aviation. On the other hand, social infrastructure facilities include medical and education which are more important from a societal point of view.[5]

4.1.4. A well developed network of transport and communication is a basic infrastructural prerequisite for rapid economic development. Adequacy of infrastructure in the transport and communication sector is crucial for attracting investment. The ongoing economic reforms, therefore, attach high priority to development of transport and communication infrastructure. The Industrial Policy 1996 accords special priority to infrastructural development which in turn would facilitate flow of funds for large investment in the industrial sector.[1] Development of transportation infrastructure is also essential for marketing of agricultural products and helps the farmers to get fair price by transporting these produces to far off destinations.

4.2. Present State of Transport Infrastructure in Orissa

4.2.1. In Orissa, the planners were of the view that the private sector cannot be relied upon to make investment in this area. Hence, it was decided that the State should assume the sole responsibility and use public sector investments for the provision of infrastructural facilities. A lion's share of total plan outlay has been devoted to the development of infrastructure. This signifies its priority in plan allocation. A substantial portion (around 45 per cent) of the total outlay on infrastructure has gone to the development of economic infrastructure. Within economic infrastructure, power and transport have received the largest share.[7] Both Central and State Governments have assumed the leadership role in creating necessary infrastructural facilities. On a comparative basis, the Government of Orissa has played an increasingly greater role in the development of infrastructure.

Road Infrastructure in Orissa

4.2.2. In absence of adequate internal rail linkages, roads are the major means of transportation in the State. The total road length in the State was 2,37,104 kms. as on 31.03.2002. The surfaced road length per 1000 square km of area was 333 kms. as compared to the all India average of 363 kms. during 1998-99. The roads of different categories in the State include 3,190 kms. of National Highways, 30 kms. of Express Highways, 4,870 kms. of State Highways, 3727 kms. of Major District Roads (MDR), 4,545 kms. of Other District Roads (ODR), 4,670 kms. of Classified Village Roads (CVR), 24,852 kms. of village roads, 20,372 kms. of Panchayat Samiti roads, 1,39,973 kms. of GP roads, 7,030 kms. of forest roads, 17,480 kms. of municipal roads, 6,277 kms. of irrigation roads and 88 kms. of GRIDCO roads.[8]

4.2.3. All-weather connectivity to every village is necessary for improving the quality of life and economic conditions in rural areas. Rural connectivity has been identified as one of the basic minimum services for development of agriculture and the rural economy and the State Government has accorded high priority to this sector. According to estimates available with the planning commission, about 40 per cent of villages in Orissa have all-weather connectivity as compared to 60 per cent at the national level. The Pradhan Mantri Gram Sadak Yojana (PMGSY) sponsored by the Central Government aims at improving all-weather rural connectivity. Under this scheme, all the villages with more than 1000 population will be connected with all-weather roads by March 2003 and all the villages with more than 500 population by March 2007. Government of India have sanctioned 139 packages for 2000-01 consisting of 1110 kms. of black-topped road, 426 kms. of concrete road and 1262 C.D. works at a cost of Rs.175.00 crore. During 2001-02, an amount of Rs. 71.36 crore has been proposed under PMGSY. With a view to improving road infrastructure World Bank have sanctioned 2.9 million U.S. dollars for project preparation on work of Orissa State Road Projects. It is proposed to take up upgradation and maintenance of 198 km and heavy maintenance of 1210 km road at a cost of Rs. 800 crore out of which world bank loan would be Rs.560 crores.[9]

National Highways

4.2.4. The total number of highways in the State has increased to twelve covering a total length of 3190.39 kms passing through 25 districts of Orissa. Out of 3190.39 kms., a portion of NH 5 (385 kms.) and total N.H.60 (52 kms.) totaling to 437 kms. have been handed over to National Highway Authority of India (NHAI) for maintenance and improvement under Golden Quadrilateral Project with effect from 1.4.1999. The NHAI took up survey and investigation of N.H. 5 and N.H. 60 for converting the road to four-lane carriageway. The stretch of N.H. 5 from Cuttack to Bhubaneswar measuring 27.80 kms. was widened to four lane under World Bank assistance at an estimated cost of Rs.218.41 crores and opened to traffic on 2.9.2000. The stretches from 27.80 kms. to 61.00 kms. of N.H. 5 has been taken up for widening to four lane since February 2000 with a project cost of Rs. 137.60 crore and is targeted for completion by February 2003.

4.2.5. It has been proposed to upgrade existing State highways comprising of 1483.28 kms. to National Highways in view of their importance. The proposal has been placed before the Ministry of Road Transport and Highways, Government of India for approval. Besides this, the Government of Orissa have started preliminary works for providing a coastal highway connecting the important locations along the coast line of Bay of Bengal linking Andhra Pradesh in the South and West Bengal in the North. The proposed coastline road will extend over a length of about 574 kms. from Gopalpur in Ganjam district of Orissa to Digha in Medinapur district of West Bengal. This road is envisaged to be executed with assistance from the Government of Norway.[10]

Rail Transport Infrastructure in Orissa

4.2.6. Railways have a major role in goods and passenger movement and have considerable impact on the socio-economic development of different regions of the country. Orissa has so far remained backward in the field of development of railways. The existing railway lines pass through the fringes of the State leaving the central areas untouched. The inadequacy is one of the factors which has had an adverse impact on the pace of infrastructural and industrial development in the State. The State had 2,385 kms. of railway route (broad gauge 2,247 kms. and narrow gauge 144 kms) as on 31.03.2001. The railway route length in the State per thousand sq. km. of area comes to 15.3 kms. By 1999-2000, a length of 329 km was electrified. There are 274 railway stations in the State.

4.2.7. The State Government have been pursuing proposals relating to the expansion of the railway network in the State through the Rail Coordination Directorate which is functioning under the administrative control of the transport department. The directorate also functions as a liaisoning agency between the State Government and Railway authorities for development of rail communication and movement of freight and essential commodities. Two railway divisions of South Eastern Railways are located in Orissa with headquarters at Khurda Road and Sambalpur and a new railway zone namely East Coast Zone has been functioning at Bhubaneswar since 1996.

4.2.8. During the year 2000-2001 efforts were made for development and expansion of railway network in the State. The Talcher-Sambalpur railway line (174 kms.) has since been completed and opened to traffic. Another two projects, i.e., Daitari-Bansapani (155 kms.) and Lanjigarh Road - Junagarh (54 kms.) which were sanctioned during 1992-94 with estimated project cost of Rs. 694.98 crore are going to be completed shortly. The other ongoing projects are Koraput-Rayagada (164 kms.), Khurda Road-Bolangir (289 kms.), Haridaspur-Paradeep (78 kms.) and Angul-Sukinda Road (90 kms.). The estimated project cost of these four projects is Rs.1354.36 crore. The work of gauge conversion and doubling of different railway lines is in progress. Gauge conversion of Rupsa-Bangiriposi (89 kms.) and Nuapada-Gunpur (90 kms.) were sanctioned in 1995-96 and 1997-98 with estimated cost of Rs.80.00 crore and Rs. 66.35 crore respectively. Similarly, doubling of 8 rail projects with estimated project cost of Rs.749.77 crore are in progress. Electrification of Kharagpur-Nimopura-Bhubaneswar and Bhubaneswar-Visakhapatnam tracks is in progress with an estimated project cost of Rs. 617.48 crores.[11]

Civil Aviation Infrastructure

4.2.9. In view of Orissa's geographical, tourist and commercial importance, the Government of India, in the Ministry of Civil Aviation have taken up expansion and modernisation of Bhubaneswar Airport. The State Government have provided 68.3 acres of land free of cost and the development work of the airport is in progress. Flights from Bhubaneswar to cities like Delhi, Kolkata, Chennai, Hyderabad and Mumbai are available consequent upon declaration of Bhubaneswar Airport as customs airport. An air cargo complex started functioning at the airport in August 1995 under the Air Customs Division, Bhubaneswar to facilitate export and import by air. At present, there are 13 airstrips and 16 helipads in the State for landing of State Government aircrafts and helicopters and efforts are being made for black topping of all the air strips to make them fit for all weather operation. During 2000-01, an amount of Rs. 43.50 lakh was earmarked for maintenance and development of airstrips/helipads while Rs.113.84 lakh has been proposed for 2001-02.[12]

Port Infrastructure in Orissa

4.2.10. Orissa, situated in the east coast of the country have 3 operable ports, of which Paradeep is the only major port and Gopalpur and Dhamra are minor ports.

The Port of Paradeep

4.2.11. Paradeep is one of the 12 major ports of India and the only major port located in Orissa. It is the main out-let and in-let of the sea-borne trade of the eastern part of the country spread over States such as Orissa, Andhra Pradesh, Madhya Pradesh, Uttar Pradesh, Bihar and West Bengal . The natural resources and industrial products of this widespread hinterland are immense and the value of the mineral trade of the country passing through the port of Paradeep is considerably higher than many other major ports of India. During 2000-2001, 130.52 lakh MT of goods were exported and 68.40 lakh MT of goods were imported through the port. An amount of Rs. 1096.58 crore was invested during 1999-2000 and 4,116 persons were employed in the port during 2000-01.[13]

Gopalpur Minor Port

4.2.12. Gopalpur port a fair weather port located 160 kms from Paradeep developed by the State Government with an investment of Rs.

35.95 crore which has been opened to traffic from 1987. This port operates for about 5 months i.e. from October to March. Mainly ilmenite, fertilizer and wheat move through the port. During 2000-01, 1.34 lakh MT ilmenite was exported through the port as against 1.54 lakh MT during 1999-00. Ilmenite was the only cargo handled by this port during the last three years while no cargo has been imported through this port for the last three years. An amount of Rs. 2.75 crore was collected as revenue during the year 2000-01 and employment of about 1000 persons round the year and for about 3000 persons for five months in the year was created. This Port obtained grant of Rs. 50.00 lakh during 1999-00 and Rs. 190.00 lakh during 2000-01 from NFCR for repair/restoration work of damages caused by the 1999 cyclone.[14]

4.2.13. Keeping in view the overall economic development of the State and the incentives to Special Economic Zones (SEZs) in the 2002-07 Exim Policy, Tata Steel has decided to use the land which was acquired for a steel plant at Gopalpur. In the meantime the Central Government had approved the proposal of declaring Gopalpur as a SEZ on 19th March 2001. The proposed SEZ will be located near Gopalpur over 3200 acre of land. The pre-feasibility report for the project had been prepared by Tata Economic Consultancy Services on behalf of the company. The feasibility report is being prepared by KPMG. This is going to be a chemical and metallurgical SEZ where a number of industries, mostly in the field of Alumina/Aluminium, chrome, iron and beach sand are likely to be established. TISCO is the facilitator for the SEZ with the Government of Orissa as the main sponsorer. In March 2001, the State Government has decided to develop the port in a joint venture with Adani Export Limited (AEL) of Gujarat. As per the MOU, the port would be developed on build-own-operate-transfer (BOOT) basis and would be operated for a period of 30 years. The project is estimated to cost Rs.20 billion. The port will be totally mechanised and will be of international standards AEL plans to initially invest Rs.500 million. This will be followed by another investment of Rs.6 billion to upgrade the seasonal port to an all-weather one.[15]

Dhamra Port

4.2.14. Dhamra minor port is situated between Haldia and Paradeep. The State Government has decided to develop it as a mega port through private investment. Accordingly an agreement has been signed with M/s International Sea Port Ltd. (ISPL) of Singapore and ICICI the lead financier of the project in April, 1998 for the expansion and modernisation of the existing port at Dhamra at a cost of Rs.14.02 billion. The port was to be developed on a build-own-operate-share- transfer (BOOST) basis with a concession period of 34 years, including the four-years construction period. This further can be extendable by a period of 10 years at a time.[16] After the State Government ratification of the Concession Agreement (CA) with the ISPL and ICICI, one Andhra Pradesh based ferro-alloys and hydel company GMR industries has evinced interest to pick up equity in the Rs.1,476 crore Dhamra Port Project. Dhamra Port, once expanded, would become one of India's largest bulk cargo handling ports and will be able to handle internationally contemporary ships. It is also expected that the port would provide an integrated set of services to large bulk cargo users. The port after development will handle ships weighing upto 1.5 lakh tonne. The port will have mechanised loading and unloading facilities for coal, coking coal and iron ore and per hour handling capacity would be 4,000 tonne to 6,000 tonne. It will also have 2.5 million metric tonne stock hoarding capacity while there will be a 62.5 km rail link between Bhadrak and Dhamra.[17]

Inland Water Transport (IWT)

4.2.15. The State Government is providing inland water transport services through motorised launches in different inaccessible areas. Ministry of Surface Transport, Government of India extends support and assistance for improvement of inland waterways, navigation control, etc. The Directorate of Inland Water Transport (DIWT), Orissa is the nodal agency for the operation of motor launch services. At present, 20 mechanised launches and 5 country boats are running on 8 different water routes namely Chandabali to Aradi, Rajnagar and Talchuan, Balugaon to Krishnaprasad, Kalijai, Nuapada and Satapada and Nuagarh to Sribantapur. The route Nuagarh-Sribantapur was suspended temporarily during 2000-01 due to damage of motor launches by the super cyclone of October 1999. The DIWT is also entrusted with the work of registration of inland vessels, investigation of new water routes for navigation and imparting crew training to fresh in-service personnel at the Crew Training Institute, Chandabali. During 2000-01, it has invested Rs.23.98 lakh and provided carriage to 2,52,215 passengers with a revenue collection of Rs.17.21 lakh as against investment of Rs.29.91 lakh, carriage of 2,06,726 passenger and revenue collection of Rs.13.85 lakh during 1999-00.

4.3. Other Infrastructural Facilities in Orissa

Postal and Telecom Infrastructure

4.3.1. There were 8,145 post offices in the State in 2000-01 out of which 7,542 post offices, i.e.,93 per cent were located in rural areas and the remaining 603 (7 per cent) in urban areas. The number of post offices per 100 sq.km in Orissa is 5.2 and the average number of post offices available in the State per lakh population comes to 22.2. Premium postal services such as speed post, express parcel post, mass mailing services, corporate money order service and satellite mail service are available in the State. The telecommunication service network has undergone a major expansion in the State in the nineties. In 1994-95, there were 656 telephone exchange, 26 Departmental Telegraph Offices and 1,15,520 telephone connections in operation. By 2000-01, the number of telephone exchanges, telegraph offices and telephone connections in the State have been increased to 990, 30 and 5,26,416 respectively. The number of telephone connections per 1000 persons was 3.5 as against the all India average of 9.0 in 1994-95, which increased to 14.34 by 2000-01. All the telephone exchanges are electronic. The Subscriber Trunk Dialing (STD) service is now available at 915 stations spread over all the 30 districts. A 1000 line node is available at Bhubaneswar, which caters to the Internet subscribers of Orissa on local call basis.[18]

Financial Sector Infrastructure

4.3.2. The role of a well-developed financial infrastructure in stimulating and sustaining economic growth is well recognised. A network of financial institutions helps the economy to deploy its savings more efficiently. There are 30 commercial banks with 1380 branches and 9 Regional Rural Banks (RRBs) with 834 branches in the State. There is one branch for around 16.6 thousand persons. While the aggregate deposits have increased by 111 per cent between 1996-97 to 2000-01, the gross bank credit has increased by about 79 per cent. The Credit-Deposit (C-D) ratio steadily declined from 48.99 in 1996-97 to 39.75 in 1999-00 and increased marginally to 41.46 during 2000-01. This was much less than the all India average of 58.33. In 2000-01, the States with better Credit-Deposit ratio than Orissa included Tamil Nadu (90.60), Maharashtra (85.39), Delhi (82.89), Andhra Pradesh (63.28), Karnataka (59.33), Gujarat (49.43), Madhya Pradesh (48.33), Rajasthan (48.18), West Bengal (44.09) and Kerala (43.05).[19]

4.3.3. Orissa has a three tier co-operative credit structure in rural areas for extending short and medium term loans with Orissa State Co-operative Bank (OSCB) at the apex level, Central Co-operative Banks (CCB) at the district level and primary agricultural co-operative societies (PACS) at the base level. There are 2525 PACs, 218 large size agricultural and multipurpose societies (LAMPs) and 6 Farmers's Service Societies (FSSs) extending short and medium term agricultural loans to cultivators. To provide long term loans, there is a two-tier structure in the State with Orissa State Co-operative Agricultural Rural Development Bank (OSCARD) at the apex level and Co-operative Agricultural Rural Development (CARD) Banks at the base level. At present there are 53 CARD Banks functioning mostly at the sub-divisional level to advance long-term agricultural credit for purposes like land shaping, purchase of tractors, power tillers, pump sets etc. In the urban areas, urban co-operative banks, employees credit co-operative societies etc. are functioning which provide loans to traders and salary and wage earners. The aggregate deposit and gross credit of Orissa State Co-operative Bank during 2000-01 was Rs.554.76 crore and Rs.800.00 crore with a credit-deposit ratio of 144.21 per cent in comparison to all India average of 87.01 per cent.[20]

4.3.4. Banks extend loan facilities to priority sectors in accordance with the annual credit plan formulated for each district by the District Level Co-ordination Committee (DLCC) for the district. During 2000-01, against the target of Rs.1821.59 crore, loan assistance of Rs.1829.93 crore was provided by the Banks under agriculture, industry and services sectors, with achievement of 100.46 per cent of the target fixed. Out of the total investment of Rs.1829.93 crore, services sector received the lion's share of 46.34 per cent, followed by agriculture sector 42.80 per cent and industry sector 10.86 per cent. The achievement for agriculture industry and services sectors was 78.46 per cent, 75.23 per cent and 151.64 per cent respectively against the respective targets fixed in the credit plan. During 2000-01, commercial banks, RRBs and co-operative banks have provided loan assistance of Rs.118.64 crore to 81,721 beneficiary families as against Rs.92.30 crore to 48,448 families in 1999-2000 under different anti-poverty programmes.

4.3.5. Banks are providing credit facilities under housing schemes, for rehabilitation of sick industrial units, under Prime Minister's Rozgar Yojana (PMRY) under National Project of Bio-Gas Development etc. During 2000-01, banks have disbursed Rs.18.43 crore to 2,096 persons under national housing scheme, Rs.1.80 crore to 653 persons under Home Loan Scheme and Rs.61.02 crore in favour of 11,469 persons under Golden Jubilee Rural Housing Scheme. Under PMRY, during 2000-01, against the target to cover 12,150 beneficiaries and an amount of Rs.51.53 crore was disbursed to 7,770 beneficiaries. In different districts of the State 1,169 Self Help Groups (SHGs) have taken up economic activity with a coverage of 13,449 members with subsidy and credit to the tune of Rs.10.78 crore and Rs.16.55 crore respectively. Besides one new scheme namely "Mission Shakti" was launched on 8th March 2001, i.e., International Women's Day with an aim to promote one lakh Self Help Groups (Women) within a period of four years and the target for credit linkage has been set for 10,500 SHGs, during 2001-02.

4.3.6. The Orissa State Financial Corporation (OSFC) was set-up in March 1956 and it started commercial operations from 1957-58. The corporation provides financial assistance for setting up of small and medium scale industries, construction of hostels and nursing homes, acquisition of transport vehicles etc. It also provides financial support for modernisation, expansion and rehabilitation of sick industrial units. Since inception of operations upto 31.03.2001 the corporation has disbursed Rs.1064.32 crore to 26,513 units. During 2000-01, the corporation disbursed an amount of Rs.115.12 crore to 1,146 units as against Rs.82.79 crore covering 584 units in 1999-2000. Out of the total investment of Rs.115.12 crore during 2000-01, the flow of assistance to backward districts constituted 13.07 per cent, 15.12 per cent to no industry districts and 71.81 per cent to other districts. The total flow of assistance to no industry districts and backward districts increased from Rs. 24.81 crore during 1999-2000 to Rs. 32.45 crore in 2000-01.[21]

Power Sector Infrastructure

4.3.7. Energy otherwise known as power is one of the prime movers of any developed economy. Adequate and reliable availability of power is indispensable for sustained growth of the economy. The primary objectives in this sector are optimum utilisation of the power generated, substantial reduction of transmission and distribution losses, maximising generation from the existing capacity and further addition of units to generate more power for meeting the increasing demand for power in coming years. Presently, the power supply position in Orissa is quite satisfactory for meeting its own demand. However, optimum utilisation of existing capacity and generation from new units will undoubtedly enable the State to sell power outside the State and thereby earn substantial revenue.[22]

4.3.8. Orissa has the distinction of being the pioneering State in power sector reform. With the enactment of Orissa Electricity Reform Act, 1995, the erstwhile Orissa State Electricity Board (OSEB) was restructured and an independent regulatory commission was established to improve the overall efficiency of the system and to protect the interest of consumers. The functions of OSEB were entrusted to two new corporations namely (i) Grid Corporation of Orissa (GRIDCO) and (ii) Orissa Hydro Power Corporation (OHPC) on 1st April 1996. The existing transmission and distribution system was transferred to GRIDCO and all hydro power stations including projects under construction were transferred to OHPC. Orissa Power Generation Corporation (OPGC), which was incorporated in 1984, is looking after the thermal power projects in the State. The distribution function of GRIDCO was privatized in the year 1999 and was entrusted to four private distribution companies, such as (i) Central Electricity Supply Company of Orissa Ltd.(CESCO), (ii) North-Eastern Electricity Supply Company of Orissa Ltd. (NESCO), (iii) Western Electricity Supply Company of Orissa Ltd. (WESCO) and (iv) Southern Electricity Supply Company of Orissa Ltd. (SOUTHCO).

4.3.9. The demand for power in the State has been growing up steadily due to increasing industrialisation, urbanisation and rural electrification.

The estimated demand for power has increased from 1,136 MW during 1996-97 to 1340 MW during 2000-01, registering an increase of 17.96 per cent over the period. The State has 46,989 inhabited villages, out of which 35,362 villages have been electrified by the end of 2000-01, representing coverage of 75.26 per cent. It has been proposed to electrify 6000 villages by conventional methods and the remaining villages by non-conventional methods during the ninth plan period. There are 19,491 tribal villages in the State out of which 10,466 (53.70 per cent) have been electrified by the end of 1999-2000.

4.3.10. The government have accorded very high priority to private sector investment for power generation. Accordingly it has been planned to add additional generating capacity by supporting two thermal power projects in the private sector (i) AES IB Valley Corporation Units V and VI (500 MW) and (ii) Kalinga Power Corporation Ltd.(KPCL) Units I and II at Duburi (500 MW). Two mega projects, one by Consolidated Electric Power Asia (CEPA) at Hirma (4320 MW) and another by NTPC at Talcher (2000 MW) are also on the anvil.

4.4. Infrastructure Facilities in Orissa vis-a-vis India

4.4.1. Table 4.1 exhibits the level of infrastructural development in the State in comparison to that of India in terms of various socio-economic indicators like length of road per 1000 sq.km. area, registered motor vehicle, villages connected with all weather roads, railway route length, number of post office, number of telephone connection, banks per thousand population, milk production, etc. It may be observed that the basic infrastructure in the State is lagging far behind in comparison to that of India in terms of many indicators such as percentage of villages electrified, per capita government expenditure on education, health and family welfare, per capital milk production in the State, etc. As far as banking facilities are concerned, there is one bank office for every 17 thousand of population per bank in Orissa as against 15 thousand people at the all-India level. From the above analysis it is clear that there has been inadequate development of socio-economic infrastructure in the state.

Table 4.1
Infrastructure Facilities in Orissa vis-à-vis India

Sl.No.	Facilities	Orissa	India
1.	Length of roads per 1000 sq.km. area (1996-97)	1687 km.	750km
2.	Registered Motor Vehicles per 1000 persons (1996-97)	21	40
3.	Percentage of villages connected with all-weather roads (1995-96)	40	48
4.	Railway route length per 1000 sq.km. of area (1997-98)	14.04 km	19.01 km
5.	Railway route length per one lakh of population (1997-98)	6.21 km	6.56 km
6.	No. of post offices per 100 sq.km.(1997-98)	5.2 (5)	4.7(5)
7.	Average number of post offices per one lakh population (1997-98)	23	16
8.	No. of telephone connections per 1000 persons (1998-99)	4	7
9.	Percentage of villages covered under telephone services (1998-99)	44	NA
10.	Percentage of villages electrified up to March 1999.	73.43	84.4
11.	Banking : Population in '000 covered per Bank Office as on March 2000.	17	15
12.	Banking : Credit-Deposit(C-D) Ratio as on March 2000.	39.75	57.05
13.	Education : Per Capita Govt. Expenditure on Education, Art and Culture in Rs.(1998-99)	Rs.354.40	Rs.456.10
14.	Health & Family Welfare : Per capita Govt. Expenditure on Medical, Public Health and Family Welfare (1998-99)	Rs.76.20	Rs.110.80
15.	Milk Producton : Per Capital Milk Production in Kg. (1994-95)	17.5 kg	70 kg

Source : Government of Orissa; Economic Survey, 1999-2000, Bureau of Economics and Statistics, Orissa, Bhubaneswar.

4.5. Policy Initiatives the Government of Orissa for the Development of Special Economic Zones

4.5.1. Realising the importance of Special Economic Zones (SEZs) for the overall economic development of the State, the Government of Orissa has formulated a draft for development of SEZs in the State. The policy based on the model policy of the Government of India and policies of State Government of Andhra Pradesh and Maharashtra aims at catalysing development of infrastructure in selected areas and create model centres for global business. The Central Government has already approved establishment of two SEZs in the State at Paradeep and Gopalpur. According to the draft, these two sites have to compete with three other SEZs on the East Coast. The document has identified lack of capital, market and infrastructure as major handicaps for establishment of SEZs. However, mineral resources and efficient ports were the major strengths of Orissa.

4.5.2. The draft proposes to exempt developers, industrial units and establishments in the SEZ from all State and local taxes and levies. It also prescribes exemption of stamp duty and registration charges for transfer of land to the SEZ developer and other deals like lease, rent, mortgage and loan etc. The proposed SEZs intends to offer complete freedom for conducting business. This will have a development commissioner representing the State and Central Government for discharging the roles of regulation, facilitation and promotion within the SEZ. The draft also promises single window facility for approval and clearance of units to be located there.

4.5.3. For provision of electricity, the draft said, initially bulk power from Grid Corporation of Orissa (GRIDCO), NTPC or Independent Power Producers (IPPs) could be wheeled upto SEZ with the developer of the complex vested with the authority to fix tariff. In the next phase, SEZ developer could set up a power plant either within the SEZ or at pit-head with wheeling arrangement to take the electricity to the complex. Similarly, industrial units could also be allowed to go for captive power plants with option to sell power to external clients. The draft has proposed exemption of electricity duty and tax on sale of power within the SEZ. Besides, subject to approval of Orissa Electricity Regulatory Commission (OERC), the State Government has agreed to facilitate grant of separate license to the SEZ developer for generation and distribution of power within the complex on exclusive basis. The document further States that, SEZ will provide more opportunity to make profitable use of the minerals available in the State. Thus the units coming up within the SEZ will get priority in allocation of mineral leases.[23]

4.6. Summary

4.6.1. The development of infrastructure is a necessary precondition for rapid industrialisation and it creates a base on which the superstructure of economic activities could be built-up. Technically improved infrastructure embraces a build up of adequate transport facilities that enables the markets to interact quickly and makes domestic raw materials available at a tolerable economic cost as well. The country's highest reserve of mineral resources are in Orissa. The reserve of coal was the highest at 51,571 MT followed by iron ore 3567 MT, bauxite 1733 MT and limestone 1032 MT. The mineral deposits of Orissa in respect of chromite, bauxite, iron ore, limestone were about 98.39 per cent, 59.53 per cent, 27.99 per cent and 1.35 per cent respectively.

4.6.2. The total road length in the State was 2,37,104 kms as on 31.3.2002. The surfaced road length per 1000 sq.km of area was 333 kms as compared to the all-India average of 363 kms. About 40 per cent of villages in Orissa have all-weather connectivity as compared to 60 per cent at the national level. The State had 2,385 kms of railway route which is 15.3 kms per thousand sq.km. The State have 3 operable ports. Paradeep is the only major port whereas Gopalpur and Dhamara are the fair-weather minor ports. Similarly, there were 8,145 post offices in the State as on 31.3.2001 of which 7542 (93 per cent) post-offices were located in rural areas and the rest 603 (7 per cent) were in urban areas.

4.6.3. Economic backwardness of Orissa is indicated by symptoms like excessive dependence on agriculture leading to high incidence of rural unemployment, absence of large scale urbanization, low industrial productivity, low level of infrastructure development and high percentage of population living below poverty line. Absence of necessary infrastructure has been the main factor for the low level of industrial and other development activities in Orissa. At the initial stage of economic liberalisation in 1991, Orissa ranked among the top three states in the country in attracting Foreign Direct Investment (FDI). The total investment proposed to be made in Orissa stood at over Rs. One lakh crore. But, most of these projects have fizzled out at the very drawing board stage because of slow progress in getting land and various statutory clearances and mostly the poor infrastructural facilities. Orissa is lagging far behind as compared to India in terms of many infrastructural indicators like percentage of villages electrified, per capita government expenditure on education, health and family welfare, etc. Various social and economical infrastructural facilities should be developed in the State both by the government and allowing private players for the overall development of the State in the coming years.

References

1. *Census of India-2001,* Directorate of Census Operations, Orissa.
2. Government of Orissa; *Economic Survey 2001-02,* Directorate of Economics and Statistics, Orissa, Bhubaneswar.
3. "The India Infrastructure Report : Policy Imperatives for Growth and Welfare" Report of the Expert Group on the commercialisation of the Infrastructure Project, Vol. II,submitted to Ministry of Finance, Government of India on June 22,1996.
4. "The Infrastructure Sector: Sound Foundation to Build Upon", *Yojana,* Vol. 42, No. 1, New Delhi, January 1998, (Editorial).
5. Sahoo, S., Role of Infrastructure in Economic Development : The Indian Case, An Unpublished Ph.D. Thesis Submitted to Deptt. of Humanities and Social Sciences, IIT Kanpur, July 1998.
6. Government of Orissa, *Economic Survey 2001-02, op.cit.,* 12/1.
7. Tripathy, P.C. "Interface between Infrastructure and Economic Development", *The Orissa Journal of Commerce,* Vol. XXI, No. 1, 1997, p. 10.
8. Government of Orissa, *Economic Survey 2001-02,* op.cit., p. 12/1.
9. *Ibid.,* p. 12/2.
10. *Ibid.,* p. 12/3.
11. *Ibid.,* p. 12/7.
12. *Ibid.,* p. 12/10.
13. Annual Administration Report, Paradeep Port Trust, 2000-01.
14. "Minor Ports" A report on the progress of some minor ports published in Indian Infrastructure, Vol. 3, No. 12, New Delhi, July 2001, p. 27.
15. "SEZ Sops Bring Cheer to Tata Steel" *The Hindu Business Line,* Vol. 9, No. 92, Visakhapatnam, April 3, 2002, p. 4.
16. "Company may boost Port Prospects," *The New Indian Express,* Vol. 6, No. 229, Bhubaneswar, September 30, 2002, p. 3.
17. "State-ICICI End Dhamara Impase", *Hindustan Times,* Vol. LXXVIII, No. 238, New Delhi, September 6, 2002, p. 3.
18. Government of Orissa, *Economic Survey 2001-02, op.cit.,* p. 12/10.
19. *Ibid.,* p.13/1.

20. *Ibid.*, p.13/2.
21. *Ibid.*, p.13/7.
22. *Ibid.*, p.11/1.
23. Satapathy, D., "Orissa Formulates Draft for Development of SEZs", *The Business Standard*, Kolkata, June, 20, 2002, p. III.

5

History, Growth and Achievement of Paradeep Port, Policy Guidelines of the Government, Opportunities and Challenges

5.1. Introduction

5.1.1. The hospitable land of Orissa had a glorious maritime history and tradition. Being situated on the shore of the Bay of Bengal and having enjoyed all the privileges to develop her maritime activities, Orissa from the time immemorial had her reputation as a sea faring country. It is said, the people of Kalinga, i.e., Orissa were the pioneers in colonising the far off lands of Sri Lanka, Java, Sumatra, Bali, Indonesia, Burma, Siam and other places. Trade relations with numerous South Eastern, Far Eastern and Western countries made Orissa commercially and materially rich and prosperous. Material prosperity, subsequently burst into cultural prosperity in and around Kalinga in ancient times. Orissa's export items included spices, diamonds and such other precious metals and these items were mainly exported to the Roman Empire. From the account of Cosmos, who belonged to the 6th Century A.D., it is known that the king of Ceylon used to purchase elephants from India, mainly from Kalinga. The Kalinga fabric had a good international market, especially of royal use. Kalinga rice and the list of varieties were suitable for king's dietry.[1]

5.2. Maritime History of Orissa

5.2.1. The factors that motivated maritime activities were many. The main factor was the lure of foreign trade, but other factors such as spirit of adventure, the establishment of colonies and kingdoms and the spread of religion and culture were also equally important. The importance of the sea as a career of great maritime trade and the allied activities has been depicted in numerous sculptural arts of Orissa, Eastern India and the countries of the South-East Asia.[2] The modern Bay of Bengal was known as the "Kalinga Sea". This was dominated by the traders of Kalinga (Orissa) for maritime activities. "The Kalinga Sea" served as the sole vehicle of overseas trade and other relations of not only Kalinga, but also of the South-Eastern India. The Kalingan overseas trade was continuously carried on through many flourishing ports like Tamarlipti (modern Tamluk in the modern Midnapore district of West Bengal), Che-li-to-la (modern Puri), Paloura-Dantapura (modern Palour in Ganjam) and Pittunda.[3]

5.2.2. During Ganga rule we find reference of some growing trade centres like Kalinga Pattanam and Visakhapatnam etc. A number of ports existed in Orissa during this period which bear testimony of her flourishing maritime trade with different foreign countries. The main ports of Orissa from which the Kalinga ships plied were 'Mausolin' (Masulipatnam), Kalingapatnam, Chilka, Puri, Chitropala, Hijli, Tamralipti, Harishpur and Balasore. The maritime trade with the Indian Archipelago, Burma and other islands brought a vast amount of wealth to Kalinga. The glories and prosperity of the ancient Orissa was probably due to her foreign trade with the distant lands.[4] The Arab and Persian writers state that in the ninth and tenth centuries A.D., Orissa carried on brisk maritime trade with South-East Asia.

5.2.3. So long the Hindu Kingdom of Orissa was independent and Hindu Kings gave encouragement and offered royal patronage, the maritime trade was flourishing and considerably added to the national wealth of the country. With the advent of the Muslims of Orissa (from the year 1568) change took place not only in the political condition of the country but also in its social and economic condition. The lack of the royal patronage, the indifference of the Muslim power to the prosperity of some ports, away from the headquarters of the Muslim Governor and the control of some important port and strategic coast areas by the Muslim administrations exclusively for the aggrandisement of the Mughal Empire without any regard to the former privilege enjoyed by the people, presented a new atmosphere in the maritime activities of the country.[5] After the

Muslim conquest of Orissa during the time of Akbar, the centre of gravity changed. Some of the southern ports of Orissa including Chilka and Chitropala, lost their former glories. The northern ports, particularly Balasore, Pipili and Harishpur came to much more prominence than before. The reason for such change is attributed to the change in the political regime.

5.2.4. Thomas Bowery an English traveller who travelled India during 1669-1679 A.D. gives a valuable description of shipping and maritime trade on the East Coast of India. The sea coast in Ganjam was favourable for navigation and the bulk of trade through the ports of this area was encouraging. The most important items of export were paddy, raw rice and boiled rice. The Rushikulya river was a good means of internal navigation. Ports of northern Orissa had attracted the attention of the Europeans in the early parts of 17th Century, i.e., after the great famine of 1866. The ports of Balasore, Dhamara and Chudamani were engaged in exporting rice and salt only. Balasore had ports at Dhamara, Churman, Srata, Lychumpor and Subarnarekha. The District of Puri had ports at Puri, Davee, Sahandu, Metchua, Futtypus, Nudia and on Chilka. There was a port of false point and it was alleged at one stage that the government neglected all ports and offered top priority to the port of false point because this was vital for military movements.[6]

5.2.5. During the early part of nineteenth Century, when the British decided to conquer Orissa, their absolute need for the conquest was to link Bengal with Madras through the coastal belt of Orissa. With the march of time and advent to British Rule, the maritime heritage of Orissa suffered a setback. The Britishers developed Visakhapatnam in Andhra Pradesh, Madras and Calcutta and completely neglected port development in Orissa. Towards the close of the nineteenth century, the portal activities of northern Orissa improved very much. Foreign ships used to visit more regularly. The British Indian Steam Company made false point a regular port of call. Similarly, the French Merchants used to load rice and oil seed from the ports at Balasore and Sail to Harve Bordex and other parts of France. Even, the American ships made the Balasore ports their common ports of call.[7]

5.2.6. The nature of foreign trade had deep impact on the economic life of the people. Orissa exported food grains and other agricultural commodities. Towards the close, in the exports list of commodities were included lac, wax, ivory, hides, timber, jute, coconut and dried fish. But the greatest burden was on the export of rice and the import items included metals, gunny bags and other manufactured goods. After independence, there was urgent need for planned economic development of the economy with the objective of guaranteeing high standard of living and peace to the millions. Shipping was accorded due priority in the realm of national plan.

5.3. The Port of Paradeep—Past and Present

5.3.1. Paradeep is one of the major ports of India and is the main out-let and in-let of the sea-borne trade of the eastern part of the country. It spreads over states such as Orissa, Bihar and West Bengal. The natural resources and industrial products of this wide spread hinterland are immense and the value of the mineral trade of the country passing through the port of Paradeep is considerably higher than many other major ports of India.

5.3.2. Paradeep port is situated at latitude 20°-15'-55.44" N longitude 86°-40'-34.62" E about 8 kilometres to the south of Mahanadi and 10 kilometres West-South-West of false point light house. Its distance via sea route from Calcutta, Vizag and Chennai is 210,260 and 598 nautical miles respectively. The port is 122 kms from Bhubaneswar, the capital of Orissa and 90 kms from Cuttack.[8]

5.3.3. The port of Paradeep, the pride of Orissa and one of the deep water major ports of India had a glorious history stretched from Puranas to British rule in India. The area is named after Shriparashara, the celebrated monk of India. Monk Parashara was directed to meditate for years together to inculcate, knowledge and enlightenment. He was in search of a dense forest with natural beauty away from the human activities and disturbances. After a great search, he selected the confluence point of river Mahanadi as the area was blessed with God gifted beauty and solitude. He engaged himself in meditation for many years and by the influence of such sacred activities, the entire area was filled with divinity. After the return of monk Parashara, the area was named as "Paradweepa" (i.e., sacred island).[9] The port of Paradeep is mainly situated on an island surrounded by Bay of Bengal confluence point of river Mahanadi and Atharabanki creek. In due course of time the public Paralance has named the area as Paradeep.

5.3.4. During the medieval period, the area was a centre of Buddhist activities. Puspagiri University of Buddhism at Lalitgiri, Udaygiri 'and Ratnagiri at a distance of about sixty kilometres from Paradeep was visited by many foreign tourists and nearby ports like Chelitala, Hariharpur played important role for the voyage of such tourists. From 5th to 9th century such area was actively used for the Alma mater activities of Mahayanic Tantra and Yoga based on principles of Buddhism.

5.3.5. With the decline of Buddhism in Orissa, the area could not play significant role for about eight centuries. During the Seventeenth century, Sendha Dynasty started ruling the area and emerged as a mighty sea power. "Sendha", title was awarded by the Raja of Dhobaigurh to Mallik Somonth in the year, 1645 A.D. as the later by his unwanted courage and physical prowess took a frantic bull by the horns and brought an end to it. Kings of Sendha dynasty ruled the area for two hundred thirty years. In the year 1876, Burdhwan Maharaja took the possession of Kujang and the administration of the area was taken over by the Anchal Adhikari, Government of Orissa, Kujang in the year 1952.[10] Maritime activities around Paradeep was recorded in history during the period 1600 to 1800 A.D. The port of Hariharpur rose to eminence as an effective port and boat building centre. Later Batighar and Hukitola were ports of operation used by French, Portuguese and English Traders. Batighar, popularly known as false point light house is about one a half century old. Such port was used mainly for export of rice and spices. The historical light-house near the port have been serving mariners of east-coast by disseminating marine signals for safe voyage. Hukitola was a prominent port for small vessels and anchorage point for big vessels.

5.3.6. In 1948, the Port (Technical) Committee formed by Government of India recommended to investigate the feasibility of establishing a sheltered deep sea port on the east coast between Vizag and Calcutta After the independence, Port of Dhaka was separated from the maritime map of India and to compensate such loss, it was required for another port in the east coast. Central Water and Power Commission (CWPC) was requested by Government of Orissa to explore the possibility of commissioning a port in the Mahanadi river delta. CWPC recommended for a port at Paradeep on Mahanadi river in the year 1950.[11]

5.3.7. Central Water and Power Research Station, Pune conducted a model study during 1954 to prefer between two alternatives viz. an estuarine harbour and a coastal harbour. Such study continued upto 1958 and recommended for a lagoon type harbour. Meanwhile during 1956, Mr. I.G.Chacke, Officer-on-Special Duty (minor ports) studied the feasibility of investments of funds for the development of Paradeep port under Second Five Year Plan. He suggested to declare Paradeep as minor port. In the same year, Kinoshitra and Company of Japan after detail study through Tokyo University recommended for the harbour just south of Mahanadi. In 1958, the Intermediate Port Development Committee of Government of India accepted the report of Mr.Chacke and Paradeep was declared as a minor port. Port of Paradeep started as a fair-weather anchorage port for export of iron ore through lighters to take iron ore to the ship at the anchorage.[12] M/s Rendel, Palmer and Trifton, a consulting engineering firm of United Kingdom, popularly known as 'RPT' recommended for a lagoon type deep water port at Paradeep. After one year study report was submitted in June 1962 and Government of Orissa started the construction work on the 15th March, 1964 and was completed on the 16th September, 1965.

5.3.8. On 3rd January, 1962, Pandit Jawaharlal Nehru, the first Prime Minister of Independent India laid the foundation stone of the port and dedicated the endeavour to the people of India with the following enunciation "Willed by the people, I commend you, to this another National Adventure". Government of India took over the management of port from Government of Orissa on 1st June, 1965. The port was declared open on 12th March, 1966. The Government of India declared Paradeep as the Eighth Major Port of India under the Major Port Act, 1963 on 18th April, 1966 making it the first major port in the East Coast commissioned in independent India. The first Trust Board was formed on 1st November, 1967.[13]

5.3.9. The first stage construction work completed with the completion of one mechanised iron ore berth for 60,000 DWT vessel, a turning circle of 400 mtrs diameter and an approach channel and 2 (two) breakwaters. The port was declared open to navigation with the entry of the Naval Vessel INS INVESTIGATOR on 12.03.1966. M/V Chios was the first merchant vessel to have sailed from the harbour with 14,430 MT of the iron ore on 26.11.66. From that day, the port has never looked back and shipping operation has been constantly increasing and emerging as a major bulk handling port in the sub-continent while 86 vessels were handled in the year 1967-68, during 1999-2000, 745 vessels were handled and during 2000-01 the number is well over 1000.[14]

5.4. Port Facilities at Paradeep Port

5.4.1. (i) ***Navigational Facilities :*** The port has an artificial lagoon type harbour protected by two rubbel mound breakwaters and approached by the dredged channel. The approach channel is 2020 M long and 190 M wide. The entrance channel is 500 M long and 160 M wide. There is one turning basin of 520 M diameter.

5.4.2. (ii) ***Berthing Facilities*** : There was only one berth when the port commenced its operation in 1966. As trade grew more berths were added. One more berth was added in 1975 and four more berths were added during the years 1984-85. By the year 1995 the port had eight berths consisting of one for handling POL products, one dedicated berth for handling raw materials of Oswal Chemical and Fertilisers Ltd., one iron ore berth, one for handling raw-materials of Paradeep Phosphates Ltd. and the rest meant for general cargo. The 9th berth came into operation in the year 2000. Night navigation was started in the year 1998. The port added four more berths in September 2001 taking the total number of berths to thirteen. Thus while the number of berths has gone up from nine to thirteen, the capacity of the port has jumped from 14 million ton to 37 million ton.[15]

The mechanised loading plant at the iron ore berth has been modified by the port to load both iron ore and thermal coal and is the only such plant in the country. The admissible draught at these berths range from 11.0 to 14.0 mtrs and can accommodate maximum size of vessels of 65,000 to 85,000 DWT. The port started as a mono-commodity port handling only iron ore. However, the port got specialised over the years in handling other dry and liquid bulk cargoes. The handling of varied nature of cargoes like thermal coal, coking coal, hard coke, limestone, other ores and alloys, iron and steel materials, raw materials and finished fertiliser, food grains and POL products testifies the personalised services that the port renders to its users. During 1999-2000, notwithstanding the effect of the super cyclone, an all time record traffic of 13.64 million tonnes was handled in the port. The quantum of traffic handled reach at 19.90 million tonnes in 2000-01.[16]

5.4.3. (iii) ***Railway Facilities*** : The railway operation within the port area are carried out by port's own railway system consisting of a route length of 6.8 kms and a track length of 55 kms. A rail borne traffic of 120.78 lakh tonnes was handled during 2000-01.

5.4.4. (iv) ***Storage Facilities*** : There are 5 transit sheds of 16,280 sqms area having a capacity of 36,000 MTs. Besides, there are 4 warehouses of 8,966 sqms area having a capacity of 21,600 MTs. At present, 2,34,700 sqms of open stacking area is available for storage of more than 13 lakh tonnes of different cargo. These stackyards are connected with rail and road.

5.4.5. (v) ***The Mechanised Coal Handling Plant*** : To cope up with the buoyant traffic, number of capacity yielding developmental works have been taken up by the port. A Rs. 703 crores Asian Development Bank aided project for handling 20 million tonnes of thermal coal for its coal-cum-sea transportation to the coal fired thermal plants in South India where an unloading port at Ennore in Tamilnadu has already commissioned.Of the 285 million US$ loan sanctioned by the ADB, the Paradeep component accounts for 134 million US$. The total cost of the plant which includes the loan component as well as contribution from the port's own resources stands at Rs.703 crores excluding interest during construction.[17]

The mechanised coal handling system is the first system in which the cargo can be unloaded from a moving train to be loaded directly on to a ship waiting at the berth. The plant provides for enormous flexibility. In case the ship is not there or the ship at berth is chartered by a different party, the cargo can be diverted to the stack yards which have the capacity of storing 6.5 lakh MT at a time. The stacking is done by two powerful stackers with a capacity of 4000 tonne per hour each and 57 meter long boom. The coal so stacked can be reclaimed, when the need comes for loading them on to the ship, by two equally powerful reclaimers with 9.5 meter diameter bucket wheel so that the coal can be moved to the berth where two ship loaders of matching capacity with 38 meter long booms can do the loading on to the ship. The process involves conveyor belts extending upto 9 kilometre of length in all comprising two main streams, and a total of 16 sub-streams which give the plant total flexibility to load from any plot located anywhere in the stackyard to either of the ships berthed at the port. There are two 14 metre deep berths where simultaneous loading of two ships can go on each at a rate of 4000 MT per hour yielding a total capacity of 20 million tonne per annum. Vessels of the size 65,000 DWT can now be loaded at these berths but the size can go upto 85,000 DWT after some additional dredging in the channel.[18]

5.5. Hinterlands Potentials of Paradeep Port

5.5.1. The Paradeep port has an extensive and rich hinterland. It commands a hinterland of about 100,000 sq.kms. rich in mineral, forest and industrial products. The Luthra Committee has mentioned that almost the entire state of Orissa, partly Southern Bihar and Eastern Madhya Pradesh comprises the hinterland of Paradeep port. It is linked with two major industrial belts of the State such as one comprising Ranchi-Rourkela-Bonai-Talcher-Cuttack-Paradeep and the other connecting Banspani-Nayagarh-Gandhamardan-Tomka-Daitari-Jajpur-Cuttack Paradeep. Paradeep's hinterland includes the country's largest iron and manganese ore reserves in Keonjhar and Sundargarh districts, the largest chromite and nickel deposit of Cuttack and Dhenkanal districts and the Talcher coal field. The potentiality of the various minerals deposits of the Paradeep hinterland can be summarised as follows.[19]

Table 5.1
Mineral Reserves in the Hinterland of Paradeep Port

Mineral	*Occurrence*	*Reserves in million tonnes*	*Distance from Paradeep by rail/road*	*Remarks*
Iron ore	Daitari-Tomka	60	150 km	NH 5-A link
	Banspani-Barbil	1000	300 km	(Banspani-Jakhpura-Paradeep)
	Kendrapara	100	350 km	Rail link (Bimlagarh-Talcher-Paradeep)
	Gandhamardan	100	250 km	Rail link (Banspani Jakhapura-Paradeep)

(Contd...)

(Contd., Table 5.1)

Mineral	*Occurrence*	*Reserves in million tonnes*	*Distance from Paradeep by rail/road*	*Remarks*
Manganese ore	Barbil-Koira area	20	300 km	Rail link
Chromite ore	Kaliapani, Kalarangi (Cuttack, Dhenkanal Dist)	6	190 km	NH 5-A
	Boula-Nansahi (Keonjhar Dist.)	2	260 km	By road and rail
Nickel ore	Kansa area	38	180 km	NH5-A
Coal	Talcher (Non-coking coal)	600	215 km	Rail

Source: "Paradeep Port" Special Volume Inaugurated on Port Day, 1995.

5.6. Peripheral Industrial Development at Paradeep Port

5.6.1. Paradeep port has been instrumental in the development of mineral based industries and the mines at Daitari, Barjanda, Manlangoli, etc. The industrial products in turn have helped in boosting the traffic at the port. Paradeep plays a significant role in strengthening the infrastructure for development of various industries around the port area.

The importance of Paradeep in developing metallurgical industries can be attributed to the availability of various minerals ranging from iron ore chromite, nickel, manganese, etc. to coal within the hinterland of Paradeep port. The infrastructure facilities available at Paradeep port for establishment of various metallurgical industries are uncomparable and include (a) port facilities like draft, handling capacity, berth cargoes, (b) land, topography of area, soil conditions, climatology, (c) transport facilities, (d) water supply, (e) power supply, etc.

5.6.2. The strategic location of Paradeep is suitable for the development of metallurgical industries like[20] –

(i) Integrated Steel Plant

- (a) Slag cement plant to utilise slag from integrated steel plant.
- (b) Slag wool plant to utilise slag from integrated steel plant.

(ii) Sponge iron complex.

(iii) Zinc smelter plant based on imported concentrate.

(iv) Calcium Carbide plant based on high grade limestone.

(v) Ferro-alloy industry for manufacture of ferromolybdenum, ferro-tungsten etc.

(vi) Tin industry based on imported concentrate.

(vii) Carbon paste plant.

5.6.3. The Port of Paradeep now goes for importing coking coal due to its shortage on the one hand and urgent need for augmenting steel production in the country on the other. Paradeep is in the offing to enter into the industrial activity and will become instrumental in ushering in an era of economic prosperity for the State of Orissa. Generally a well developed port provides ample scope for the location of export oriented industries and industries dependent on imported bulk raw materials and components. Port based industries dependent on imported raw materials have the advantage of saving the transportation cost over the factory situated inland. Distribution of finished products of the port-based industries is also easier and cheaper items for export can be directly loaded into ships for exports.

5.6.4. A port-based fertilizer plant Paradeep Phosphates Ltd. (PPL) has been commissioned since 1985 to produce 1.5 million tonnes of DAP per annum. In addition Oswal Chemical and Fertilizers Ltd. have also set up a fertilizer complex in 1999 to manufacture 2 million tonnes of phosphatic fertilizer per annum. The work for 9 million tons capacity Paradeep Refinery by Indian Oil Corporation is already in progress. The investment will be over Rs. 8000 crores with additional investment of Rs. 800 crores for marketing installation and about Rs. 580 crores for proposed pipeline. This will be the country's first zero-residue refinery and also country's first IGCC (Integrated Gassification Combined Cycle) unit for power generation.[21]

5.7. Outstanding Achievement of the Port in 2000-01

5.7.1. Recovering from the shock of the 1999 super cyclone Paradeep Port Trust has consolidated itself by establishing several milestones during the year 2000-01.

- An all time record of 199.00 lakh tonnes of total traffic was handled at the port surpassing the previous record of 136.36 lakh tonnes handled in 1999-2000.

- An all time record of 68.48 lakh tonnes of import cargo was handled exceeding the previous record of 47.76 lakh tonnes handled in 1999-2000.
- An all time record of 130.52 lakh tonnes of export traffic was handled at the port surpassing the previous record of 88.60 lakh tonnes handled in 1999-2000.
- An all time record of 915 number of vessels were handled during the year as compared to 741 numbers handled in 1999-2000.
- A record quantity of 9.55 lakh tonnes of POL traffic was exported outperforming the previous record of 9.21 lakh tonnes exported during 1999-2000.
- New cargoes : The following cargo was handled for the first time at the port during the year.

(Figures in tonnes)

Cargo	*Export / Import*	*Quantity*
Sulphuric Acid	Import	1,20,590

- Commodity-wise record annual exports/imports were achieved in the following.

(Figures in tonnes)

Cargo	*Exp/Imp*	*Record Qty*	*Previous Record*	
			Quantity	*Year*
Iron ore	Export	29,92,153	27,07,125	1995-96
Thermal coal	Export	82,07,553	63,70,063	1998-99
Rock phosphate	Import	20,82,713	4,31,051	1999-00
Coking coal	Import	16,91,180	16,77,384	1995-96
Ammonia	Import	3,21,091	1,85,636	1998-99
Sulphur	Import	5,42,623	1,57,188	1999-00

Operational Performance of the Port in 2000-01

	2000-01	1999-2000
Vessels handled (in nos)	915	741
Total NRT (in lakhs)	109.36	77.09
Total GRT (in lakhs)	207.32	143.64
Total DWT (in lakhs)	332.29	259.02
Traffic Handled (in lakh tonnes)		
Exports	130.52	88.60
Imports	68.48	47.76
Container	-	-
Transhipment	-	-
Total	199.00	136.36
Operational Performance		
Average waiting (in days)	1.41	1.14
Average turnround time (in days)	4.16	3.89
Average berthday output (in tonnes)		
Liquid bulk	8,450	7,492
Dry bulk (mech)*	12,033	10,131
Dry bulk (conv)	7,255	6,467
Break bulk	2,669	2,647
Overall	8,503	7,106

includes iron ore, thermal coal, sulphur, rock phosphate and mop handled mechanically.

NRT : Net Registered Tonnage.

GRT : Gross Registered Tonnage.

DWT : Dead Weight Tonnage.

Source : Annual Administration Report, Paradeep Port Trust, 2000-01.

5.7.2. The table highlights the operational performance of the port in 2000-01 as compared to 1999-2000. During 2000-01, there are 915 vessels sailed from the port, as compared to 741 vessels in the previous year. Similarly the G.R.T. and N.R.T. of the vessels sailed during 2000-01 were 207.32 lakhs and 109.36 lakhs respectively. The corresponding figures for 1999-2000 were 143.64 lakhs and 77.09 lakhs respectively. 199.00 lakh tonnes of cargo was handled at this port during the year 2000-01 as compared to

136.36 lakh tonnes in 1999-2000. While the average waiting days in 2000-01 was 1.41. The comparative figure of 1999-2000 was 1.14. So far as turn-around time is concerned the number of days in 2000-01 was 4.16, the corresponding figure for 1999-2000 were 3.89. Thus, the analysis reveals the improved performance of Paradeep Port in 2000-01 over 1999-2000 as compared in terms of indicators like ships sailed, G.R.T. and N.R.T. of vessels and the volume of cargo handled.

5.8. Achievement in Quality Dimension : ISO 9002 Certificate

5.8.1. Recently the quality management system of the port has been accessed and approved in accordance with the requirement of ISO 9002 with respect to the scope "Management of Deep Water Sea-Port and related Services activities" by Indian Register Quality Systems. The port is aiming next to achieve ISO 14000 certification. The future of the port is very bright if the report of RITES titled VISION-2020 is of any indication. Paradeep has been projected as the leader among the Indian ports.[22]

5.9. Policy Guidelines of the Government

5.9.1. Infrastructure being a sine-qua-non of economic development, its development is not a luxury but a necessity. Like every other development activity, infrastructural development has several players and it cannot be taken as a responsibility of a single institution/ministry. It casts responsibilities on various institutions, ministries, policy makers, industrialists, financiers and banking institutions. The extent to which a country can achieve a coordinated and integrated programme with the help of the various players will determine the speed at which infrastructure development will take place.[23]

5.9.2. Recognizing the importance of infrastructure sector, the Government of India formulates policies from time to time with a view to meeting the future challenges. In October 1996, the Ministry of Surface Transport issued guidelines on privatisation. Under the guidelines specific areas were identified for private participation, including liquid bulk, break bulk, multipurpose and specialised cargo berths container terminals, warehousing, and storage facilities, handling equipment, captive power plants, dry ducking and ship repair facilities and captive facilities for port based industries.

5.9.3. Another policy initiative followed the Port Laws (amendment) Act, 1997. The policy called for setting up of Tariff Authority for Major

Ports (TAMP), an independent regulatory body to fix tariffs at the major ports. In June 1998, the ministry made some modifications to the Act of 1997. It allowed joint ventures and foreign collaborations between a major port and foreign ports, between a major port and a company / consortium, between a major port and minor port, and bilateral arrangements with a foreign government.

5.9.4. In December, 1998, foreign direct investment (FDI) in the sector was increased from 74 per cent to 100 per cent with automatic approval. This was followed by proposal by the government in May 2000 to make amendments to the Major Port Trusts Act, 1963 in order to enable major port authorities to enter into private and joint ventures for creating additional port capacity. The Government of India has extended a variety of incentives to developers and lenders funding port projects. These include:[24]

- A 10-year tax holiday for the development of ports. This can be availed of in the first 20 years of operation.
- Reduction in import duties on construction of plant and equipment.
- Tax concession of 40 per cent to financial institutions on income from financing port projects.
- Income tax exemption on earnings of infrastructure funds investing in infrastructure projects.
- Subscription to equity shares and debentures issued by infrastructure companies eligible for 20 per cent income tax deduction upto a limit of Rs.70,000 a year.

5.10. Corporatisation and Paradeep Port

5.10.1. Most of the ports in the country are presently run as trusts and have very little accountability. They have been showing net surpluses by ignoring prudential norms. Depreciation is either underprovided or not provided at all. In an effort to make the ports more accountable, the Union Government is exploring the option of corporation. Under this, the port trust is converted into an economically independent company run by a professional board of directors under the Companies Act. The idea behind corporatisation is to lower costs, increase productivity and quality of service as well as enforce greater accountability and transparency in port functioning. This, in turn, should facilitate better access to the capital markets and strategic investor funds. It would also help in adapting the market changes.[25]

5.10.2. The Central Government has decided to corporatise major ports including Paradeep port which has the potential to develop into a mega port with a cargo handling capacity of over 100 million tonnes. The ports, i.e., all major ports require Rs. 40,000 crores to raise the cargo handling capacity to 850 MT by 2012 by constructing about 400 additional berths. But only Rs.12,000 crores would be available from plan funds and the internal resources of the ports for investment in the port development. The remaining Rs.28,000 crores would have to come from the private sector or from the capital markets.[26]

5.11. Future Prospects of Paradeep Port

5.11.1. Paradeep port is a growing port and is expected to grow further. The oil refinery is likely to add about 9 million tonne cargo besides giving a fillip to growth of industry and export in the region. The State Government has also shown keen interest in development of industries around Paradeep port. The Central Government had declared to establish a "Special Economic Zone" near Paradeep. An area of about 10,000 acres had been identified close to the Paradeep port for development of the SEZ with an investment of more than Rs. 250 crore.The other features of Paradeep SEZ site are;[27]

- The State highway-12 (Paradeep-Cuttack) passes touching the Northern boundary of the SEZ. The NH 5 and mining areas of Sukinda and Daitari passes through the SEZ site.
- The single broad gauge line of South Eastern Railway (Paradeep-Cuttack) passes by the Southern boundary of the SEZ site.
- Paradeep Phosphates Ltd., Oswal Chemicals and Fertilisers Ltd., are also located nearby.
- The site is also very close to river Mahanadi, one of the biggest rivers in Eastern India, Taladanda Canal carrying irrigation water passes by the Northern boundary of the site.

5.11.2. An MOU has been signed between Industrial Development Corporation of Orissa (IDCO) and Bang Pakong Industrial Park (BPIP) for developing 7000 hectares of land for setting up of an industrial park at Paradeep. The port has the distinction of having very peaceful industrial relation. Paradeep port has got the natural advantage of a soft soil bed, i.e., absence of rock surface up to 40 metres below the mean sea level thus enabling the port to go for even deeper berths to accommodate any size of ships. The port has a mineral rich hinterland providing appreciable incentive for major growth. There is also a massive growth in export of iron ore and the Daitari-Bansapani railway line when completed is expected to give a further boost to export of iron ore through the port. The port is in the process of inviting Build-Operate- Transfer (BOT) bids for a clean cargo berth in its Southern side for handling of food items and containers.[28]

5.11.3. Paradeep Port was basically established to export the mineral resources plentily available in the State. But, today when the port is celebrating its 40 years of establishment, its aim have multifaceted. Mega industrial houses such as Steel Authority of India Ltd. (SAIL), Tata Iron and Steel Company(TISCO), National Aluminium Company (NALCO), Paradeep Phosphates Ltd.(PPL), Oswal Fertilisers, Indian Oil Corporation Ltd.(IOCL), Bharat Petroleum Corporation Ltd.(BPCL), Mahanadi Coal Field Ltd.(MCL), Nilachal Ispat Nigam Ltd.(NINL), IMFA and Electricity Boards of Tamil Nadu, Karnataka, and Andhra Pradesh are depending on this Port for import and export purpose.[29]

5.11.4. The Indian Ports Association, while updating the master plan of Paradeep port, has projected a traffic of 34, 64 and 82 million tonnes by the years 2002, 2007 and 2012 respectively. M/s RITES, in their study titled "Perspective Plan for Indian Port Sector-Vision 2020", have also projected a capacity requirement of 37.68 MT, 64.18 MT and 103.44 MT for the port by the years 2001-2002, 2006-2007 and 2019-20 respectively. Paradeep port is thus poised for massive expansion in the coming years and will become one of the biggest bulk handling ports in the country and one of the busiest major ports.[30]

5.12. Summary

5.12.1. Paradeep, one of the deep water major ports of India situated in the State of Orissa. The foundation stone was laid by Pandit Jawaharlal Nehru, on 3rd January 1962. Government of India took over the charge on 1st June 1965 and declared it as the eighth major port of India. There are thirteen berths (including four berths added in September, 2001) to handle the cargoes up to the capacity of 37 million tonnes. The port has all the modern mechanised facilities and 80 per cent of the jobs are mechanised. The mechanisation process got a boost following the commissioning of Rs.900 crore mechanised coal handling plant on September 11 with assistance from Asian Development Bank (ADB). The port has its own railway facilities.

5.12.2. The port has established several milestones during the year 2000-01 in exporting iron ore and thermal coal, at the same time importing rock phosphate, coking coal, ammonia and sulphur, etc. The total export of the port was 130.52 lakh MT in 2000-01 (including foreign 37.93 lakh MT and coastal 92.59 lakh MT) import was 68.40 lakh MT which includes foreign import of 60.15 lakh MT and coastal import of 8.33 lakh MT for the same year. The number of persons employed in 2000-01 stood at 4116. The average waiting days and average turn-around time in 2000-01 was 1.41 days and 4.16 days respectively.

5.12.3. Paradeep port plays a significant role in strengthening the infrastructure for development of various industries around the port area. The government's declaration for establishment of a SEZ and the mega oil refinery commissioned by IOCL near the port would hopefully increase the importance of the port. The steps like the privatisation and corporatisation of ports, mechanisation and automation of port related activities etc., are considered moves in right direction of reform for enhancing its productivity and profitability. This would hopefully enable Paradeep port to become an active participant in the growth process of the country in general and the poorest State, Orissa in particular.

References

1 Panigrahi, K.C. : *History of Orissa*, Kitab Mahal, Cuttack,1981.

2. *Ibid.*

3. Behera,D.,Orissa's Overseas Relations, *Orissa Review*, December,1987,p.24

4. *Ibid.*

5. Ray, B.C. : *Orissa Under the Mughals*, Chapter-IX, Shipping and Maritime Activities.

6. *Ibid.*

7. Jena, K.C.The Ascendancy of the British Raj in Orissa, Letter of T.E.. Revenshaw of secretary of Government of Bengal No. 276, 20 July 1874, General Administration Report of Orissa Division for 1873-74.

8. "Port of Paradeep" A Brochure Published by The Port Authority in August, 1999.

9. "Port of Paradeep" A Special Volume of *Shipping and Marine Industries Journal*, Vol. 24, Mumbai, May 2001, p. 61.

10. *Ibid.*, p. 63
11. *Ibid.*, p. 46.
12. *Ibid.*, p. 46.
13. *Annual Administration Report*, Paradeep Port Trust, 2000-01.
14. *Ibid.*, p. 41.
15. "Paradeep Port", A Special Brochure Published on the Occasion of Port Day,1999.
16. *Annual Administration Report*, Paradeep Port Trust, 2000-01.
17. Mahapatra, S.K., (Chairman,Paradeep Port Trust), "A Big Day for Paradeep Port", *The New Indian Express*, Bhubaneswar, September 11, 2001, p. 5.
18. *Ibid.*
19. "Port of Paradeep", Special Volume of *Shipping and Marine Industries Journal*, *op.cit.*, p.59.
20. "Eastern Business Review-Focus-Infrastructure", *Business Standard*, Vol. XXVIII, No. 28, Kolkata, April 30, 2002, p. 5.
21. *Ibid.*
22. *Annual Administration Report*, Paradeep Port Trust, 2000-01.
23. Narain, Y., "New Initiatives in Infrastructure Sector", *Yojana*, Vol. 42, No. 1, New Delhi, January, 1998, p. 5.
24. "Port Policy - Opening up the Sector in Phases", *Indian Infrastructure*, Vol. 3, No. 12, New Delhi, July, 2001, p. 23.
25. "Major Ports to be Corporatised", *The Hindu Business Line*, Chennai, August 23, 2001. p. 1.
26. "Paradeep Port Starts Corporatisation", *The New Indian Express*, Bhubaneswar, June 24, 2000, p. 5.
27. "Centre Approves Economic Zones", *Hindustan Times*,Vol. LXVIII, No. 255, New Delhi, September 26, 2002.
28. "Paradeep Port Over the Years", *The New Indian Express*, Bhubaneswar, September 11,2001, p. 5.
29. "Orissa: A State Survey", *Business Standard*, Vol. XXVIII, No. 126, Kolkata, August 31, 2002, p. IV.
30. "Port Sector-Coping with Growth", *Indian Infrastructure*,Vol. 3, No. 12, New Delhi, July 2001, p. 22.

6

Operational Analysis of Paradeep Port (1986-87 to 2000-01)

6.1. Introduction

6.1.1. This chapter incorporates the empirical analysis of collected data pertaining to Paradeep port from the period 1986-87 to 2000-01. In view of gauging the impact of economic reforms on the performance of the port, the analysis has been made on the bases of pre- and post-reform period besides encompassing the analysis for the total period of the study. The parameters like cargo traffic handled, performance of ships, distribution of non-working time, traffic handled by different modes of transport and flag-wise distribution of cargo, etc., have been analysed. The physical performance indicators such as berth day output, berth occupancy, average ship turn-around time, utilisation of cargo handling equipment, pre-berthing delay have been discussed. Further the operational performance indicators like operating ratio, current ratio, stores consumption and class wise staff strength including the particulars of accidents at the port during the study period have been studied in detail in this chapter.

6.2. Traffic Handled at Paradeep Port

6.2.1. Table 6.1 reveals the trend of cargo traffic handled (overseas and coastal) at Paradeep port during the period 1986-87 to 2000-01. This has been shown in Fig. 6.1. The traffic unloaded at the port is regarded as traffic imported and traffic loaded as traffic exported as per the nomenclature by the Department of Shipping, Government of India. During the period the overseas traffic unloaded varies from 19.98 lakh tonnes in 1986-87 to

60.15 lakh tonnes in 2000-01, registering more than 300 per cent rise in traffic unloaded during the period. The average annual growth of overseas traffic unloaded was 33.32 lakh tonnes. The pre-reform period average annual growth was 27.68 lakh tonnes as against 33.22 lakh tonnes in the post-reform period, which speaks about the favourable impact of reforms on the performance of the port. The overseas traffic loaded at the port shows a fluctuating trend during the period. During the pre-reform period, in 1994-95, the port loaded the highest traffic of 24.40 lakh tonnes and the lowest of 17.92 lakh tonnes in 1992-93 at an average annual growth of 21.47 lakh tonnes. In the post-reform period, in 2000-01, the port loaded a record volume of overseas cargo of 37.93 lakh tonnes at an average annual increase of 21.12 lakh tonnes.

6.2.2. After the super cyclone of 1999, the port revived its operation and added some new berths to its capacity in 2000 and 2001. The total overseas cargo handled at the port depicts a fluctuating trend in both pre- and post-reform periods. The average overseas traffic handled in the pre-reform period was 49.15 lakh tonnes which was increased to 65.73 lakh tonnes per annum in the post-reform period. The average of overseas traffic was 54.67 lakh tonnes per annum during the whole period. Similarly in the case of coastal trade the unloaded traffic in the pre-reform period was meagre. In the post-reform period, it was 1.26 tonnes in 1996-97 which was increased to the highest of 8.33 lakh tonnes in 2000-01. The average annual traffic in the post-reform period was 4.35 lakh tonnes as against 0.229 lakh tonnes in the pre-reform period. The coastal traffic loaded at Paradeep port was significant during this period. There has been consistent increase in the loading of coastal traffic in both pre- and post-reform period except a marginal decline in 1988-89. In absolute terms, coastal traffic loaded has increased from 6.56 lakh tonnes in 1986-87 to 69.27 lakh tonnes in 1999-2000 and it jumped to 92.59 lakh tonnes in 2000-01. This has been exhibited in Fig. 6.2.The traffic handled at the port was 40.57 lakh tonnes per annum during the whole study period. But in the post-reform period, the average traffic handled per annum was 72.97 lakh tonnes which is significantly higher than the average annual traffic of 24.37 lakh tonnes in the pre-reform period. The total coastal traffic also shows an increasing trend throughout the study period except marginal decline in 1988-89. The post-reform period average annual coastal traffic was 77.32 lakh tonnes as against 24.59 lakh tonnes in the pre-reform period. The total average annual growth of coastal traffic in the said period was 42.17 lakh tonnes.

6.2.3. The reason of increase in coastal trade in the post-reform period can be attributed to the development of minor ports by different State Governments with private sector participation and the increasing efficiency of the port with additional berth facilities. The total overseas and coastal traffic during the study period witnessed an increasing trend except in 1998-99. The average annual growth of total traffic handled during the period was 96.85 lakh tonnes. In the pre-reform period, the average annual growth was 73.74 lakh tonnes, which registered nearly two times growth of 143.05 lakh tonnes in the post-reform period. The overall growth of traffic (overseas and coastal) handled at the port is because of the liberalised export-import (EXIM) policy of Government of India and more particularly the implementation of the recommendations of the Rakesh Mohan Committee Report on infrastructure. In addition, the port has added two new berths in 1995, one in 2000 and four in 2001. The new berths include a mechanised coal handling plant to handle more traffic from the port. Due to the addition of the new berths in 2000 and 2001, the percentage change in traffic handled reached at 45.93 per cent over the previous year's traffic.

6.3. Performance of Cargo Ships at Paradeep Port

6.3.1. Table 6.2 reveals the performance of cargo ships at the port during the period 1986-87 to 2000-01. The number of ships sailed at the port during the period increased from 237 in 1987-88 to 886 in 2000-01 with an average of 445 ships per annum. The cargo handled at the port also rose from 4851671 tonnes in 1986-87 to 19807945 tonnes in 2000-01, registering an average annual growth of 9,5876.06 lakh tonnes during the study period. The average turn-around time shows a fluctuating trend and varies from the lowest of 3.89 days in 1999-00 to the highest of 9.44 days in 1989-90. The average annual turn-around time for the whole study period was 6 days and declined to 4.44 days in the post-reform period as against 6.78 days in the pre-reform period. The lower the turn-around time the higher would be the productivity of the port. The average stay at berth

Table 6.1

Cargo Traffic Handled at Paradeep Port (Loaded and Unloaded) during the Period 1986-87 to 2000-01

(In lakh tonnes)

	Study Period	Overseas			Coastal			Overseas and Coastal			Per cent change over previous period
		Unloaded	Loaded	Total	Unloaded	Loaded	Total	Unloaded	Loaded	Total	
Pre-reform Period	1986-87	19.98	21.95	41.93	0.03	6.56	6.59	20.01	28.51	48.52	0.00
	1987-88	22.48	19.23	41.71	0.04	10.12	10.16	22.52	29.35	51.87	6.90
	1988-89	27.77	22.75	50.52	-	9.80	9.80	27.77	32.55	60.32	16.29
	1989-90	24.60	24.32	48.92	-	12.92	12.92	24.60	37.24	61.84	2.52
	1990-91	28.39	21.01	49.40	-	19.44	19.44	28.39	40.45	68.84	11.32
	1991-92	28.80	20.48	49.28	-	23.69	23.69	28.80	44.17	72.97	5.99
	1992-93	24.28	17.92	42.20	-	33.86	33.86	24.28	51.78	76.06	4.23
	1993-94	25.77	20.64	46.41	0.04	36.82	36.86	25.81	57.46	83.27	9.47
	1994-95	33.38	24.40	57.78	1.53	41.90	43.43	34.91	66.30	101.21	21.54
	1995-96	41.35	22.00	63.25	0.65	48.59	49.24	42.00	70.59	112.59	11.24
	Average	**27.68**	**21.47**	**49.15**	**0.229**	**24.37**	**24.59**	**27.90**	**45.84**	**73.74**	
Post-reform Period	1996-97	37.33	18.18	55.51	1.26	59.03	60.29	38.59	77.21	115.80	2.85
	1997-98	43.79	16.76	60.55	1.09	71.38	72.47	44.88	88.14	133.02	14.87
	1998-99	39.39	13.43	52.82	5.68	72.58	78.26	45.07	86.01	131.08	-1.45
	1999-00	42.37	19.33	61.70	5.39	69.27	74.66	47.76	88.60	136.36	4.02
	2000-01	60.15	37.93	98.08	8.33	92.59	100.92	68.48	130.52	199.00	45.93
	Average	**44.60**	**21.12**	**65.73**	**4.35**	**72.97**	**77.32**	**48.95**	**94.09**	**143.05**	
	Whole Period Average	**33.32**	**21.35**	**54.67**	**1.60**	**40.57**	**42.17**	**34.92**	**61.92**	**96.85**	

Source : Annual Administration Reports, Paradeep Port Trust.

Fig. 6.1

Overseas and Coastal Traffic Handled at Paradeep Port during 1986-87 to 2000-01

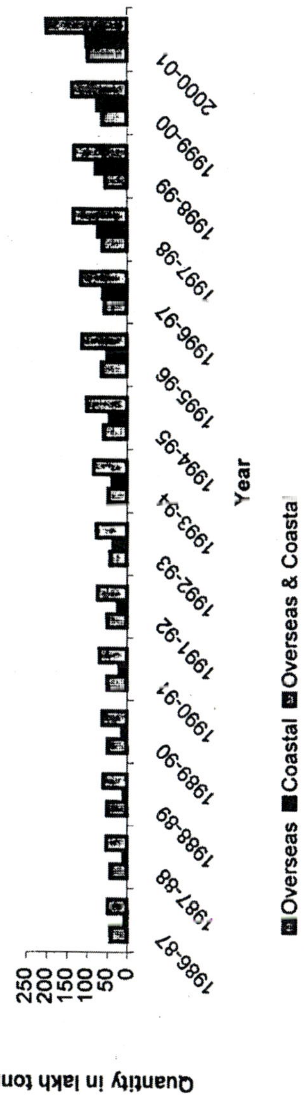

Fig. 6.2
Import and Export of Traffic Handled at Paradeep Port during 1986-87 to 2000-01

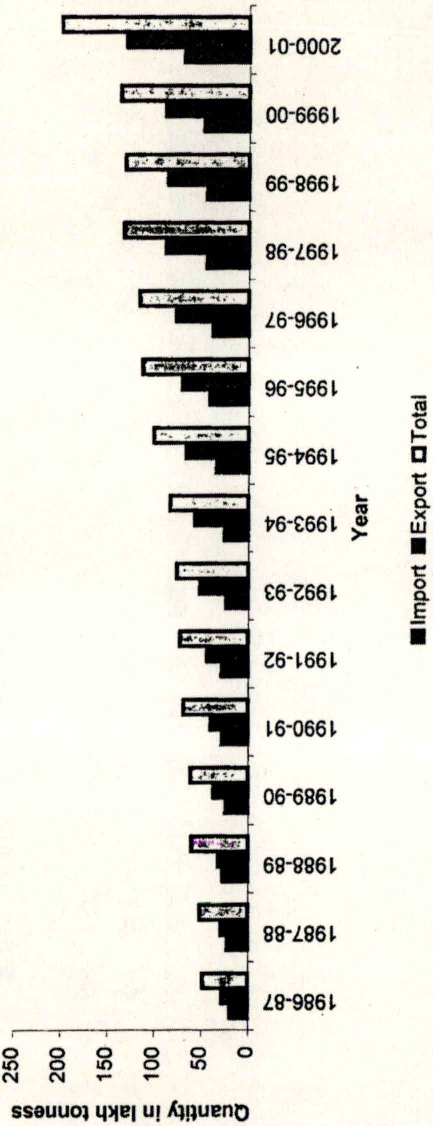

also exhibits a fluctuating trend. The average annual stay at berth during the pre-reform period was 4.80 days which was decreased to 4.17 days in the post-reform period as against the average of 2.91 days in the whole study period. The average working time at the port also varies from the lowest of 0.71 days in 1987-88 to the highest of 5.22 days in 1990-91. The average working time in the pre-reform period was 3.68 days which then slipped down to 2.56 days in the post-reform period as against the annual average of 3.30 days during the whole period. Average pre-berthing time also shows declining trend with slight fluctuation in 1989-90 and 1995-96. In the post-reform period the average pre-berthing time was 1.40 days as against 2.16 days in the pre-reform period and 1.90 days in the total study period.

6.3.2. The low pre-berthing time is one of the contributory factors of higher productivity of the port. Similarly the average non-working time shows downward trend during the study period. The average non-working time or the idle time in the post-reform period declined to 1.02 days as against 1.33 days in the pre-reform period and 1.22 days during the whole study period. Average parcel size shows a fluctuating trend during the period under study. The average parcel size in the post-reform period slipped down marginally to 20,391.8 tonnes as against 23,218.6 tonnes in the pre-reform period and 22,276.33 tonnes during the total study period. The average output per ship berth day shows an increasing trend over the period. The average output per ship berth day increased from 4,322 tonnes in 1986-87 to 8503 tonnes in 2000-01 against the average of 5578.06 tonnes per year. During the post-reform period it was increased to 7055.8 tonnes as against 4,839.2 tonnes in the pre-reform period. Similarly the percentage of non-working time at berth varies from 16.80 days in 1988-89 to 30.19 days in 2000-01. The average non-working time was increased to 28.60 days in the post-reform period as against 24.06 days in the pre-reform period and 25.57 days during the total study period. The foregoing analysis of various parameters like number of ships sailed, cargo handled, average turn-around time, non-working times indicate the state of higher performance of the port in the post-reform period compared to pre-reform period.

Table 6.2

Performance of Cargo Ships at Paradeep Port during 1986-87 to 2000-01

	Study Period	*No. of ships sailed*	*Cargo Handled (Tonnes)*	*Average Turn-around time (Days)*	*Average stay at Berth (Days)*	*Average working time (Days)*	*Average pre-berthing time (Days)*	*Average non-working time (Days)*	*Average parcel size (Tonnes)*	*Average output per ship berth-day (Tonnes)*	*Percentage of non-working time at berth*
Pre-reform period	1986-87	270	4851671	8.25	4.32	2.56	4.21	1.53	22402	4322	23.26
	1987-88	237	5146897	5.40	4.61	0.71	4:07	1.19	21902	4748	22.58
	1988-89	273	5898538	6.70	4.99	4.69	1.60	0.96	21606	4330	16.80
	1989-90	244	6246202	9.44	6.39	4.68	2.73	1.71	25599	4005	26.78
	1990-91	264	6778105	8.15	6.14	5.22	1.58	1.47	25675	4173	22.02
	1991-92	315	7297902	6.13	4.72	4.39	1.19	1.44	23168	4924	26.06
	1992-93	315	7365663	6.09	4.55	3.67	1.36	1.37	23383	5134	27.22
	1993-94	329	7971821	5.78	4.60	3.55	1.03	1.35	24230	5263	27.63
	1994-95	432	9856652	5.65	4.10	3.84	1.36	1.23	22816	5564	24.28
	1995-96	523	11194738	6.287	3.609	3.503	2.487	1.091	21405	5929	24.00
	Average	**320**	**7260818.9**	**6.78**	**4.80**	**3.68**	**2.16**	**1.33**	**23218.6**	**4839.2**	**24.06**
Post-reform period	1996-97	557	11487446	4.943	3.220	2.918	1.627	1.167	20624	6406	28.57
	1997-98	643	13287656	5.122	3.305	3.013	1.666	1.300	20665	6252	30.15
	1998-99	678	13096959	4.112	2.754	2.638	1.200	0.887	19317	7012	25.16
	1999-2000	712	13525822	3.89	2.67	2.43	1.14	0.99	18997	7106	28.97
	2000-2001	886	19807945	4.16	2.63	1.84	1.41	0.79	22356	8503	30.19
	Average	**695**	**14241165**	**4.44**	**2.91**	**2.56**	**1.40**	**1.02**	**20391.8**	**7055.8**	**28.60**
	Whole period Avg.	**445**	**95876.06**	**6.00**	**4.17**	**3.30**	**1.90**	**1.22**	**22276.33**	**5578.06**	**25.57**

Source : Annual Administration Reports, Paradeep Port Trust.

6.4. Trends of Traffic at Major Ports of India and Share of Paradeep Port

6.4.1. Table 6.3 reflects the total traffic handled by major ports in the country and the proportion of traffic handled by Paradeep port during the period of 1986-87 to 2000-01. Traffic handled by all major ports as well as Paradeep port shows increasing trend during the study period. The traffic of all major ports in 1986-87 was 124.37 million tonnes. At the same time, the traffic at Paradeep port was 4.85 million tonnes, recording a 3.90 per cent of the total traffic of all major ports in the country. In 2000-01 the port of Paradeep handles 19.90 million tonnes of traffic (7.07 per cent of total traffic) as against 281.13 million tonnes of traffic at all major ports. The average annual traffic at all major ports during the study period stood at 193.46 million tonnes. In the pre-reform period the average annual traffic of all major ports stood at 161.85 million tonnes which rose to 256.68 million tonnes in the post-reform period. This is due to the emphasis laid by Government of India on infrastructure sector in accordance with the implementation of the recommendations of the Rakesh Mohan Committee Report on infrastructure. Further, from time to time, the Government of India provided sops and incentives for the development of port infrastructure by way of industrial policies and Five Year Plans.

6.4.2. Similarly, the average annual traffic at Paradeep port during the pre-reform period was 7.37 million tonnes which has been doubled showing 14.30 million tonnes of average traffic in the post-reform period. The average traffic handled by the port during the study period stood at 9.68 million tonnes. The average percentage of share of traffic at Paradeep port during the study period was 5.00 per cent as against 4.55 per cent in the pre-reform period which increased to 5.57 per cent in the post-reform period. The percentage share of traffic at Paradeep port declined marginally in 1999-2000 due to the devastating super-cyclone of October 29 & 30, 1999, that severely affected most of the districts of Orissa and Paradeep port as well. Inspite of the severity of the super-cyclone, the port operations were restored within 5 days with the efforts of the administration. A three-phase recovery plan of near normalcy within 15 days, full normalcy within a month and rebuilding and restoration was taken up successfully. The reason for the percentage increase in the traffic at Paradeep port can be attributed to the addition of seven new berths with a mechanised coal handling plant and reduced turn-around time and pre-berthing time at the port during the post-reform period.

Table 6.3
Trends of Traffic at Paradeep Port and its Percentage Share among Major Ports of India

(In Million Tonnes)

	Study Period	*Paradeep Port*	*All Major Ports*	*Share of Traffic of Paradeep Port (In per cent)*
Pre-reform period	1986-87	4.85	124.37	3.90
	1987-88	5.19	134.60	3.85
	1988-89	6.03	147.06	4.10
	1989-90	6.18	147.57	4.18
	1990-91	6.88	151.67	4.53
	1991-92	7.30	156.64	4.66
	1992-93	7.60	166.50	4.56
	1993-94	8.33	179.02	4.65
	1994-95	10.12	195.89	5.16
	1995-96	11.26	215.21	5.23
	Average	**7.37**	**161.85**	**4.55**
Post-reform period	1996-97	11.58	226.97	5.10
	1997-98	13.30	251.66	5.28
	1998-99	13.11	251.74	5.20
	1999-2000	13.63	271.92	5.01
	2000-2001	19.90	281.13	7.07
	Average	**14.30**	**256.68**	**5.57**
Whole Period Average		**9.68**	**193.46**	**5.00**

Source: Government of India, *Basic Port Statistics of India 1999-2000,* Ministry of Surface Transport, New Delhi.

6.5. Berth-day Output at Paradeep Port

6.5.1. The port of Paradeep handles mainly iron ore, coal, hard coke, limestone, chromium ore, charge chrome, fertiliser raw materials, iron and steel and scraps. Table 6.4 highlights the commodity wise berth-day output during the period of 1986-87 to 2000-01. This has also been described in Fig. 6.3. Berth-day output describes total tonnage handled distributed over the total number of berth-days. The higher the berth-day output the better the productivity of the port. The iron ore berth gives the highest berth-day output among commodities handled at the port. The iron ore berth-day output exhibits fluctuating trend during the study period. During the pre-reform period the output was highest of 19,790 tonnes in 1994-95 and the lowest of 10,943 tonnes in 1986-87. Similarly, during the post-reform period the output was highest of 18,593 tonnes in 2000-01 and the lowest of 14,873 tonnes in 1997-98. The average annual berth-day output for the whole period was 16,464.13 tonnes. The post-reform period average berth-day output was 16,939 tonnes per annum as against 16,226.7 tonnes per annum in the pre-reform period.

6.5.2. Since Orissa contains the highest amount of iron ore in the country and Paradeep port is the sole outlet for export of iron-ore from the State, the port of Paradeep handles and gives the highest output per berth-day of iron ores. In case of coal, the second highest berth-day output at the port shows rising trend from 3559 tonnes in 1986-87 to 9082 tonnes in 2000-01. The average annual berth-day output of coal during the whole period was 6,433.53 tonnes. The post-reform period average berth-day output of coal was 8,814 tonnes as against 5243.3 tonnes in the pre-reform period. In the mean time, the addition of some new coal handling berths and the increasing demand for coal both export and imports are responsible for higher growth of berth-day output at the port and more particularly in the post-reform period. Hard coke berth-day output has witnessed slower growth with fluctuating trend during the period. The average berth-day output of hard coke for the whole period was 2,308.86 tonnes. In the pre-reform period the average berth-day output was 2,035.5 tonnes which was increased to 2,855.6 tonnes in the post-reform period. In case of limestone, the berthday output shows declining trend in the first three years of the study period but, after that it shows fluctuating trend. The average berth-day output of limestone for the total study period was 5,364.66 tonnes per annum. The pre-reform period average berth-day output of limestone was 4,808.9 tonnes which was increased considerably to 6,476.2 tonnes in the post-reform period. The chrome ore and charge chrome shows fluctuating trend registering the average berth-day output of 2,432.26 tonnes per annum in the whole study period. In the post-reform period the annual average berth-day output of chrome ore and charge chrome was 2,821 tonnes as against 2,237.9 tonnes in the pre-reform period.

6.5.3. The port of Paradeep has started handling raw materials for fertiliser from 1991-92 after the establishment of two fertiliser plants namely, Paradeep Phosphates Ltd. and Oswal Fertilisers at Paradeep. The average berth day output of fertiliser of the whole period was 6,079.4 tonnes per annum. In the pre-reform period, the average berth-day output of fertiliser

Table 6.4

Commodity-wise Berth-Day Output at Paradeep Port during 1986-87 to 2000-01

	Study period	Iron ore	Coal	Hard coke	Lime-stone	Ch.Ore/ Ch.Chrome	Fertilizer raw material	Iron & Steel	Scrap	Overall
Pre-reform Period	1986-87	10,943	3,559	1435	4380	1995	-	1398	682	-
	1987-88	14,081	4,825	2548	4352	2194	-	1770	950	-
	1988-89	17,913	4,586	1599	3867	2242	-	1629	1017	4322
	1989-90	13,188	4,163	1406	3819	1742	-	1284	1061	4005
	1990-91	16,419	4,744	1568	4489	2094	-	700	801	4181
	1991-92	16,728	5,412	1534	4833	2058	7416	875	-	4924
	1992-93	18,189	5,993	2002	5048	2413	6927	925	-	5134
	1993-94	18,081	6,170	2499	6265	2463	8993	2126	-	5263
	1994-95	19,790	6,158	2814	6106	2586	5518	1276	-	5564
	1995-96	16,935	6,823	2950	4930	2592	4622	-	-	5929
	Average	**16,226.7**	**5,243.3**	**2,035.5**	**4,808.9**	**2,237.9**	**6,695.2**			**4,915.25**
Post-reform Period	1996-97	17,835	7,728	3016	6935	2312	5647	-	-	6405
	1997-98	14,873	8,378	2791	6701	2473	3583	-	-	6252
	1998-99	17,950	9,654	2896	6346	2721	4892	-	-	7012
	1999-00	15,444	9,228	2738	5175	3216	5342	-	-	7106
	2000-01	18,593	9,082	2837	7224	3383	7854	-	-	8503
	Average	**16,939**	**8,814**	**2,855.6**	**6,476.2**	**2821**	**5,463.6**	-	-	**7,055.6**
Whole Period Average		**16,464.1**	**6,433.5**	**2,308.8**	**5,364.6**	**2,432.2**	**6,079.4**	-	-	**5,738.4**

Source : Annual Administration Reports, Paradeep Port Trust.

Fig. 6.3
Overall Berth-Day Output at Paradeep Port during 1986-87 to 2000-01

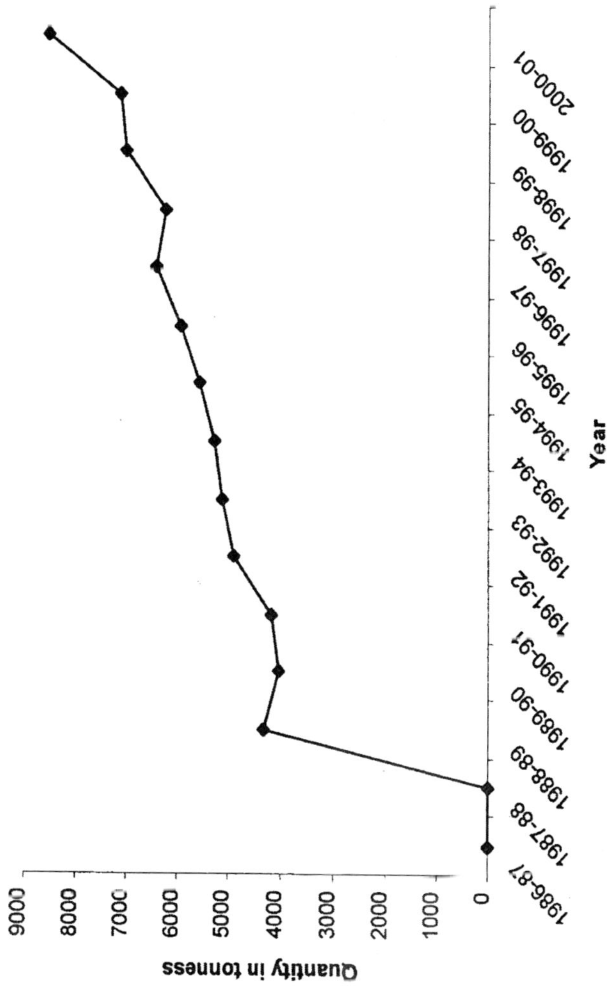

was 6,695.2 tonnes as against 5,463.6 tonnes in the post-reform period. The decline in the average berth-day output of fertiliser was due to the commencement of activities of the minor ports in the post-reform era. The port had handled scrap till 1990-91 and iron and steel till 1994-95 after which the handling of the said commodities were stopped. The Table has also revealed the rising trend of overall berth-day output during the study period. The overall berth-day output figures are not available for the period 1986-87 and 1988-89. It was 4,322 tonnes in 1988-89 and increased to 8,503 in 2000-01. The average overall output per berth-day during whole period was 5,738.46 tonnes, whereas the corresponding figures in the post-reform period was 7055.6 tonnes as against 4,915.25 tonnes in the pre-reform period. The cause of increasing berth-day output in the post-reform era is due to the use of mechanised cargo handling equipment by the port ; increased demand for the commodities in the coastal and overseas markets and the establishment of more industries due to healthy industrial climate created by the Government in the State.

6.6. Labour Productivity of Major Commodities Handled by the Port

6.6.1. Table 6.5 highlights the labour productivity of major commodities handled by the port during the period 1986-87 to 2000-01. The labour productivity of coking coal depicts an increasing trend with marginal fluctuations over the period. In 1987-88, the productivity was 465 tonnes per hook shift which was increased to 865 tonnes per hook shift in 2000-01. The average annual productivity for the whole period stood at 641.71 tonnes per hook shift. The labour productivity in the pre-reform period was 550.55 tonnes per hook shift, which had been increased to 805.8 tonnes per hook shift in the post-reform period. Similarly in case of thermal coal, the labour productivity reached 918 tonnes per hook shift as against 358 tonnes per hook shift in 1987-88. The average productivity per annum in the whole study period was 578 tonnes per hook shift. In the post-reform period, the average productivity increased significantly to 799.2 tonnes per hook shift, as against 455.11 tonnes per hook shift in the pre-reform period. Labour productivity for hard coke shows a fluctuating trend and registers an average annual growth of 365.28 tonnes per hook shift. In the pre-reform period the average productivity was 319.66 tonnes per hook shift, which rose to 447.4 tonnes per hook shift in the post-reform period. In case of limestone, fluctuating trend is also noticed. The labour productivity was 368 tonnes per hook shift in 1987-88 which was increased to 710 tonnes per hook shift in 2000-01. The average annual productivity of limestone was 529.57 tonnes per hook shift in the whole study period. The average annual productivity of limestone in the pre-reform period was 452.77 tonnes per hook shift, which was increased to 667.8 tonnes per hook shift in the post-reform period.

6.6.2. The labour productivity for Chrome-ore, Charge Chrome, Ferro chrome and Ferro Manganese also shows fluctuating trends during the study period. The average annual productivity for the whole study period was 526.42 tonnes per hook shift. In the post-reform period it was 636.2 tonnes per hook shift as against 465.44 tonnes per hook shift in the pre-reform period. In the case of fertiliser raw materials the figures show a slow growth of 203 tonnes to 247 tonnes per hook shift in the pre-reform period with average annual productivity of 220 tonnes per hook shift. But in the post-reform period it reached 551 tonnes per hook shift in 2000-01 with average annual productivity of 417.25 tonnes per hook shift. The average annual growth for the total study period stood at 285.75 tonnes per hook shift. The overall labour productivity shows an increasing trend during the period except in 1988-89 and 1989-90. This has been explained in graphical form in Fig. 6.4. The overall productivity varies from 233 tonnes per hook shift in 1986-87 to 800 tonnes per hook shift in 2000-01 and the average annual productivity of 515.06 tonnes per hook shift during the study period.

6.6.3. Similarly the overall average annual productivity was 727.2 tonnes per hook shift in the post-reform period which is significantly higher than 409 tonnes per hook shift in the pre-reform period. The peaceful working environment due to sound labour management relation has resulted in raising the overall labour productivity at the port. More significantly, in the post-reform period the pro-labour policy of the government, the use of machines with advanced technology and safety measures provided by the port are the plausible reasons for the growth of productivity of all commodities. In addition, the commissioning of specialised berths with mechanised handling facilities for each product has enhanced the labour productivity at the port during the post-reform period.

Table 6.5

Labour Productivity of Major Commodities at Paradeep Port during 1986-87 to 2000-01

(In tonnes/hook shift)

	Study Period	*Coking coal*	*Thermal coal*	*Hard Coke*	*Lime stone*	*Ch.ore/Ch.ch-rome/Ferro chrome/Ferro manganese*	*Fertiliser raw materials*	*H.R. Coil*	*Scrap*	*Overall*
Pre-reform period	1986-87	-	-	-	-	-	-	-	-	233
	1987-88	465	358	357	368	441	80	273	95.5	335
	1988-89	459	359	229	321	357	-	244	101	316
	1989-90	423	331	290	364	345	245	165	108	313
	1990-91	598	392	268	413	365	213	108	98	363
	1991-92	556	452	310	433	464	203	160	-	443
	1992-93	573	533	326	488	515	214	153	-	491
	1993-94	591	542	329	595	554	275	252	-	507
	1994-95	658	523	375	584	609	283	211	-	529
	1995-96	632	606	393	509	539	247	-	-	560
	Average	**550.55**	**455.11**	**319.66**	**452.77**	**465.44**	**220**			**409**
Post-reform Period	1996-97	785	647	466	681	578	307	-	-	632
	1997-98	797	700	370	664	612	268	-	-	663
	1998-99	849	873	462	708	676	-	-	-	798
	1999-00	733	858	444	576	544	543	501	-	743
	2000-01	865	918	495	710	771	551	584	-	800
	Average	**805.8**	**799.2**	**447.4**	**667.8**	**636.2**	**417.25**			**727.2**
	Whole Period Average	**641.71**	**578**	**365.28**	**529.57**	**526.42**	**285.75**			**515.06**

Source : Annual Administration Reports, Paradeep Port Trust.

Fig. 6.4
Overall Labour Productivity at Paradeep Port during 1986-87 to 2000-01

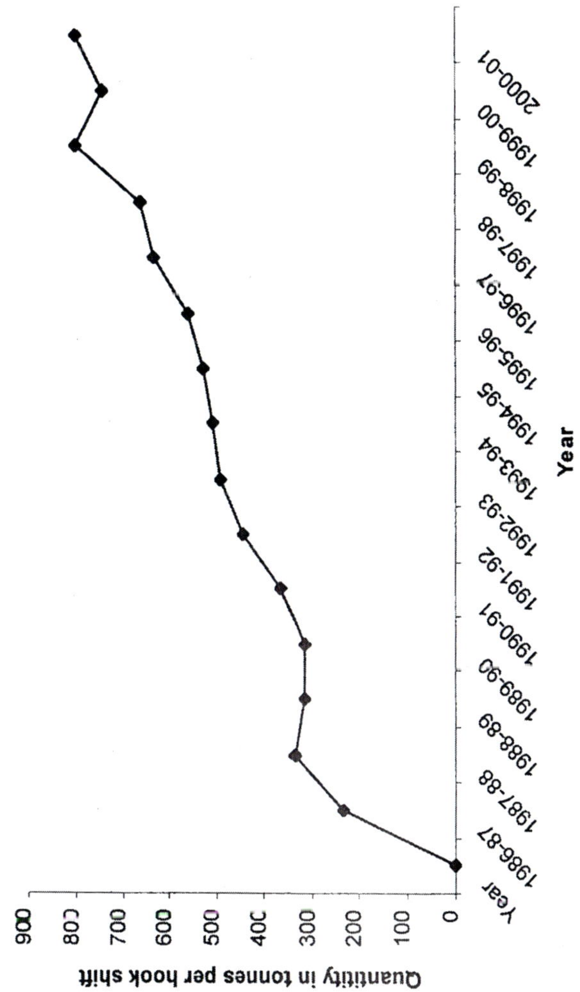

6.7. Average Ship Turn-around Time (ASTA) for Major Commodity-wise Vessels at Paradeep Port

6.7.1. Average ship turn-around time means, the average time spent by a ship since its entry into the port till its departure. Average ship turn-around (ASTA) time is an important indicator of performance in a port. The average ship turn-around time at Indian ports are much higher than the ports of other developed countries which should have been less to make the port more efficient and productive. The average ship turn-around time for Indian ports varies from four to seven days, whereas for Singapore it is six to eight hours only. A longer ASTA period means that ships calling on Indian ports have to pay a higher ship detention cost, which ranges from $ 15,000 to $ 20,000 per day per ship. In Table 6.6 the average turn-around time of ship for iron ore varies from the lowest of 2.62 days in 1988-89 to the highest of 8.18 days in 1986-87 (as seen in the Fig. 6.5). The average annual turn-around time for the whole study period was 4.33 days. Similarly, the average annual turn-around period in the pre-reform period stood at 4.28 days, as against 4.43 days in the post-reform period. The marginal increase of turn-around time in the post-reform period does not imply that the efficiency of the port has declined. The increase was due to the entering of more number of ships and handling of large sized bulks of traffic in the port.

6.7.2. Similarly in case of cocking coal, there has been gradual fall in average ship turn-around time for six years from 12.72 days in 1989-90 to 6.14 days in 1994-95 and further it was declined to 3.72 days in 2000-01. The average annual turn-around time during the whole period was 6.77 days. The pre-reform period registers 7.95 days of ASTA which fell significantly to 4.40 days in the post-reform period. In case of thermal coal, there was reduction in ASTA time during the period starting from 8.19 days in 1988-89 to 3.29 days in 2000-01. The average annual turn-around time during the period of thirteen years for thermal coal was 5.57 days. In the pre-reform period the average turn-around time was 6.68 days which declined considerably to 3.79 days in the post-reform period. In the pre-reform period, the average turn-around time for fertilisers raw materials varies from the highest of 7.47 days in 1990-91 to the lowest of 1.52 days in 1989-90. The average turn-around time for fertiliser raw material in the pre-reform period was 3.09 days per annum. This is due to less number of

Table 6.6

Average Ship Turn-around Time for Major Commodity-wise Vessels at Paradeep Port during 1986-87 to 2000-01

(In days)

	Type of vessels → / *Study period*	*Iron ore*	*Coking coal*	*Thermal coal*	*Fertilizer raw-materials*	*Ch.ore/ Ch.chrome/ Ferro manganese/ Ferro chrome*	*Iron & Steel*	*Overall*
Pre-reform period	1986-87	8.18	9.02	-	1.84	6.57	8.83	8.25
	1987-88	3.52	7.03	-	1.59	5.32	2.79	5.4
	1988-89	2.62	9.15	8.19	1.69	8.30	3.50	6.75
	1989-90	4.90	12.72	8.56	1.52	10.51	6.82	9.44
	1990-91	3.59	8.77	7.96	7.47	7.96	10.95	8.15
	1991-92	3.15	6.80	6.59	2.15	8.98	9.15	6.13
	1992-93	3.22	6.11	5.34	2.72	7.24	13.60	6.09
	1993-94	3.85	6.12	5.35	2.17	5.50	10.09	5.78
	1994-95	3.73	6.14	5.76	4.44	6.77	15.83	5.65
	1995-96	6.05	7.69	5.71	5.35	8.60	-	6.29
	Average	**4.28**	**7.95**	**6.68**	**3.09**	**7.57**	-	**6.79**
Post-reform period	1996-97	4.22	4.86	4.22	3.76	5.97	-	4.94
	1997-98	4.99	4.77	4.12	7.25	5.23	-	5.12
	1998-99	4.01	4.33	3.88	4.87	4.58	-	4.11
	1999-00	4.79	4.33	3.44	4.62	4.45	-	3.89
	2000-01	4.16	3.72	3.29	7.80	5.02	-	4.16
	Average	**4.43**	**4.40**	**3.79**	**5.66**	**5.05**	-	**4.44**
	Whole Period Avg.	**4.33**	**6.77**	**5.57**	**3.95**	**6.73**	-	**6.01**

Source : Annual Administration Reports, Paradeep Port Trust.

Fig. 6.5
Average Ship Turn-around Time at Paradeep Port during 1986-87 to 2000-01

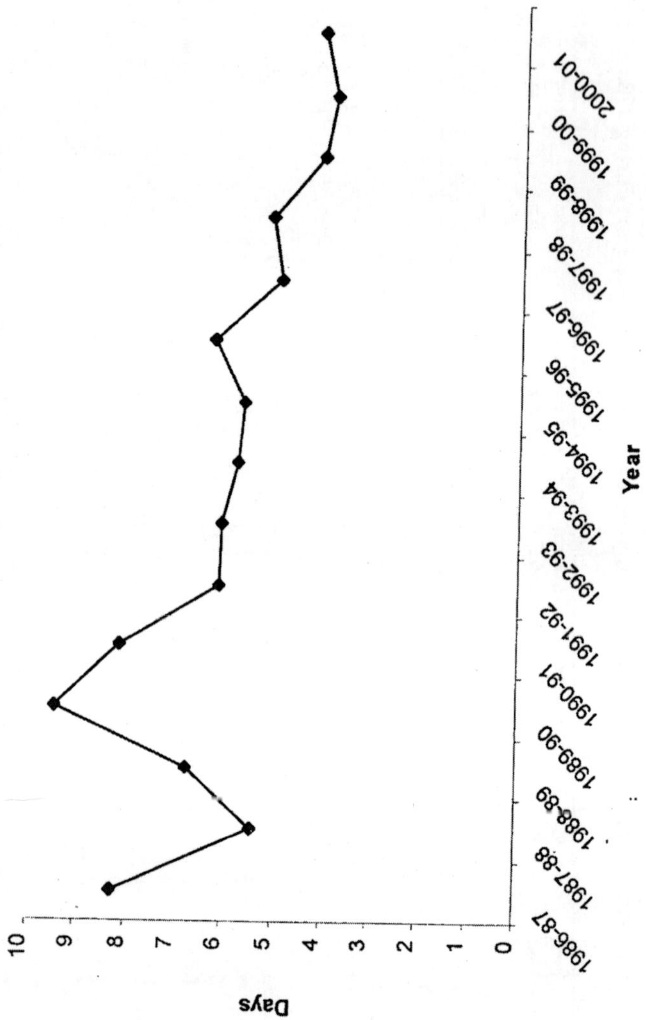

ships entering into the port during this period. But in the post-reform period the average annual turn-around time of fertiliser raw material shows an increasing trend of 5.66 days against the average annual turn-around days of 3.95 days during the whole period.

6.7.3. Chrome ore, charge chrome, Ferro Manganese, manganese ore, Ferro Chromes show fluctuating trends during the study period. The average turn-around time for the whole period was 6.73. In the pre-reform period the average turn-around time was 7.57 days which reduced to 5.05 days in the post-reform period. For iron and steel no figures were available after 1994-95. The overall average turn-around time of all commodities also shows fluctuating trend but declines considerably from 8.25 days in 1986-87 to 4.16 days in 2000-01. The average turn-around time for the whole period was 6.01 days. The pre-reform period average turn-around time stood at 6.79 days which was reduced to 4.44 days in the post-reform period. The efficient utilisation of port capacity, mechanised handling facility, developed storage facility, well equipped rail and road connectivity and overall port-management are the contributory factors for reducing the average turn-around time in the post-reform period. The establishment of mega fertiliser plant Oswal Fertilisers & Chemicals Ltd. and significant increase in import of fertiliser raw materials by the existing public sector fertiliser unit Paradeep Phosphate Ltd. to compete in international market contributed much for setting up more fertiliser berth and higher activities.

6.8. Berth Occupancy

6.8.1. Berth occupancy reflects the time for which a berth is occupied by ships. So higher the berth occupancy period in a year, higher is the productivity of the port. Table 6.7 highlights the berth occupancy of the port during the period from 1986-87 to 2000-01. This has also been explained in Fig. 6.6. The number of days available at different berths was 2190 days in 1986-87 and remained constant for six years till 1991-92. From 1993-94 it started showing higher berth occupancy year after year. It reached the occupancy of 3266 days in 1997-98 and further in 1999-2000 it went up to 3441 days. In 2000-01, it showed a marginal decline and reached 3274 days. The average annual berthdays available for the total study period was 2537.2 days. In the post-reform period the average annual berth day available was increased to 3161.2 days as against 2225.3 days during the pre-reform period. The increasing trend of available days in the post-reform period is due to addition of seven new berths in this period. All these berths are mechanised and highly efficient in operation. Similarly, the number of days occupied by the ships in the port during the period shows fluctuating trend. The number of days occupied in the pre-reform period was highest of 2123 days in 1995-96 as against the lowest of 1121 days in 1987-88.

Table 6.7
Berth Occupancy at Paradeep Port during 1986-87 to 2000-01

	Study Period	*No. of days available*	*No. of days occupied*	*Percentage of occupancy*
Pre-reform Period	1986-87	2190	1361	62
	1987-88	2190	1121	51
	1988-89	2190	1405	64
	1989-90	2190	1538	70
	1990-91	2190	1444	66
	1991-92	2190	1303	59
	1992-93	2171	1449	69
	1993-94	2232	1519	68
	1994-95	2239	1720	77
	1995-96	2471	2123	86
	Average	**2225.3**	**1498.3**	**67.2**
Post-reform Period	1996-97	2920	1933	66
	1997-98	3266	2139	65
	1998-99	2905	1942	67
	1999-00	3441	1964	63
	2000-01	3274	2277	70
	Average	**3161.2**	**2051**	**64.9**
Whole Period Avg.		**2537.2**	**1682.5**	**66.3**

Source : Annual Administration Reports, Paradeep Port Trust.

6.8.2. The average annual days occupied by the ships in the pre-reform period stood at 1498.3 days which rose considerably to 2051 days during the post-reform period. The average annual days of occupancy for the total study period was 1682.5 days. The percentage of occupancy

Fig. 6.6

Berth Occupancy at Paradeep Port during 1986-87 to 2000-01

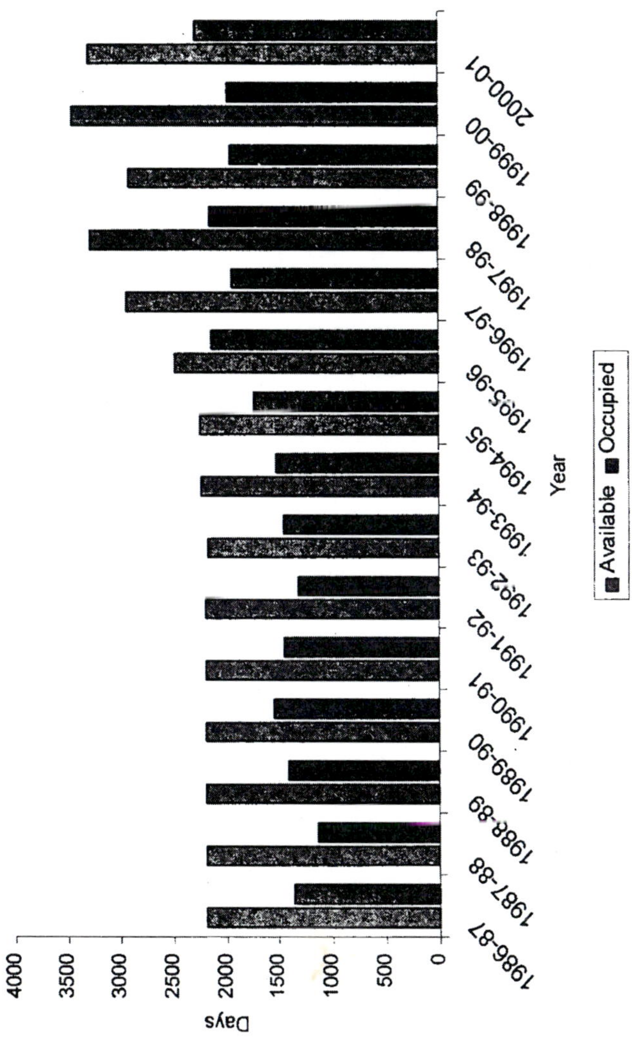

during the period also witnessed fluctuating trend from the highest of 86 per cent in 1995-96 and lowest of 51 per cent in 1987-88. The average annual percentage of occupancy in the pre-reform period was 67.2 per cent as against 64.9 per cent in the post-reform period. The whole period average percentage of occupancy stood at 66.3 per cent. During the post-reform period total number of berths reached 13 from 6 in the pre-reform period. Though the number of berths are added to the port in the post-reform period and the number of ships also increased, but, not to that extent to occupy the berths. Thus, the percentage of occupancy declines marginally in this period.

6.9. Utilisation of Cargo Handling Equipment at Paradeep Port

6.9.1. Proper utilisation of cargo handling equipment at the port is one of the important factors of productivity. Table 6.8 explains about the utilisation of cargo handling equipment at the port during 1986-87 to 2000-01. The port mainly uses wharf cranes, pay loaders, mobile cranes and fork lifts during the study period. From 1997-98 the port has started the use of diesel locos including the above equipment. Throughout the study period, the port has used 4 number of wharf cranes. On an average, the total number of hours available (gross) in the whole period stood at 34,976 hours as against 34,915.2 hours in the pre-reform period and 35,097.6 hours in the post-reform period. The average of net available working hours during the study period was found to be 28,757.07 hours as against 29,238.6 hours in the pre-reform period but declined to 27,794.01 hours in the post-reform period. Similarly the average annual availability of wharf crane in the pre-reform period was 83.74 per cent which was reduced to 79.19 per cent in the post-reform period. The average working time of the equipment was also reduced from 10,624.3 hours in the pre-reform period to 6,589.21 hours in the post-reform period. On an average, the utilisation of the equipment during the whole study period comes to 32.26 per cent as against 36.33 per cent in the pre-reform period and declined to 23.70 per cent per annum in the post reform period.

6.9.2. Similarly in the case of pay loader, the number of equipment in 1987-88 was only two which was increased to three in 1989-90 and in 1992-93 further increased to four and remained constant in the rest of the years of the study period. The gross total number of hours available in the whole period came to be 27,459.9 hours as against 26,897.8 hours per

Table 6.8

Utilisation of Cargo Handling Equipment at Paradeep Port during 1986-87 to 2000-01

	Study Period	WHARF CRANE						PAY LOADER					
		No. of Equip-ment	*Total no. of hrs. available*	*Available working hr (Net)*	*% of availa-bility*	*Actual working time*	*% of utilisa-tion*	*No. of Equip-ment*	*Total no. of hrs. available*	*Available working hr (Net)*	*% of availa-bility*	*Actual working time*	*% of utilisa-tion*
Pre-reform period	1986-87	4	35,040	29,218	83.38	7972	27.28	2	19,954	15,538	91.64	7,376	47.47
	1987-88	4	35,136	31,316.5	89.12	4790	15.30	2	17,568	15,365.5	87.46	5,740	43.86
	1988-89	4	35,040	26,451	75.48	8548.5	32.31	2	22,608	15,972	70.64	8,143.5	46.72
	1989-90	4	35,040	24,127.40	68.85	9487.45	39.32	3	26,280	17,550.35	66.78	8,746.30	49.83
	1990-91	4	35,040	32,161.30	91.78	11,189.00	34.79	3	26,280	19,742.10	75.12	8,241.05	41.74
	1991-92	4	35,136	29,262.51	83.28	24,339.12	83.17	3	26,952	16.759.32	62.18	1.4,860	88.66
	1992-93	4	35,040	28,963.50	82.65	16513.35	57.01	4	28,656	18,198.15	63.50	9,592.45	52.71
	1993-94	4	35,040	29,921.55	85.39	7644.00	25.54	4	35,040	25,197	71.90	5,193.15	20.61
	1994-95	4	33,504	31,076.10	92.75	7784.45	25.04	4	33,504	18,732.25	55.91	5,584.6	29.81
	1995-96	4	35,136	29,888.05	85.06	7975.2	26.69	4	35,136	20,663.3	58.80	4,895.7	23.69
	Average		**34,915.2**	**29,238.6**	**83.74**	**10624.3**	**36.64**		**26,897.8**	**18371.8**	**68.30**	**7937.26**	**43.20**
Post-reform period	1996-97	4	35,136	25,374.25	72.21	6819.15	26.87	4	35,136	25,151	71.58	4,602.7	18.30
	1997-98	4	35,136	22,660	65	7875	35	4	35,136	21,283	61	4,099	19
	1998-99	4	35,040	28,974.45	82.69	4,499.00	15.53	4	17,520	15,834.40	90.38	2,151.35	13.59
	1999-00	4	35,136	32,580.93	92.73	6,874.66	21.10	4	30,264	26,036.50	86.03	2,428.42	9.33
	2000-01	4	35,040	29,380.43	83.85	6,878.25	23.41	4	24,864	19,437	78.17	2,750.33	14.15
	Average		**35,097**	**27,794.01**	**79.19**	**6,589.21**	**23.70**		**28,584**	**21,548.38**	**75.38**	**3,206.36**	**14.87**
	Whole Period Avg.		**34,976**	**28,757.07**	**82.21**	**9279.27**	**32.26**		**27,459.9**	**19,430.66**	**70.76**	**6360.3**	**32.73**

(Contd.)

Table 6.8 (Contd.)

Period	MOBILE CRANE						FORK LIFT						DIESEL LOCOS					
	1	*2*	*3*	*4*	*5*	*6*	*7*	*8*	*9*	*10*	*11*	*12*	*13*	*14*	*15*	*16*	*17*	*18*
Pre - reform period	5	44,627	41,236	92.4	6232	15.11	12	1,12,28	1,03,105	91.82	7805	7.56						
	5	45,527	43,744.5	96.08	6184	14.14	12	1,12,72	1,06,200.5	94.20	5301	4.99						
	5	43,800	41,396.5	94.51	6433.5	15.54	12	1,05,12	97,459	92.71	9411.5	9.65						
	6	52,560	33,833.25	64.37	6276.40	18.55	12	1,05,12	59,985.05	57.06	6763.30	11.27						
	6	46,728	35,577.30	76.13	5439.40	15.28	12	93,600	53,822.00	57.50	8,613.05	16						
	5	43,920	28,797.15	65.56	25558.30	88.75	10	76,104	56,627	74.40	51,328.29	90.64						
	5	38,237	26,168.40	68.43	14248.30	54.44	12	90,816	80,984.25	89.17	43895.30	54.20						
	4	39,384	29,337.00	74.48	3477.7	11.85	8	96,288	70,631.30	73.35	8150.3	11.53						
	4	33,504	4,120.30	12.29	3043.8	73.88	8	67,008	59,054	88.12	4972.5	8.42						
	5	43,920	21,003.25	47.82	3350.65	15.95	8	70,272	59,064	84.05	32.5	7.5						
	Avg.	**43,220.7**	**30,521.36**	**70.61**	**8024.4**	**26.29**	-	**92,934**	**74,693.20**	**80.37**	**14,627.27**	**19.58**						
Post - reform period	4	36,136	17,548.45	49.94	3164.2	18.03	8	70,272	67,520.30	96.08	8376.6	9.44						
	4	35,136	17,230	49	2398	14	10	83,952	76,487	91	3441	5	7	61,152	40,201	66	21,198	55
	4	26,280	21,608.15	82.22	1778.30	8.21	10	87,600	87,200.45	99.54	4,422.05	5.07	8	56,880	51,710	90.91	22,905	44.29
	4	28,152	20,570.83	73.07	2311.33	11.24	10	87,840	87,479.50	99.59	3,080.00	3.52	7	61,488	57,269	93.13	21,475	37.49
	4	35,040	32,936.50	93.99	2823.50	8.57	10	87,600	85,630.50	97.75	3,435.00	4.01	7	61,320	47,128	76.85	31,6292	67.11
	Average	**32,148.8**	**21,978.78**	**68.36**	**2495.06**	**11.35**		**83,452.**	**45,983.37**	**96.79**	**4,550.93**	**5.40**		**60,210**	**49,077**	**81.50**	**24,481.75**	**49.88**
	Whole Period Avg.	**39530.06**	**27673.83**	**70.00**	**6181.28**	**22.33**		**89,773.**	**76,750**	**85.49**	**11,268.5**	**14.68**						

1. No. of equipment 2. Total no. of hrs. available 3. Available working hr.(net) 4. % of availability 5. Actual working time 6. % of utilisation 7. No. of equipment 8. Total no. of hrs. available 9. Available working hr.(net) 10. % of availability 11. Actual working time 12. % of utilisation 13. No. of equipment 14. Total no. of hrs. available 15. Available working hr.(net) 16. % of availability 17. Actual working time 18. % of utilisation

Source : Annual Administration Reports, Paradeep Port Trust.

annum in the pre-reform period which was increased marginally to 28,584 hours in the post-reform period. Similarly the net available working hours were increased from 18,371.8 hours per annum in the pre-reform period to 21,548.38 hours per annum in the post-reform period as against 19,430.66 hours in the total study period. The availability of equipment in the post-reform period stood at 75.38 per cent per annum as against 68.30 per cent per annum in the pre-reform period and 70.76 per cent per annum in the whole study period. The actual working time at the port was reduced from 7,937.26 hours per annum in the pre-reform period to 3,206.36 hours in the post-reform period. On an average the utilisation of the equipment also declined from 43.20 per cent in the pre-reform period to 14.87 per cent in the post reform period against 32.73 per cent per annum in the whole period. During the four years of post-reform period for diesel locos, the actual working time came out to be 24,481.75 hours per annum against the available working time of 49,077 hours per annum and the total working time of 60,210 hours available per annum. The port has used 49.88 per cent actual working time and 81.50 per cent available working hours out of total hours at the port during the study period.

6.9.3. Similarly in case of mobile cranes, the number fluctuates between 4 and 6 in the pre-reform period and remained constant at 4 number of cranes during the post-reform period. The availability of mobile crane increased from 70.61 per cent per annum in the pre-reform period to 68.36 per cent in the post-reform period as against 70.00 per cent in the total study period. The actual working time declined to 2,495.06 hours per annum in the post-reform period from 8,024.4 hours in the pre-reform period and 6,181.28 hours per annum during the whole study period. The percentage of utilisation also shows a reduced average of 11.35 per cent in the post-reform period as against 26.29 per cent in the pre-reform period and 22.33 per cent in the whole study period.

6.9.4. There were 12 fork lifts working at the port till 1990-91. It was reduced to 8 fork lifts during 1993-94 to 1996-97 and again increased to 10 fork lifts from 1997-98. The total number of hours available at the port during the whole period on an average came to 89,773.6 hours. In the pre-reform period, the total number of hours available were 92,934 hours per annum which were reduced to 83,452.8 hours per annum in the post-reform period. Similarly, the net available working hours at the port for the equipment during the total study period stood at 76,750 hours per annum as against 74,693.2 hours per annum in the pre-reform period and was reduced to 80,863.5 hours per annum during the post-reform period. The availability of the equipment also shows an increasing trend during the post-reform period of 96.89 per cent as against 80.37 per cent in the pre-reform period and 85.49 per cent during the whole period. The actual working time and the utilisation of the equipment depict a declining trend of average 4,550.93 hours and 5.62 per cent during the post-reform period as against 14,627.27 hours and 19.58 per cent in the pre-reform period. From 1997-98, the port used 7 diesel locos which were increased to 8 tin 1998-99 and again were reduced to 7 till 2000-01. The use of diesel locos in the post-reform period has increased efficiency and productivity in the operations of the port.

6.10. Distribution of Non-working Time at Berths

6.10.1. Table 6.9 analyses the distribution of non-working time at berths according to various reasons like non-availability of equipment, working berth, absence of workers, equipment breakdown, shed congestion, lack of cargo, strike and stoppages, adverse weather condition, power failure, hatch-opening, closing and storing, waiting for sailing ships, etc. During the study period, the two factors such as non-availability of working berth and strike and stoppages reflect no idle time at berths. The absence of workers which varies from the highest of 720 hours in 1988-89 to the lowest of 7 hours in 1997-98 shows a perceptible declining trend, more particularly during the post-reform period. The average annual absence of workers reduced to 28.38 hours during the post-reform period from 266.42 hours during the pre-reform period as against the average of the total period of 187.07 hours. The reason for such improvement may be attributed to different welfare measures taken by the port authority during the post-reform period which have motivated employees for their regular attendance in duties. The cause of non-availability of equipment during the post-reform period reduced significantly to 26 hours in 1996-97 as against the 374.19 hours per annum during the pre-reform period. Equipment breakdown in the post-reform period stood at 572.08 hours per annum as against 409.19 hours per annum during the pre-reform period and 463.48 hours per annum during the whole period. The use of more mechanised equipment by the port and increasing volume of traffic caused more

Table 6.9

Distribution of Non-Working Time at Berth According to Reasons during 1986-87 to 2000-01

	1	2	3	4	5	6	7	8	9	10	11	12	13	14	15	16
Pre - reform period	1986-87	172	-	435.5	381	876.37	-	536.16	-	609.46	237.13	-	-	586.43	2235.5	5897.56
	1987-88	197	-	63.28	2.58	915.97	2.50	370.37	-	421.25	191.43	90.42	-	528.21	3025.6	5611.69
	1988-89	228	-	720	603	368	-	628	-	406	570	-	-	661.00	1327.0	5283.00
	1989-90	222	-	408.50	795.16	69.33	-	705.12	-	946.16	305.59	2253.37	1065.18	1841.0	829.47	10020.53
	1990-91	231	-	673	590	447	-	808	-	1022	290	1915	1006	2219	1314	10284
	1991-92	246	-	282	144	352	-	603	-	873	271	1743	1019	1123	2340	8750
	1992-93	275	-	11	120	170	-	1470	-	769	359	1759	1074	934	2382	9048
	1993-94	298	-	32	380	213	-	1880	-	527	526	1546	1176	1355	2079	9684
	1994-95	341	-	8.41	614.18	152.57	-	3026	-	493.22	243.48	1243.24	1313.47	17.02	3198.5	10312.18
	1995-96	360	-	30.58	112.08	527.69	53.50	2044.8	-	623.28	270.94	1359.89	1106.99	-	3295.3	9425.13
	Average	**257**	-	**266.42**	**374.19**	**409.19**	-	**1207.1**	-	**669.03**	**326.45**	**1488.74**	**1108.66**	**1029.4**	**2202.6**	**8431.6**
Post-reform period	1996-97	370	-	48	26	551	-	2049	-	407	337	443	1442	54	4968	10365
	1997-98	643	-	7	-	1070	-	-	-	682	1002	-	1193	4882	4205	13041
	1998-99	678	-	7.91	-	338.42	-	-	-	453.42	173.91	-	2186.91	1289.8	3642.7	8093.12
	1999-00	712	-	19	-	243	-	-	-	391	249	-	2336	1463	5135	9,836
	2000-01	886	-	60	-	658	88	-	-	335	461	-	2851	2318	5464	12,235
	Average	**658**	-	**28.38**	-	**572.08**	-	-	-	**453.68**	**444.58**	-	**2001.78**	**2001.3**	**4682.9**	**10714.02**
Whole period Avg.		**391**	-	**187.07**	-	**463.48**	-	-	-	**597.24**	**365.82**	-	**1,480.79**	**1376.5**	**3029.4**	**9192.4**

1. Study period, 2. No. of ships, 3. Non-avail of working berths 4. Absence of workers 5. Equipment non-availability 6. Equipment break-down, 7. Shed congestion, 8. Lack of cargo, 9. Strike and Stoppages 10. Adverse weather condition 11. Power failure, 12. Hatch opening/Closing/storing 13. Waiting for sailing 14. Ship A/C* 15. Others 16. Total.

*Ships A/c includes shippers A/c.

Source : Annual Administration Reports, Paradeep Port Trust.

breakdown of equipment. The non-working time at berths due to shed congestion was low in the study period. In 2000-01, the port experienced a 88 hours of shed congestion as against 2.50 hours and 53.50 hours during 1987-88 and 1995-96 respectively. Non-working time at berth also got reduced due to lack of cargo during the post-reform period and recorded 2049 hours in 1996-97 as against 1207.14 hours per annum during the pre-reform period.

6.10.2. Similarly the non-working time at the port due to adverse weather condition was 597.24 hours per annum during the entire study period as against the 669.03 hours per annum during the pre-reform period. Further it was declined to 453.68 hours during the post-reform period. Though weather condition is an uncontrollable factor, the port authorities have taken adequate measures to reduce the impact of adverse weather conditions to the minimum. The power failure is an important factor that creates non-working time at berths. During the post-reform period, the non-working time due to power failure was increased to 444.58 hours per annum as against 326.45 hours per annum in the pre-reform period and 365.82 hours during the total study period. Figures relating to hatch-opening, closing and storing were not available during the post-reform period except 443 hours in 1996-97 as against the 1488.74 hours per annum during the pre-reform period. The non-working time due to waiting for sailing have increased phenomenally to 2001.78 hours per annum during the post-reform period from 1108.66 hours in the pre-reform period and 1480.79 hours during the whole study period. Ships accounts including shippers accounts and other reasons also showed higher average of 2001.36 hours and 4682.95 hours during the post-reform period as against 1029.40 hours and 2202.65 hours during the pre-reform period respectively. On an average, the total non-working time due to different reasons also increased from 8,431.6 hours in the pre-reform period to 10,714.02 hours in the post-reform period as against 9192.4 hours during the whole study period.

6.11. Distribution of Pre-berthing Delay at Paradeep Port

6.11.1. Table 6.10 portrays the pre-berthing delay at Paradeep port during 1986-87 to 2000-01. Pre-berthing delay means the time for which a ship waits before getting entry into a berth. So lesser the pre-berthing delay more will be the productivity of the port and vice-versa. The Table 6.6 explains the pre-berthing delay time according to various reasons like non-availability of berths, non-availability of tugs and crafts, non-availability of pilot and crew, delay due to strikes, night navigation, draft restriction, weather constraints, ships and shipper's account and agent's accounts, etc. The number of ships rose from 237 in 1987-88 to 886 in 2000-01 showing gradual increase during the study period. The average number of ships sailed during the pre-reform period was 320 ships which became more than double to 695 ships in the post-reform period. This is due to the expansion of the berths and use of mechanised equipments to handle the cargo and increase in the demand for this mode of transport in the post-reform period. The prime reason for pre-berthing delay in the port was due to non-availability of berth. It was highest of 21238.80 hours in 1995-96 and lowest of 3618 hours in 1999-2000. The pre-berthing delay for the whole period was 7990.82 hours per annum. In the pre-reform period it was 9012.5 hours per annum which declined considerably to 5947.48 hours in the post-reform period. The increase in the performance resulting from reduction of pre-berthing delay was due to addition of seven new berths in the post-reform period. There was absolutely no delay due to non-availability of tugs and crafts, non-availability of pilot and crew and strikes during the period except 112 hours and 66 hours of delays for non-availability of tugs and crafts and strikes respectively during 1999-2000. This indicates the emergence of conducive environment for the future development of the port. Another reason of delay is night navigation. The delay due to night navigation in the pre-reform period was 635.22 hours per annum which was increased to 1211.84 hours in the post-reform period. The delay for the whole period was 827.42 hours per annum. The increase in the delay in the post-reform period was due to more number of ships sailed at the port.

6.11.2. At present, the port provides night navigation facility up to 2100 hours and it is to be extended to all vessels round the clock in near future. During 2000-01, the port provided night navigational shipping movement facility for 295 ships. Similarly, ship's account and shipper's account also shows an increasing time of 11495.02 hours per annum in the post-reform period as compared to 605.48 hours per annum in the pre-reform period and 4235.32 hours during the whole period. Unpreparedness of receiver shipper, weather constraints and agents account constituted the other reasons which accounted for 4,576.66 hours of delay per annum

Table 6.10
Distribution of Pre-berthing Delay According to Reason at Pardeep Port during 1986-87 to 2000-01

(in hours)

	Study Period	*No. of Ships*	*Non-availability of berth*	*Non-availability of Tugs/ Crafts*	*Non-availability of Pilot/ Cargo*	*Strike*	*Night Navi-gation*	*Draft Restri-ction*	*Ship's Accou-nts**	*Others**	*Total*
Pre-reform period	1986-87	270	4372.36	-	-	-	516.20	-	848.56	732.43	6469.55
	1987-88	237	1979.76	-	-	-	503.28	-	741.84	785.52	4010.40
	1988-89	273	7597.92	-	-	-	531.84	-	1329.60	1025.04	10484.40
	1989-90	244	13005.36	-	-	-	330.24	-	915.36	1694.40	15975.36
	1990-91	264	7360	-	-	-	515	-	699	1376	10050
	1991-92	315	7123.44	-	-	-	817.10	-	209.52	682.22	8832.28
	1992-93	315	8804	-	-	-	663	-	381	444	10292
	1993-94	329	6671.04	-	-	-	779.76	-	214.08	510.72	8175.60
	1994-95	432	11958.24	-	-	-	965.04	-	188.40	1042.80	14154.48
	1995-96	523	21238.80	-	-	-	730.80	-	527.52	8725.44	31222.56
	Average	**320**	**9012.5**	-	-	-	**635.22**	-	**605.48**	**1701.85**	**11966.66**
Post-reform period	1996-97	557	7100	-	-	-	1096	-	130	13524	21850
	1997-98	643	8439.18	-	-	-	1274.81	285.33	12859.21	2859.86	25718.39
	1998-99	678	3876.23	-	-	-	1172.42	11.17	12736.93	1741.46	19538.21
	1999-2000	712	3618	112	-	66	1293	-	11058	3329	19476
	2000-2001	886	6704	-	-	-	1223	-	20691	1429	30047
	Average	**695**	**5947.48**	-	-	-	**1211.84**	-	**11495.02**	**4576.66**	**23325.92**
	Whole Period Average	**445**	**7990.82**	-	-	-	**827.42**	-	**4235.32**	**2660.12**	**15753.08**

* Others include receiver shipper not ready, weather constraints, agent's account. ** Ship's account includes shipper's account.

Source : Annual Administration Reports Paradeep Port Trust.

in the post-reform period as against 1701.85 hours per annum in the pre-reform period. These are the obvious but unavoidable reasons causing delay with the increase in number of ships sailing at the port.

6.12. Share of Total Traffic Carried by Indian Ships and Foreign Ships at Paradeep Port

6.12.1. Table 6.11 reflects the picture of share of traffic handled by Indian ships and foreign ships during the study period of 1986-87 to 2000-01. The total number of vessels called at port during the study period reached 915 in 2000-01 from 285 vessels in 1986-87. The number of ships per annum in the post-reform period rose to nearly 724 ships from 359 ships during the pre-reform period against 480 ships during the total study period. The number of Indian ships also varies from 95 ships in 1988-89 to 470 ships in 2000-01. The average number of Indian ships called at the port during the pre-reform period stood at 167 ships which was doubled, i.e., above 400 ships during the post-reform period as against the average of 245 ships during the whole study period. So far as foreign ships are concerned, while fluctuating trend is noticed in the pre-reform period, the post-reform period has witnessed gradual rise in the foreign ships operating at the port. The number of foreign ships varies between the lowest of 155 ships in 1990-91 to 445 ships in 2000-01. The average number of foreign ships called at the port during the whole study period comes to nearly 236 ships as against 192 in the pre-reform period and 324 during the post-reform period. The percentage of total traffic carried by Indian ships varies from the lowest of 45.42 per cent in 1988-89 to the highest of 65.85 per cent in 1997-98. Out of the total, on an average traffic handled by Indian ships during pre-reform period came out to be 55.84 per cent and in the post-reform period nearly 60.55 per cent. But during the whole period, Indian ships had handled 57.41 per cent of the total traffic.

6.12.2. Consequently, declining trend is noticed in respect of traffic handled by foreign ships is evident from the fact that while the share of total traffic handled by foreign ships was 44.15 per cent in pre-reform period declined to 39.44 per cent in the post-reform period. Foreign ships share in post-reform period has been low when compared with the figure of 42.58 per cent of the whole study period. In the post-reform period, the number of both the Indian ships and foreign ships had increased because of the establishment of new minor ports by the coastal States in India with

Table 6.11

Share of Traffic Carried by Indian Ships and Foreign Ships at the Port during 1986-87 to 2000-01

Period	*Study period*	*Total No. of vessels called at port*	*Indian ships*	*Foreign ships*	*% of total traffic carried by Indian ships*	*% of total traffic carried by foreign ships*
Pre-reform period	1986-87	285	97	188	46	54
Pre-reform period	1987-88	325	104	221	57	43
Pre-reform period	1988-89	304	95	209	45.42	54.58
Pre-reform period	1989-90	258	96	162	47.52	52.48
Pre-reform period	1990-91	278	123	155	50.35	49.65
Pre-reform period	1991-92	336	165	171	58.51	41.49
Pre-reform period	1992-93	366	197	169	64.56	35.44
Pre-reform period	1993-94	405	244	161	62.72	37.28
Pre-reform period	1994-95	483	232	251	62.02	37.98
Pre-reform period	1995-96	550	319	231	64.34	35.66
Pre-reform period	**Average**	**359**	**167.2**	**191.8**	**55.84**	**44.15**
Post-reform period	1996-97	592	342	250	61.53	38.47
Post-reform period	1997-98	676	393	283	65.85	34.15
Post-reform period	1998-99	695	388	307	64.41	35.59
Post-reform period	1999-00	741	406	335	61.04	38.96
Post-reform period	2000-01	915	470	445	49.93	50.07
Post-reform period	**Average**	723.8	**399.8**	**324**	**60.55**	**39.44**
	Whole Period Average	480.6	**244.73**	**235.86**	**57.41**	**42.58**

Source : Annual Administration Reports, Paradeep Port Trust.

private participation and establishment of two new fertiliser plants, for which there was import of raw materials from foreign countries. Further, the increase in the export of fertilisers from the region has enhanced demand for more number of ships. Similarly, due to establishment of more thermal units of existing power stations in Orissa during the post-reform period, there has been increase in the demand for thermal coal which are imported from Australia.

6.13. Traffic Handled by Railway at Paradeep Port

6.13.1. The major share of traffic at Paradeep port is handled through railways compared to other modes of transport like road and pipeline. Table 6.12 indicates the inward and outward rail traffic handled by the port during the study period of 1986-87 to 2000-01. Since Orissa is endowed with vast natural resources of various minerals, the port acts as a connectivity point between the users of the mineral resources and the source (for export purpose) showed an upward fluctuating trend. The inward rail traffic of 21.71 lakh tonnes in 1986-87 reached 103.27 lakh tonnes during 2000-01 (as seen in Fig. 6.7). The share of inward rail traffic to total rail traffic was increased from 61.51 per cent in 1987-88 to 85.50 per cent during 2000-01. The inward traffic during the whole study period stoods at 49.59 lakh tonnes per annum as against 36.74 lakh tonnes in the pre-reform period. During the post-reform period it increased considerably to 75.30 lakh tonnes, i.e., more than double of pre-reform period. The inward rail traffic was increased from the lowest of 54.49 per cent in 1988-89 to the highest of 85.50 per cent in 2000-01. Similarly the outward rail traffic also reflects a fluctuating trend varying between 10.71 lakh tonnes in 1986-87 to 18.69 lakh tonnes in 1997-98. The average outward rail traffic during the whole study period was found to be 15.85 lakh tonnes per annum. In the post-reform period, the outward rail traffic increased marginally to 17.62 lakh tonnes per annum as against 14.97 lakh tonnes per annum in the pre-reform period. The outward traffic also varied during the study period registering the highest of 45.51 per cent in 1988-89 and the lowest of 14.50 per cent in 2000-01.

Table 6.12
Traffic Handled by Railway during 1986-87 to 2000-01

(In lakh tonnes)

	Study period	*Inward rail traffic*	*Outward rail traffic*	*Total rail traffic*
Pre-reform Period	1986-87	21.71	10.71	32.42
		(66.96)	(33.04)	(100)
	1987-88	24.57	15.37	39.94
		(61.51)	(38.49)	(100)
	1988-89	20.61	17.22	37.83
		(54.49)	(45.51)	(100)
	1989-90	26.96	16.48	43.44
		(62.06)	(37.94)	(100)
	1990-91	36.12	16.98	53.10
		(68.02)	(31.98)	(100)
	1991-92	39.28	14.76	54.04
		(72.68)	(27.32)	(100)
	1992-93	44.28	11.58	55.86
		(79.27)	(20.73)	(100)
	1993-94	48.15	13.77	61.92
		(77.76)	(22.24)	(100)
	1994-95	53.43	15.46	68.89
		(77.56)	(22.44)	(100)
	1995-96	56.30	17.14	73.44
		(76.66)	(23.34)	(100)
	Average	**36.74**	**14.97**	**52.08**
Post-reform Period	1996-97	61.99	16.21	78.20
		(79.27)	(20.73)	(100)
	1997-98	72.71	18.69	91.40
		(79.55)	(20.45)	(100)
	1998-99	71.72	18.58	90.30
		(79.42)	(20.58)	(100)
	1999-00	66.82	17.12	83.94
		(79.60)	(20.40)	(100)
	2000-01	103.27	17.51	120.78
		(85.50)	(14.50)	(100)
	Average	**75.30**	**17.62**	**92.92**
	Whole Period Average	**49.59**	**15.85**	**65.7**

Note : Figures in the bracket indicate the percentage to the total.

Source : Annual Administration Reports, Paradeep Port Trust.

Fig. 6.7
Traffic Handled by Railway at Paradeep Port during 1986-87 to 2000-01

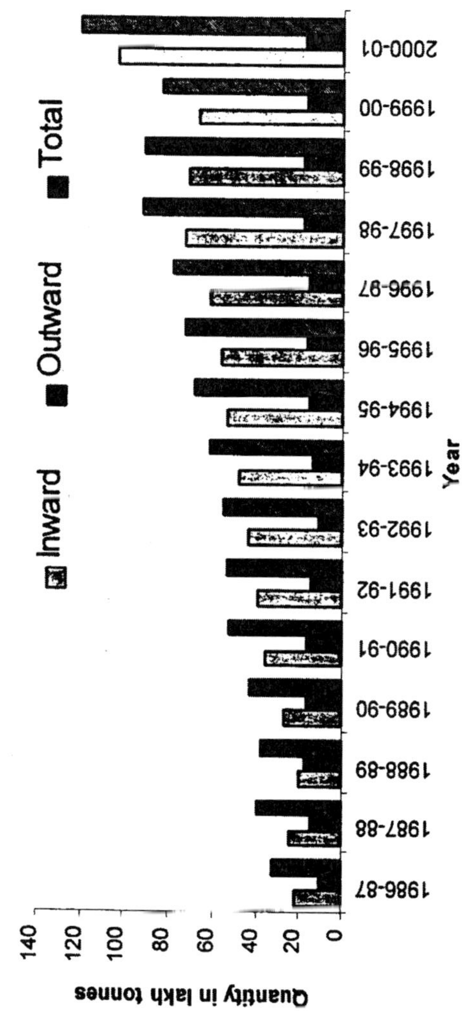

6.13.2. The unsatisfactory performance of outward rail traffic during the study period is due to lack of adequate rail connectivity to different parts of the State. The backward districts are still the untouched areas for the railways after fifty-five years of independence, even with the formulation of nine Five Year Plans for economic development. Due to poor rail connectivity, the other modes of transport such as road transport played the major role in handling the outward traffic. Due to import of less quantity of goods, the outward rail transport will be costlier compared to transportation by road. Further, as rail connectivity to various parts of the State has not yet been developed, road transport will be economical. The total rail traffic reached 120.78 lakh tonnes in 2000-01 from 32.42 lakh tonnes in 1986-87. The port has its own railway section operating within the port's area. But for handling of inward and outward traffic at the port, the port depends upon the South Eastern railway authorities. Sometimes the handling of port traffic are paralised due to non-availability of sufficient wagons for inward and outward traffic. The inward rail traffic accounted for 85 per cent of total rail traffic because for export purpose more quantities of ores, coal, etc. were transported through the port. So the rail transport mode is the cheaper and quicker mode of transport for inward traffic.

6.14. Export Cargo Received by Different Modes of Transport at Paradeep Port

6.14.1. Table 6.13 exhibits the export cargo received by different modes of transport such as rail, road, inland water transport and pipeline at the port during the period 1986-87 to 2000-01. The table reveals that, the rail mode of transport has emerged as the most significant modes from among the total modes of transport for handling cargo. The quantities of export traffic varied from the lowest of20.61 lakh tonnes in 1988-89 to the highest of 103.27 lakh tonnes in 2000-01. This has been explained in Fig. 6.8. The export traffic received by rail mode was 37.14 lakh tonnes per annum in the pre-reform period which was increased to 75.30 lakh tonnes per annum registering nearly 100 per cent rise in the post-reform period. This was also significantly higher than the whole period average annual export traffic of 49.86 lakh tonnes. The percentage share of rail mode of transport in total export cargo received remained near about same of 80 per cent during the whole study period. Similarly the export cargo received by other modes of transport was also increased from 6.8 lakh tonnes in 1986-

87 to 27.25 lakh tonnes in 2000-01. The average quantity of export cargo received in the pre-reform period was 18.79 lakh tonnes per annum which was significantly higher than the average export traffic of 8.69 tonnes per annum in the pre-reform period. The percentage share of export received by other modes varied from the lowest of 10.71 per cent in 1990-91 to the highest of 36.67 per cent in 1988-89. The export traffic per annum remained more or less unchanged during the pre, post and in the total period.

6.14.2. The port exports mainly the mineral resources such as iron ore, chrome ore, charge chrome, thermal coal etc., which need to be exported in huge quantities for attaining economies of scale in operation. So the rail mode is economical for this purpose. After the establishment of ADB aided mechanised coal handling plant the port in 2001, the port is expected to handle more export traffic in the coming years. The total export traffic also records a higher average of 94.09 lakh tonnes per annum in the post-reform period as against 45.84 lakh tonnes per annum in the pre-refom period. On an average, the export cargo received at the port by different modes of transport during the whole period was 61.92 lakh tonnes per annum. The volumes of higher traffic handled at the port during the study period had contributed significantly to operating incomes and surpluses of the port.

6.15. Import Cargo Despatched by Different Modes of Transport at Paradeep Port

6.15.1. Table 6.14 highlights the import cargo despatched by different modes of transport such as rail, road, inland water transport and pipeline. Since the rail mode is significant at the port in comparison to other modes, an analysis has been made between rail mode and other modes of transport. The quantities of import cargo traffic despatched by rail varied from the lowest of 10.71 lakh tonnes in 1986-87 to the highest of 18.69 lakh tonnes in 1997-98. This has been exhibited in Fig. 6.9. The average import traffic despatched by rail was 15.86 lakh tonnes per annum during the whole study period ; but in the post-reform period the import traffic despatched per annum was 17.62 lakh tonnes which is significantly higher than the average annual import traffic of 14.94 lakh tonnes in the pre-reform period. Though the average quantities of rail traffic had increased during the post-reform period, but the percentage share of rail traffic has declined from 68.25 per cent in 1987-88 to 25.60 per cent in 2000-01. On an average,

Table 6.13

Export Cargo Received by Different Modes of Transport at Paradeep Port during 1986-87 to 2000-01

	Study Period	*Received by Rail*		*Received by other modes (Road, Inland water transport and pipe line)*		*Total*	
		Quantity (in lakh onnes)	*Per cent*	*Quantity (in lakh tonnes)*	*Per cent*	*Quantity (in lakh tonnes)*	*Per cent*
Pre-reform Period	1986-87	21.71	76.14	6.80	23.86	28.51	100
	1987-88	24.57	83.71	4.78	16.29	29.35	100
	1988-89	20.61	63.33	11.93	36.67	32.54	100
	1989-90	26.96	72.39	10.28	27.61	37.24	100
	1990-91	36.12	89.29	4.33	10.71	40.45	100
	1991-92	39.28	88.93	4.89	11.07	44.17	100
	1992-93	44.28	85.51	7.5	14.49	51.78	100
	1993-94	48.15	83.79	9.31	16.21	57.46	100
	1994-95	53.43	80.58	12.87	19.42	66.30	100
	1995-96	56.30	79.75	14.29	20.25	70.59	100
	Average	**37.14**	**81.02**	**8.69**	**18.98**	**45.84**	-
Post-reform Period	1996-97	61.99	80.28	15.22	19.72	77.21	100
	1997-98	72.71	82.49	15.43	17.51	88.14	100
	1998-99	71.72	83.38	14.29	16.62	86.01	100
	1999-00	66.82	75.41	21.78	24.59	88.60	100
	2000-01	103.27	79.12	27.25	20.88	130.52	100
	Average	**75.30**	**80.02**	**18.79**	**19.98**	**94.09**	-
Whole Period Average		**49.86**	**80.52**	**12.06**	**19.48**	**61.92**	-

Source: Annual Administration Reports, Paradeep Port Trust.

Fig. 6.8
Export Cargo Received by Different Modes of Transport during 1986-87 to 2000-01

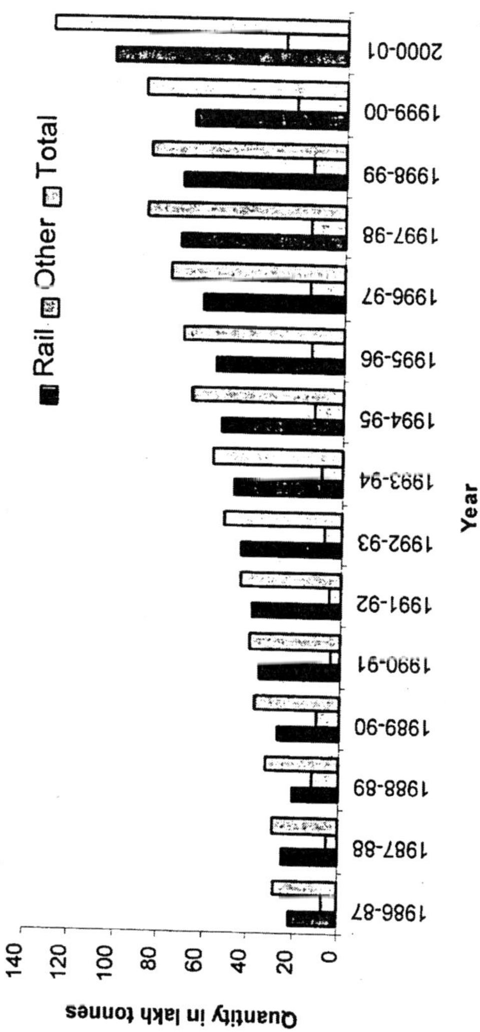

the rail traffic was 46.11 per cent per annum during the whole period under study as against 36.02 in post-reform period and 55.06 per cent in pre-reform period. Similarly, the import traffic despatched by other modes also exhibits an increasing trend during the study period. The import traffic despatched by other modes was 9.3 lakh tonnes in 1986-87 which registers a growth of more than five times to 50.89 lakh tonnes in 2000-01. The average quantity of import traffic despatched by other modes increased considerably from 12.18 lakh tonnes (44.94 per cent) in the pre-reform period to 31.29 lakh tonnes (63.98 per cent) in the post-reform period. The average traffic despatched by other modes was 18.55 lakh tonnes (50 per cent) per annum during the whole study period. In the other modes of transport, the share of road transport was significant.

6.15.2. During the study period, the volume of total import traffic showed an increasing trend with minor fluctuation. The import traffic rose up to 48.91 lakh tonnes per annum in the post-reform period from 27.13 lakh tonnes per annum in the pre-reform period. The quantity of traffic imported at Paradeep port was less than the traffic exported, thus making the port an export surplus port. As the import traffic handled at the port was less transportation by road was frequently adopted being economical. Further, rail mode of transport was not preferred due to inadequate supply of wagons by railway authorities and prevalence of well developed road connectivity during the study period.

6.16. Average Stock Holding and Stores Consumption

6.16.1. Table 6.15 portrays the consumption of stock under the study period which is also a crucial indicator of port productivity. The value of stores issued depicts consistent growth with minor fluctuations during the study period. The value of stores issued in the total study period came to be Rs. 8.22 crore per annum. The values of stores issued in the pre-reform period was Rs. 5.57 crores per annum which rose up to Rs. 13.52 crore per annum in the post-reform period. Similarly the average stock also exhibits an increasing trend till 1997-98 from 1986-87 and then declined to 24.83 crore, Rs. 23.23 crore and Rs. 22.00 crore in years 1998-99, 1999-00 and 2000-01 respectively.

During the whole study period, on an average the stores consumed were Rs. 15.81 crore per annum. In the pre-reform period the average stock was Rs. 10.92 crore which was increased to two hundred fifty per cent and

Table 6.14

Import Cargo Despatched by Different Modes of Transport at Paradeep Port during 1986-87 to 2000-01

	Study Period	Despatched by Rail		Despatched by other modes (Road, Inland water transport and pipe line)		Total	
		Quantity (in lakh tonnes)	*Per cent*	*Quantity (in lakh tonnes)*	*Per cent*	*Quantity (in lakh tonnes)*	*Per cent*
Pre-reform Period	1986-87	10.71	53.52	9.30	46.48	20.01	100
	1987-88	15.37	68.25	7.15	31.75	22.52	100
	1988-89	17.22	61.98	10.56	38.02	27.78	100
	1989-90	16.48	65.99	8.12	33.01	24.60	100
	1990-91	16.98	59.83	11.40	40.17	28.38	100
	1991-92	14.76	51.68	13.80	48.32	28.56	100
	1992-93	11.58	51.83	10.76	48.17	22.34	100
	1993-94	13.77	61.41	8.65	38.59	22.42	100
	1994-95	15.46	47.23	17.27	52.77	32.73	100
	1995-96	17.14	40.84	24.82	59.15	41.96	100
	Average	**14.94**	**55.06**	**12.18**	**44.94**	**27.13**	-
Post-reform period	1996-97	16.21	42.13	22.26	57.86	38.47	100
	1997-98	18.69	41.64	26.19	58.36	44.88	100
	1998-99	18.58	41.22	26.49	58.78	45.07	100
	1999-00	17.12	35.84	30.64	64.16	47.76	100
	2000-01	17.51	25.60	50.89	74.40	68.40	100
	Average	**17.62**	**36.02**	**31.29**	**63.98**	**48.91**	-
Whole Period Average		**15.86**	**46.11**	**18.55**	**53.89**	**34.39**	-

Source : Annual Administration Reports, Paradeep Port Trust.

Fig. 6.9
Import Cargo Despatched by Different Modes of Transport during 1986-87 to 2000-01

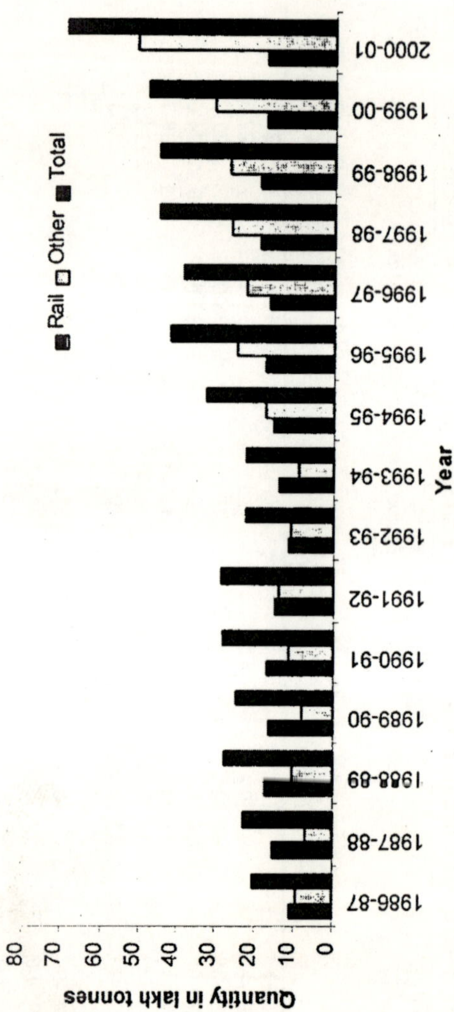

Table 6.15
Stores Consumption to Average Stock Holdinbg

(in Crores)

	Study Period	*Value of Stores issued*	*Average Stock*	*Percentage*
Pre-reform period	1986-87	4.04	3.99	101.25
	1987-88	2.53	4.51	56.10
	1988-89	3.83	5.39	71.06
	1989-90	4.04	5.68	71.13
	1990-91	4.16	6.42	64.80
	1991-92	4.94	8.5	58.12
	1992-93	6.67	11.65	57.25
	1993-94	6.34	17.45	36.33
	1994-95	7.90	20.85	37.90
	1995-96	11.32	24.84	45.58
	Average	**5.57**	**10.92**	**51.00**
Post-reform period	1996-97	13.23	27.31	48.45
	1997-98	12.56	30.72	40.89
	1998-99	12.45	24.83	50.14
	1999-2000	14.58	23.23	62.76
	2000-2001	14.82	22.00	67.36
	Average	**13.52**	**25.61**	**52.79**
	Whole period Average	**8.22**	**15.81**	**52.00**

Source : Annual Administration Reports, Paradeep Port Trust.

stood at Rs. 25.61 crore in the post-reform period. The percentage of stores consumption shows a fluctuating trend during the study period. The total study period average stores consumption was 57.94 per cent. In the post-reform period the average stores consumption was 53.92 per cent as against 59.95 per cent in the pre-reform period. In the post-reform period there was gradual increase in percentage of stores consumption in the last four years. This is due to the use of mechanised equipment and well-developed storage and berthing facilities available at the port during this period. The ADB assisted project of mechanised handling facilities for thermal coal and construction of two coal berths along with replacement of stackers by stacker-cum-reclaimer, and upgradation of ore handling plant and coal handling tippler, construction of railway lines along with stockyard were some of the major developmental works undertaken during the post-reform period for the upgradation of stores consumption at the port.

6.17. Flag-wise Distribution of Cargo Handled at Paradeep Port

6.17.1. Table 6.16 analyses the flag-wise distribution of cargo handled at the port during the study period. The port dealt with the highest of 47 number of countries in 1995-96 and 1996-97 and the lowest of 26 countries in 1986-87 and 1990-91 in overseas trade. On an average, the total number of countries dealt by the port in the whole period was 33 countries per annum. In the pre-reform period the number of countries were 32 which were increased to 37 countries in the post-reform period. The number of ships in the overseas trade varied between the lowest of 203 countries in 1990-91 to the highest of 388 countries in 2000-01. The number of ships dealt by the port in the whole period was 261 per annum. In the post-reform period the figures were 318 as against 232 in the pre-reform period. The overseas imports and exports rose significantly during this period and more particularly in the post-reform period. The volume of the total export and import trade during the period was 5,418.93 lakh tonnes per annum as against 4841.8 lakh tonnes per annum in the pre-reform period and 6573.2 lakh tonnes in the post-reform period. Similarly in case of coastal trade, the port dealt with 48 countries in total during the study period of which 19 countries in the pre-reform period and 28 countries in the post-reform period. The number of ships used for coastal traffic by the port varies from 51 in 1988-89 to 498 in 2000-01. The number of ships in the pre-reform period was 107 per annum which increased significantly to 377 ships per annum in the post-reform period.

6.17.2. The analysis reveals that the port handled less coastal import traffic in the pre-reform period which has experienced a spectacular progress in the post-reform period. In 2000-01, the port handled all time record of 833 lakh tonnes of coastal import cargo. The total coastal export has shown gradually rising trend during the study period. It varied between the lowest of 658 lakh tonnes in 1986-87 to the highest of 10,092 lakh tonnes in 2000-01. In the post-reform period the total coastal traffic showed phenomenal increase and the average annual traffic of this period was 7729.6 lakh tonnes as against 1665.8 lakh tonnes in the pre-reform period and 3887.06 lakh tonnes during the whole study period. The reasons of satisfactory performance concerning the growth of fleet and diversification of trade with different countries for overseas and coastal trade at the port may be attributed to the increasing demand of this mode of transport due to lower cost and the development of new minor ports by the different State

Table 6.16

Flagwise Distribution of Cargo Handled at Paradeep Port during 1986-87 to 2000-01

(In '000 Tonnes)

	Study Period	OVERSEAS					COASTAL				
		No. of countries	No. of ships	Imports	Exports	Total	No. of countries	No. of ships	Imports	Exports	Total
Pre-reform period	1986-87	26	204	1998	2196	4194	3	76	3	655	658
	1987-88	27	210	2225	1908	4133	3	109	1	1015	1016
	1988-89	31	249	2726	2233	4959	2	51	6	950	956
	1989-90	34	215	1756	3190	4946	-	43	-	1323	1323
	1990-91	26	203	2787	2084	4871	-	61	-	1907	1907
	1991-92	32	251	2836	2115	4951	1	74	-	2369	2369
	1992-93	28	216	2251	1782	4033	2	114	-	3357	3357
	1993-94	31	221	2234	2138	4372	2	123	4	3632	3636
	1994-95	33	269	3158	2466	5624	4	176	88	4166	4254
	1995-96	47	283	4135	2200	6335	2	240	61	4859	4920
	Average	**32**	**232**	**2610.6**	**2231.2**	**4841.8**	**2**	**107**	**27.16**	**2423.3**	**2439.6**
Post-reform period	1996-97	47	255	3733	1817	5550	4	301	114	5904	6018
	1997-98	35	299	4380	1676	6056	2	344	108	7138	7246
	1998-99	36	305	3939	1343	5282	2	373	568	7258	7826
	1999-2000	35	345	4236	1934	6170	8	370	540	6926	7466
	2000-2001	31	388	6015	3793	9808	13	498	833	9259	10092
	Average	**37**	**318**	**4460.6**	**2112.6**	**6573.2**	**6**	**377**	**432.6**	**7297**	**7729.6**
	Whole period Average	**33**	**261**	**3227.26**	**2191.6**	**5418.93**	**4**	**211.45**	**-**	**4047.86**	**4202.93**

Source : Annual Administration Reports, Paradeep Port Trust

Governments with private sector participation. The efforts by the Government in expanding the infrastructural facilities like increase in berths, mechanised cargo handling equipments, better connectivity, etc., are also contributing significantly for the improved performance of trade and allied activities in the port.

6.18. Accident at Paradeep Port

6.18.1. Table 6.17 indicates the particulars of accident at the port during the study period from 1986-87 to 2000-01. The accidents can be classified into two types, such as fatal and non-fatal. So far as fatal accident is concerned, 20 such cases were reported in port area and 23 cases in the non-port area. Similarly the non-fatal accidents in the port area were higher than the non port area. There were 307 accidents of non-fatal nature occurred in the port area, which was on an average 21 accidents in a year. In the post reform period non fatal accidents were slightly higher, i.e., 24 cases per year. But in the non-port area, there were only 27 accidents occurred out of which 26 were in the pre-reform period and one in the post-reform period. The Table also reveals that the number of accidents in port area both fatal and non-fatal are higher, i.e. 327 than the non-port area accidents which were 40 only. Similarly, in the port area accidents per year in the post-reform period were 26 as against 22 in the pre-reform period. This is due to more number of ships handled by the port during the post-reform period than in the pre-reform period. As the port authorities are taking adequate measures, the number of accidents has been reduced significantly. In case of accidents in non-port areas the number of cases had fallen drastically to only two in the post reform period as against 48 numbers in the pre-reform period, which is evidently a sign of positive developments in ensuring safety in port operation.

6.18.2. The port has started a free medical advice centre (OPD) in medical campus to examine and prescribe required medicines to the patients. Eye camps were organised by the Paradeep Branch of Lion's Club with the help of medical and paramedical staff of Paradeep Port Trust Hospital on suitable occasions. Employees, cargo handling workers (main list) and auxiliary workers were provided with necessary financial assistance to meet medical expenses in the event of acute financial hardship. As a measure of welfare, proper care was taken for the dependents of employees who died in service. Janata Personal Accident Insurance Policy has been

Table 6.17
Particulars of Accident at Paradeep Port during 1986-87 to 2000-01

(In '000 Tonnes)

	Study Period	*Fatal*		*Non-Fatal*		*Total*	
		Port	*Non-Port*	*Port*	*Non-Port*	*Port*	*Non-Port*
Pre-reform period	1986-87	-	2	10	3	10	5
	1987-88	-	-	9	4	9	4
	1988-89	1	1	16	1	17	2
	1989-90	1	3	11	2	12	5
	1990-91	2	2	7	1	9	3
	1991-92	-	2	22	3	22	5
	1992-93	-	4	23	4	23	8
	1993-94	4	2	37	1	41	3
	1994-95	-	4	36	4	36	8
	1995-96	1	2	28	3	29	5
	Average	**1.8**	**2.2**	**19.9**	**2.6**	**20.8**	**4.8**
Post-reform period	1996-97	1	1	22	1	23	2
	1997-98	3	-	15	-	18	-
	1998-99	2	-	28	-	30	-
	1999-2000	4	-	24	-	28	-
	2000-2001	1	-	29	-	30	-
	Average	**2.2**	**1**	**23.6**	**1**	**25.8**	**2**
	Whole Period Average	**2**	**2.3**	**21.13**	**2.45**	**22.46**	**4.54**

Source : Annual Administration Reports, Paradeep Port Trust.

introduced at this port for covering accident of port employees. This policy is for a sum of Rs. 5.00 lakhs and covered a period of 10 years, for which each employee pays only Rs. 350/-. The trend of less accidents, provisions of insurance for accident compensation and provision of medical facilities have direct bearing on the morale and efficiency of workers in the port.

6.19. Operating Ratio

6.19.1. Table 6.18 portrays the trends of operating expenditures and operating incomes during the study period. The operating expenditure shows increasing trend throughout the study period. Starting from Rs. 29.35 crores in 1986-87, it reached at Rs. 150.94 crores in 2000-01 registering a five fold rise in operating expenditure. This has been described in Fig. 6.10. On an average, the operating expenditure during the whole study period stood at Rs. 73.23 crores per annum. In the pre-reform period, the average annual operating expenditure was Rs. 50.84, which was increased to Rs. 118.02 crores in the post-reform period. Similarly, in the case of operating income there was phenomenal increase from Rs. 39.08 crores in 1986-87 to reach a peak value of Rs. 176.72 crores in 1997-98. In 1998-99 it declined to Rs. 172.78 crores and again increased to Rs. 184.41 crores and Rs. 262.13 crores in 1999-2000 and 2000-01 respectively. The average annual operating income in the whole period stood at Rs. 118.85 crores. Table also shows that average annual operating income in the post-reform period was more than double of incomes in the pre-reform period. The operating surplus exhibits a fluctuating trend during the period. It varies from the lowest of Rs. 9.73 crores in 1986-87 to the highest of Rs. 111.19 crores in 2000-01. The average figure of surplus per annum in the whole study period was Rs. 46.15 crores. In the pre-reform period the average annual operating surplus was Rs. 31.56 crores which was increased considerably to Rs. 75.32 crores in the post-reform period. The operating ratio also shows a fluctuating trend over the study period. It varies from the lowest of 53.84 per cent in 1990-91 to the highest of 76.02 per cent in 1987-88. The average annual operating ratio during the total study period was 61.61 per cent. In the pre-reform period the ratio was 61.69 which declined marginally to 61.54 per cent in the post-reform period. Despite increase in operating expenses, the rising trends of operating incomes and operating surplus indicate satisfactory performance of the port during the study period.

Table 6.18
Operating Expenditure to Operating Income during 1986-87 to 2000-01

(in Crores)

	Study Period	*Operating Expenditure*	*Operating Income*	*Ratio (In %)*	*Operating Surplus*
Pre-reform period	1986-87	29.35	39.08	75.10	9.73
	1987-88	31.54	41.49	76.02	9.95
	1988-89	33.66	48.28	69.72	14.62
	1989-90	36.82	60.37	61.00	23.55
	1990-91	41.06	76.26	53.84	35.2
	1991-92	50.01	79.57	62.85	29.56
	1992-93	64.50	88.38	72.98	23.88
	1993-94	64.04	112.30	57.03	48.26
	1994-95	71.32	126.91	56.20	55.59
	1995-96	86.17	151.49	56.88	65.32
	Average	**50.84**	**82.41**	**61.69**	**31.56**
Post-reform period	1996-97	99.12	162.72	60.91	63.6
	1997-98	103.31	176.72	58.46	73.41
	1998-99	113.41	172.78	65.64	59.37
	1999-2000	123.34	184.41	66.88	61.07
	2000-2001	150.94	262.13	57.58	111.19
	Average	**118.02**	**191.75**	**61.54**	**75.32**
	Whole Period Average Ratio	73.23	**118.85**	**61.61**	**46.15**

Source : Annual Administration Reports, Paradeep Port Trust.

6.20. Analysis of Current Ratio

6.20.1. Table 6.19 reveals the trends of current assets and current liabilities of the port during the study period. A ratio equal or near to 2:1, i.e., current assets double the current liabilities is considered to be satisfactory. A relatively high current ratio is an indicator that the organisation has the ability to pay its current obligations in time. On the other hand, a relatively low current ratio represents that the liquidity position of the firm is not good and the firm shall not be able to pay its current liabilities in time. However, a high current ratio may not be favourable because (i) there may be slow moving stocks. The stocks will pile up due

Fig. 6.10
Operating Expenditure, Income and Surplus of Paradeep Port during 1986-87 to 2000-01

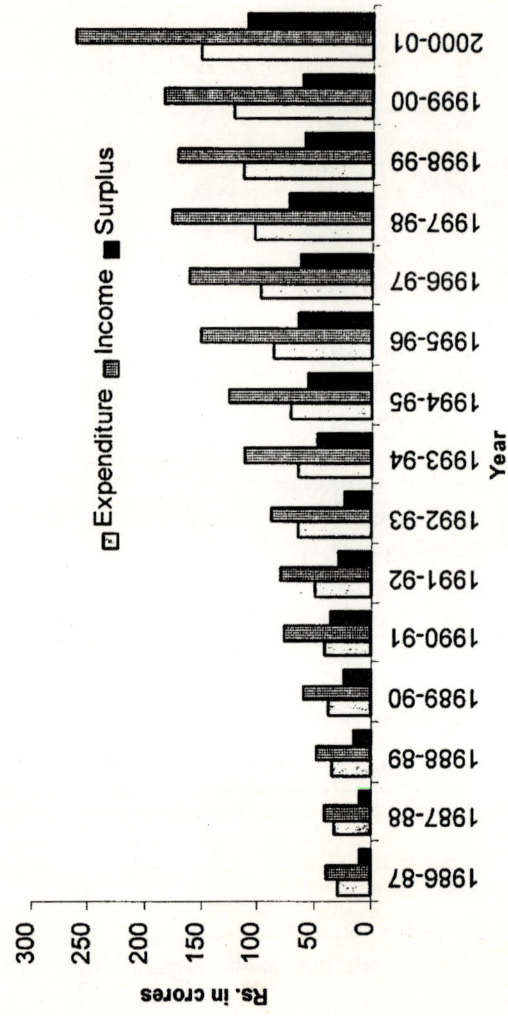

Table 6.19
Current Assets to Current Liabilities

(in Crores)

	Study Period	*Current Assets*	*Current Liabilities*	*Current Asset/Current Liabilities (In per cent)*
Pre-reform period	1986-87	68.63	84.89	80.84
	1987-88	81.11	96.14	84.37
	1988-89	102.51	109.82	93.34
	1989-90	87.12	104.04	83.74
	1990-91	81.41	103.30	78.81
	1991-92	91.62	131.94	69.44
	1992-93	106.63	170.96	62.37
	1993-94	122.66	219.85	55.79
	1994-95	163.23	240.09	67.99
	1995-96	144.82	249.03	58.15
	Average	**104.97**	**151.00**	**69.51**
Post-reform period	1996-97	163.94	268.45	61.07
	1997-98	175.41	309.00	56.77
	1998-99	177.43	353.64	50.17
	1999-00	234.15	431.08	54.31
	2000-01	356.85	587.21	60.77
	Average	**221.55**	**389.87**	**56.82**
	Whole Period Average	**143.83**	**230.62**	**62.36**

Source : Annual Administration Reports, Paradeep Port Trust.

to poor movement (ii) the figures of debtors may go up because debt collection is not satisfactory (iii) the cash or bank balance may be lying idle because of insufficient investment opportunities. On the other hand, low current ratio may be due to (i) insufficient funds to pay off liabilities and the organisation may be trading beyond its capacity. From the Table it is clear that both the current assets and current liabilities have increased significantly during the study period. The amount of current assets increased from Rs. 68.63 crores in 1986-87 to Rs. 356.85 crores in 2000-01. Similarly, the current liabilities also rose from Rs. 84.89 crores to Rs. 587.21 crore during the same period. The average of the current assets per annum during the whole study period was Rs. 143.83 crores. But in the post-reform period the average current asset per annum reached Rs. 221.55 crores as against Rs. 104.97 crore in the pre-reform period. Similarly the average current liabilities per annum during the total period under study was Rs. 230.62 crores. In the post-reform period the average current liabilities per annum was Rs. 389.87 crores which is significantly higher than the average current liabilities of Rs. 151.00 crores per annum during the pre-reform period. The ratio also shows a fluctuating trend with decline from 80.84 per cent in 1986-87 to 50.17 in 1998-99 and increased marginally to 54.31 per cent and 60.77 per cent in 1999-2000 and 2000-01 respectively.In none of this years under study, current assets were not higher even at least equal to current liabilities. This indicates lower liquidity which might affect the short-term solvency of the port.

6.21. Port Operations (Shipping) at Paradeep

6.21.1. Table 6.20 reveals the shipping activities at the port during the study period of 1986-87 to 2000-01. The total number of vessels sailed by the port varies from the lowest of 258 vessels in 1989-90 to the highest of 915 vessels in 2000-01. The average number of vessels sailed at the port during the total study period stood at 480 vessels. In the pre-reform period the average number of ships sailed by the port was 359 which had been doubled to 724 during the post-reform period. The total Gross Registered Tonnage (GRT) also registers gradual increase throughout the study period. GRT is weight of the volume occupied by the closed-in-spaces of a ship taking 100 cubic feet of such closed-in-spaces as equivalent to one vessels ton. It thus, refers to the cubic capacity of the vessels. So higher is the GRT, better would be the performance of the port. The average GRT of the port during the total study period was found to be 94.71 lakh. The post-reform period average GRT registered a rise of 146.36 lakh as against 68.89 lakhs in the pre-reform period. Similarly, the figures of average GRT shows a fluctuating trend during the study period. The total study period average stood at 19,357.46 lakh GRT as against 19,010 lakh GRT in the pre-reform period. This of course, was marginally increased to 20,052.4 lakh GRT during the post-reform period. Similarly the Net Registered Tonnage (NRT) also shows an increasing trend during the study period except with nominal fall in 1989-90. NRT refers to the earning space capacity of a ship available for the storage of cargo and accommodation of passengers. It is obtained by deducting the cubic capacity space occupied by stores, fuel, machinery, crew, etc. from the GRT. The total NRT which was 24.48 lakh tonnes in 1986-87 with some fluctuations reached at 77.09 lakh tonnes in

1999-2000 and further to 109.36 lakh tonnes in 2000-01. The average figure of NRT during the total study period was 52.77 lakhs tonnes per annum. In the post-reform period the average NRT registered a growth of 79.34 lakh tonnes as against 39.48 lakh tonnes in the pre-reform period. The average NRT also exhibits a fluctuating trend during the study period. In the pre-reform period it was 10,934.1 tonnes which was declined slightly to 10,909.8 tonnes in the post-reform period against the average of 10,926 tonnes during the whole period. The overall performance of the ships during the post-reform period was more encouraging as compared to the performance in the pre-reform period. This is due to the factors like upgradation of port facilities, addition of mechanised equipments, creation of increasing berth capacity and dredging of the port for accommodation of vessels without obstruction and delay.

Table 6.20

Port Operations (Shipping) during the Period 1986-87 to 2000-01

(In lakhs)

	Study period	*No. of vessels*	*Total GRT*	*Avg. GRT*	*Total NRT*	*Avg. NRT*
Pre-reform period	1986-87	285	41.46	14,650	24.48	9,240
	1987-88	325	48.65	14,970	28.40	8,740
	1988-89	304	51.32	16,881	31.70	10,427
	1989-90	258	51.94	20,132	23.35	9,049
	1990-91	278	59.10	21,257	35.86	12,898
	1991-92	336	66.02	19,826	38.15	11,455
	1992-93	366	76.75	21,142	44.35	12,217
	1993-94	405	82.55	20,434	50.00	12,129
	1994-95	483	98.31	20,353	57.72	11,951
	1995-96	550	112.50	20,455	61.79	11,235
	Average	**359**	**68.89**	**19,010**	**39.48**	**10,934.1**
Post-reform period	1996-97	592	115.34	19,482	65.69	11,096
	1997-98	676	131.48	19,450	73.89	10,930
	1998-99	695	134.04	19,287	70.67	10,168
	1999-00	741	143.64	19,385	77.09	10,403
	2000-01	915	207.32	22,658	109.36	11,952
	Average	**723.8**	**146.36**	**20,052.4**	**79.34**	**10,909.8**
	Whole Period Average	**480.6**	**94.71**	**19,357.46**	**52.77**	**10,926**

Note : GRT - Gross Registered Tonnage; NRT - Net Registered Tonnage

Source : Annual Administration Reports, Paradeep Port Trust.

6.22. Class-wise Staff Strength at Paradeep Port

6.22.1. Human resource is a vital resource without which an organisation could hardly achieve satisfactory productivity growth. Table 6.21 highlights the class-wise staff strength at the port during the study period of 1986-87 to 2000-2001. There are mainly four categories of employees working in this port including shore workers, other than shore workers and casual workers. The class-I staff relates to high salaried officers, whose number remained constant at 81 for nine years from 1986-87 to 1994-95 and then increased to the highest of 94 in 1996-97 which was the all time highest during the study period. But it declined to 90 in 1999-2000 and further declined to 86 in 2000-2001. Similarly the class. II staff strength remained at 110 for three years from 1986-87 to 1988-89 and was reduced to 100 till 1992-93 for four years. It reached 218 in 1996-97 and further declined to 213 in 2000-2001. This has been analysed in Fig. 6.11. The class-I and class-II employees per annum increased to 88 persons and 211 persons in the post-reform period as against the average of 81 persons and 134 persons in the pre-reform period respectively. But in case of class-III and class-IV, the average figures of the employees in the post-reform period were reduced to 1378 persons and 1016 persons from 1593 persons and 1167 persons respectively. The absolute figures of class-III employees reduced significantly from 1700 persons in 1986-87 to 1317 persons in 1997-98 and slightly increased to 1366 in 2000-01. Similarly, the number of class-IV employees reduced considerably from 1239 in 1986-87 to 884 in 1997-98, but increased significantly to 1063 in 2000-01. The total staff strength figures exhibits, an increasing trend till 1994-95 and then declined for two years, but it rose again in 1997-98 to 4227 persons the all time highest during the study period. From 1997-98 onwards till 2000-01 there has been marginal reduction reached 4116 in 2000-01. The number of employees per annum was 3140 during the pre-reform period which was increased to 3892 persons in the post-reform period as against 3391 persons during the total study period. In this age of economic reforms, there is an urgent need for rightsizing the over-manned organisation. When the port is on the way to privatisation and corporatisation, for downsizing of the existing surplus labour force, the authorities had reduced the number of class-III and class-IV low salaried class employees. However, the authorities have increased the employment of class-I and class-II officers—the higher salaried class people in the port which has nullified the beneficial effects

Table 6.21

Class-wise Staff Strength at Paradeep Port as on March 31 every year

	Study Period	*Class-I*	*Class-II*	*Class-III*	*Class-IV*	*Shore Workers*	*Other than Shore Workers*	*Casual Workers*	*Others*	*Total*
Pre-reform period	1986-87	81	110	1700	1239	-	-	-	-	3130
	1987-88	81	110	1701	1239	-	-	-	-	3131
	1988-89	81	110	1701	1239	-	-	-	-	3131
	1989-90	81	100	1591	1163	-	-	202	-	3137
	1990-91	81	100	1585	1163	-	-	230	-	3159
	1991-92	31	100	1585	1160	-	-	288	-	3214
	1992-93	81	100	1585	1160	-	-	288	-	3214
	1993-94	81	200	1498	1160	-	-	292	-	3231
	1994-95	81	200	1498	1160	-	-	292	-	3231
	1995-96	84	211	1485	985	-	-	64	-	2829
	Average	**81.3**	**134.1**	**1592.9**	**1166.8**	-	-	-	-	**3140.7**
Post-reform period	1996-97	94	218	1486	928	-	-	12	-	2738
	1997-98	85	193	1317	884	-	1476	272	-	4227
	1998-99	87	218	1369	1096	-	1427	-	-	4197
	1999-2000	90	216	1352	1107	-	1417	-	-	4182
	2000-2001	86	213	1366	1063	1004	384	-	-	4116
	Average	**88.4**	**211.6**	**1378**	**1015.6**	-	-	-	-	**3892**
	Whole Period Average	**83.66**	**159.93**	**1521.26**	**1116.4**	-	-	-	-	**3391.13**

Source : Annual Administration Reports, Paradeep Port Trust.

Fig. 6.11
Class-wise Staff Strength at Paradeep Port as on March 31 every year

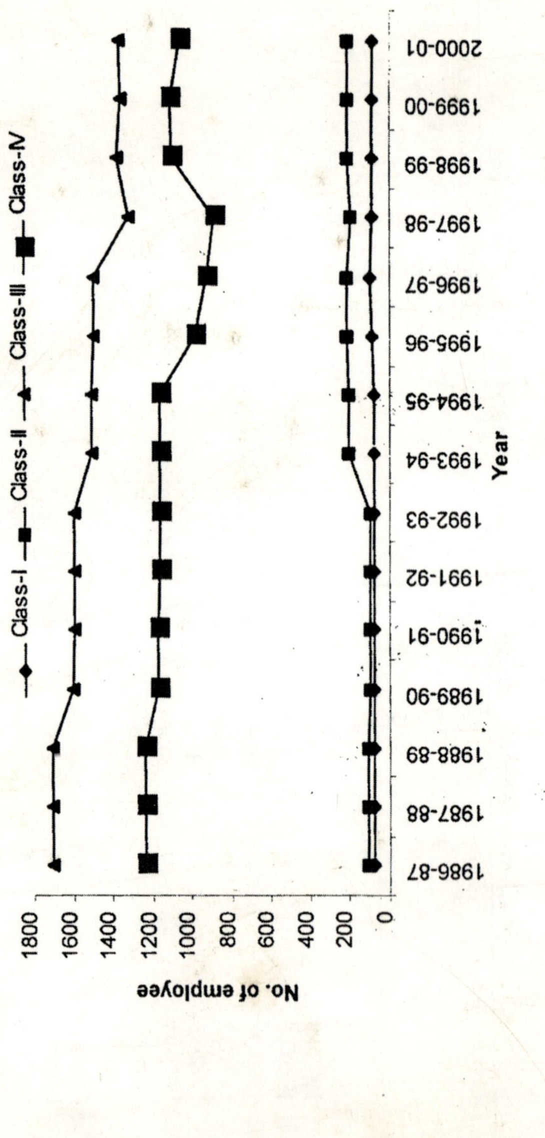

of downsizing at lower levels. Use of more mechanised equipment and consequently employment of technically trained manpower have reduced the need for more class-III and class-IV employees in the port. Reductions of class-III and class-IV employees on the one hand and increase in productivity of the port on the other speaks about the favourable impact of downsizing of surplus employees on operational efficiency and productivity of the port.

6.23. Summary

6.23.1. The foregoing analysis reveals the operating performance of Paradeep port during the period 1986-87 to 2000-01. Though the port started its operation from the year 1965, its share of traffic was not significant as compared to other ports till 1985. The trade at Paradeep port increased with the increase in trade of the country with the other countries due to adoption of liberalised and deregulated policy of the government from mid 1991. But due to inadequate infrastructural facilities of Indian ports, the port sector could not perform well. After 1996, the government put special emphasis on the development of port infrastructure by allowing the private sector to operate in this area. As a result of which the Indian ports got a push and are now competing with the other ports of the Asian region.

6.23.2. The overseas and coastal cargo traffic handled at the port during the study period depicts the overall growth of the port and more particularly the satisfactory performance of the port during the post-reform period. The total traffic loaded at the port exceeds the total traffic unloaded at the port, thus making the port an export surplus port. On an average, the total traffic unloaded during the post-reform period increased significantly to 48.95 lakh tonnes as against 27.90 lakh tonnes during the pre-reform period. Similarly the total traffic loaded during the pre- and post-reform period were 48.54 lakh tonnes and 61.92 lakh tonnes per annum respectively. During 2000-01, the port had handled 45.93 per cent more traffic over the previous years traffic. The liberalised economic policy of Government of India, implementation of India Infrastructure Report of 1996 and addition of seven new mechanised berths to the port resulted in increase of overall traffic during the post-reform period.

6.23.3. During the study period, the number of ships sailed by the port increased from 270 in 1986-87 to 886 in 2000-01. Similarly the average output per ship berth day also increased from 4322 tonnes in 1986-87 to

8503 tonnes in 2000-01. The average turn-around time, average stay at berth, average pre-berthing time and average non-working time have also declined significantly, resulting in satisfactory performance of the port in the post-reform period compared to pre-reform period.

6.23.4. The trend of traffic handled by Paradeep port was increased from 4.85 MT in 1986-87 to 11.26 MT in 1995-96 and 19.90 MT in 2000-01. The share of the port in handling traffic as compared to other major ports of India also exhibits an upward trend from 3.90 per cent in 1986-87 to 7.07 per cent in 2000-01. The reason for the increase in the share of Paradeep port in total traffic handled by all major ports of the country may be attributed to the addition of seven new berths with a mechanised coal handling plant and reduced turn-around time and pre-berthing time of the port during the post-reform period.

6.23.5. With the increase in cargo traffic at the port, the number of berths also went up to 13 in the post reform period from 6 in the pre-reform period. The output at the iron ore berth was highest which varied from 10,943 tonnes in 1986-87 to 18,593 tonnes in 2000-01. The berth-day output of other commodities such as coal, hard coke, lime-stone, chrome-ore/ charge-chrome fertiliser and raw materials have also increased during the post-reform period. The overall berth-day output for all commodities at the port also swelled to 7055-6 tonnes in the post-reform period from 4915.25 tonnes in the pre-reform period. Due to use of mechanised cargo handling equipment by the port and increased demand in the overseas and coastal markets, the berth-day output of the port has witnessed substantial rise in the study period.

6.23.6. The labour productivity of major commodities increased significantly during the post-reform period as against the pre-reform period. The overall labour productivity for all commodities also increased to 727.2 tonnes per hook shift in the post-reform period from 409 tonnes per hook shift in the pre-reform period. The peaceful working atmosphere arising out of sound industrial relation has resulted in raising overall labour productivity at the port. Commissioning of specialised berths for each product with mechanised handling facilities has enhanced the labour productivity at the port during the post-reform period.

6.23.7. The average ship turn-around (ASTA) time a crucial parameter of judging operational efficiency of the port has also declined at different berths. The overall ASTA time has declined significantly from 6.79 days per annum in the pre-reform period to 4.44 days in the post-reform period. The efficient utilisation of port capacity, mechanised handling facility, well equipped rail and road connectivity and overall port management are the contributory factors for reducing the ASTA time in the post-reform period. The establishment of mega fertiliser plant, Oswal Fertilisers and Chemicals Ltd. and significant increase in import of fertilizer raw materials by the existing public sector unit Paradeep Phosphates Ltd. to compete in international market had been responsible for setting up more fertiliser berths and activities of greater scale.

6.23.8. Due to the increase in the number of berths, the availability of berth days and berth occupancy had witnessed substantial rise during the study period. On an average, the number of days available at the port during the pre-reform period was 2225.3 days per annum, which rose to 3161.2 days in the post-reform period. Similarly, the average number of days occupied also increased from 1498.3 days per annum the pre-reform period to 2051 days per annum in the post-reform period.

6.23.9. Proper utilisation of cargo handling equipment at the port is one of the important factors of higher productivity. During the study period, the port used 5 types of cargo handling equipment such as wharf crane, pay loader, mobile crane, fork lift and diesel locos. The port started the use of the diesel locos in 1997-98 only. The use of diesel locos in the post-reform period has increased the efficiency and productivity in port operations.

6.23.10. The non-working time at the port declined considerably during the post-reform period. Due to sailing of more number of ships and more use of mechanised instruments, the equipment breakdown was quite obvious. However, the port authorities have taken adequate steps to reduce this in the post-reform period.

6.23.11. The numbers of both Indian ships and foreign ships have risen in the post-reform period at the port because of establishment of new minor ports by the coastal States in India and establishment of two new fertiliser plants, for which there was import of raw materials from foreign countries. Further, the increase in the export of fertilisers from the region has enhanced the demand for more number of ships. Similarly, due to establishment of more thermal units of existing power stations in Orissa during the post-reform period, there has been increase in the demand for thermal coal, which are imported from Australia.

6.23.12. The traffic handled by railways at Paradeep port depicts an upward trend during the study period. The inward rail traffic accounted for 85 per cent of total rail traffic in order to export more quantities of ores, coal through the port. The transportation of traffic by railways is the cheaper and quicker mode of transport for inward traffic. Due to import of less quantity of goods and inadequate railway connectivity to different parts of the State, the outward rail transport is costlier as compared to other modes of transport.

6.23.13. So far as export cargo was concerned, railways also accounted for nearly 80 per cent of total traffic. Since minerals such as iron-ore, chrome ore, thermal coal, etc., need to be exported in bulk quantities for attaining economies of scale in ports operation, the rail-mode of transport is formed to be more economical. But for import cargo despatched by different modes of transport, as the import traffic handled at the port was less, transportation by road was frequently adopted being economical. Further, rail mode of transport was not preferred due to inadequate supply of wagons by railway authorities. The stores consumption and average stockholding have increased during the study period. Due to use of mechanised equipment and well developed storage and berthing facilities available at the port, the stores consumption has increased in the post-reform period.

6.23.14. In flag-wise distribution of cargo, the port had dealt with 47 number of countries in 1995-96 and 1996-97 as against 26 countries each in 1986-87. Similarly, the total traffic has also increased in the post-reform period. Due to increasing demand of this mode of transport from cost point of view and the development of new minor ports by the different State Governments, caused the growth of fleet and diversification of trade with different countries. Further, the efforts by the government in expanding the infrastructural facilities like increase in berths, mechanised cargo handling equipment, better connectivity are also contributing significantly for the improved performance of trade in the port.

6.23.15. The number of accidents both in port and non-port areas have been reduced significantly during the post-reform period. The trend of decline in the number of accidents, provisions of insurance for accident compensation and provision of medical facilities have direct bearing on the morale and efficiency of workers in the port. The operating surplus of the port increased inspite of rise in operating expenditures and operating incomes as well during the study period. The operating surplus reached the level of Rs. 111.19 crores in 2000-01 as against Rs. 9.73 crores in 1986-87. Despite increase in operating expenses, the rising trends of operating incomes and operating surpluses indicate satisfactory performance of the port during the study period and more particularly in the post-reform period.

6.23.16. Class-wise staff strength at the port reveals the picture of downsizing of the existing surplus labour force. The port authorities have reduced the Class-III and Class-IV low-salaried class employees. However, the authorities have increased the employment of Class-I and Class-II officers the high salaried class people in the port which has nullified to some extent the beneficial effects of downsizing at lower levels. Use of more mechanised equipment and consequently employment of technically trained manpower have reduced the need for more Class-III and Class-IV employees in the port. Reduction of Class-III and Class-IV employees on the one hand and increase in productivity of the port on the other speaks about the favourable impact of downsizing of surplus employees on operational efficiency and productivity of the port.

7

Summary of the Findings and Conclusions

7.1 Introduction

7.1.1. The present study entitled "Port Infrastructure and Economic Development" is divided into two parts. The first part comprising of three chapters includes introduction, objectives and methodology of the study and significance of the study. It also exhaustively deals with various aspects of infrastructure, its role, significance with special reference to port sector, performance of ports, prospects and challenges. The second part constitutes the core of the study consists of four chapters. It encompasses the analysis of collected data supplemented by preliminary discussions on the history, growth, achievements, policy guidelines of the government, opportunities and challenges. It also highlights the state of infrastructure facilities in Orissa. The study on the empirical analysis of the progress and performance of Paradeep port covering the period from 1986-87 to 2000-01. An attempt has been made to make a comparative analysis of the operations of the port between the pre-and post-reform period. The objective was to study the impact of economic reform initiated in the early nineties and also the infrastructure sector reform started after mid-nineties on the operational efficiency and productivity of the Indian ports in general and Paradeep port in particular in terms of a number of parameters. The major findings of the study are summarised in the following paragraphs.

7.2. Role and Significance of Infrastructure in Economic Development with Special Reference to Port Infrastructure in India

7.2.1. Infrastructure is a basic need to create improved marketability, efficient resource utilisation and increased opportunities for the public to participate in the development process through which greater investment, employment and production can be realised. Power, telecommunication, roads, ports, transportation, water supply and sanitation, etc., are the components of physical or economic infrastructure. Social infrastructure includes health and human resource development. These two segments of infrastructure are interdependent and hence complementary. Infrastructure development is of two types, namely, demand driven and supply driven. Demand driven infrastructure is a must for development whereas supply driven infrastructure is desirable.

7.2.2. During the age of globalised business environment, infrastructure performance is a key factor in attracting foreign direct investment which has become an essential element in capital starved developing economies. According to a study conducted recently on infrastructure development, among 16 Asian countries, India was placed 15th, just above Vietnam. And from among 60 countries in the world, including developed countries, India ranked 58th in terms of infrastructure development. Due to inadequate infrastructural facilities India is lagging behind other countries in inviting foreign direct investment. Though the investment in the infrastructure increases in absolute figures but in terms of percentage to GDI, it exhibits a declining trend. The India Infrastructure Report estimates that the GDI in infrastructure is expected to increase from 5.5 per cent of GDP in 1995-96 to about 7 per cent in 2000-01 and 8 per cent by 2005-06. Infrastructure investment will account for 22 to 25 per cent of the GDI rising from about Rs. 60,000 crore in 1995-96 to Rs. 1,07,000 crore in 2000-01 ; Rs. 1,80,000 crore in 2005-06; Rs. 4,30,000 crore in 2010-11 and Rs. 7,40,000 in 2015-16.

7.2.3. Infrastructure services are often monopolistic in nature. They usually involve high upfront costs and long payback periods and investments are typically lumpy and bulky. They are also characterised by the existence of externalities which make it difficult for infrastructure entities to recoup investment costs and operational expenses through the levy of user charges. Consequently infrastructure services have been predominantly provided by the public sector. But during the last decade a wave of privatisation and deregulation has been sweeping infrastructure sector with the outcome of improvement in efficiency and service quality and enhanced commercialisation. The government has recognised that private sector participation including foreign investment is required to supplement the public sector efforts. Various reforms have been made in infrastructure sector and rules and procedure for investment have been liberalised in order to provide an enabling environment conducive for private participation. The role of government has changed from owner and sole provider to that of a facilitator.

7.2.4. Transport system is broadly considered as the artery and nerves covering the entire economy of the country. In a vast country like India an efficient transport system is the pre-requisite for attaining a higher level of economic development. The demand for transport services in India has been growing much faster than the rate of economic growth. The road transport services as well as railways occupy a prominent place in our economy accounting for 53.3 per cent and 31.7 per cent respectively of the total transport sector. Water transport has a share of approximately 6.5 per cent. The share of transport sector in total plan outlay has fallen from 22.10 per cent during the First Five Year Plan to 13.10 per cent during the Eighth Five Year Plan though in absolute figure the plan allocation has increased during the period. In India, we have a four-tier transport system, i.e., Railways, Roadways, Waterways and Airways.

7.2.5. In terms of area and population, the total road length in the country in April 1997 worked out to be about 64 kms for every 100 sq. kms of area and 275 kms for every one lakh population. The National Highways, which spans about 58,112 kms throughout the country cater to about 45 per cent of the total road transport demand. The government has decided to develop 4/6 lane roads connecting four metropolitan cities and North-South, East-West corridors including connectivity for all major ports with an investment of Rs. 54,000 crore to be completed by 2007.

7.2.6. The rail mode of transport has been playing an integrating role in socio-economic development of the country being emerged as the largest in Asia and the fourth largest in the world. The railways have been performing the dual role of functioning as a commercial undertaking and a provider of public utility service. Air transport equally plays a vital role in a vast country like India. Water transport is another most vital mode of transport considered to be the cheapest mode of transport. Water transports are of two types such as inland water transport and coastal or marine transport. Inland water transport (IWT) is the cheapest and one of the efficient modes of transport. Unlike in other modes of transport there is practically no investment needed and is also a labour intensive mode of transport and benefiting the weaker sections of the community. At present, there are three systems declared as National Waterways. They are NW-I Ganga-Bhagirathi Hoogly (1620 km), NW-II Brahmaputra (891 km) and NW-III West Coast Canal (205 km). Realising the significance of IWT, the government has declared certain scheme, for the development of IWT sector in the country. The States would be offered 90 per cent grant for implementation of these schemes. The states would have to contribute 10 per cent. For Sikkim and the North-East, the entire money would be provided by the Centre as grant.

7.2.7. The coastal or marine transport deals with the major and minor ports. With having a vast coastline of 6000 kms, India has now 12 major ports and 160 minor ports. More than 90 per cent of India's foreign trade in volume and 75 per cent in terms of value are conducted by sea. The investment made for port development during different plans have increased from Rs. 26 crore in the First Five Year Plan to Rs. 3216 crore in the Eighth Plan and Rs. 9428 crore in the Ninth Five Year Plan. The Ministry of Surface Transport has projected the total traffic to be handled at Indian ports by the year 2021-22 will be 1373 MT and the investment required will be Rs. 1,00,575 crore. The port capacity requirement will be 540 MT by 2005-06. Development of hub port is necessary for India because of change in technology and growing demand for operation of large sized vessels. The government has decided to develop hub ports one in the East Coast at Chennai Port and one on the West Coast at Navi Mumbai for conservation of additional cost through cargo transhipment and reduction in transit time and safer delivery through adequate supervision by Indian agencies.

7.2.8. Other infrastructural facilities like power, telecommunication, postal services, tourism, urban infrastructure, rural infrastructure and banking infrastructure, etc. have major roles to play for the overall development of the country. The government has paid attention for the development of this basic infrastructural needs by enhancing private participation resulting in qualitative delivery of service.The development of export processing zones (EPZs) and Special Economic Zones (SEZs) in the country will not only boost the export but it has perceptible impact on inflow of foreign investment and employment generation potentials in the country. So far the government has approved 13 SEZs in the country and some of the EPZs have been converted in to SEZs for a broader venture in the country. The government in its Exim Policy (2002-07) has declared a good number of incentives for attracting the private players and encouraging the State Governments to establish the SEZs in the country.

7.3. Performance of Indian Ports, Prospects and Challenges

7.3.1. India has a vast coastline of nearly 6000 kms stretching from east to west coast. Of the 12 major ports, six are located on the west coast and six on the east coast. And out of the total declared 179 minor ports, 13 are non-working ports, 120 ports belong to west coast States, 24 ports belong to east coast States and the rest 22 belong to the Union Territories. The primary responsibility for development and management of major ports rests with the Central Government. The major ports are governed by the Major Port Trust Act, 1963, which enables these ports to conduct regulatory as well as commercial functions. The State Governments administer the minor and intermediate ports. At present, the Indian ports handle 90 per cent of the country's foreign trade by volume and 70 per cent by value. Before independence, there were only 5 ports in India. The government in the independent India put emphasis on planned development through various Five Year Plans. Till the end of the Eighth Five Year Plan 227 MT of the traffic were handled as against the capacity of 220 MT at the ports. To meet the emerging challenges of growing port sector at par with international standards and also to cope-up with huge investments needs for such developments, the government had adopted policy measures aimed at opening up the port sector for private investments. Besides the objective of mobilising substantial resources, the other objectives are improvement in productivity, efficiency and quality of services, reduction in gestation period for setting up new facilities and to bring in new technology and improved management techniques for enhancing international competitiveness.

7.3.2. Under the private sector participation in major ports, the government has already identified broad areas for investment and the guidelines in respect of procedures to be followed for inviting private investors into the port sector. The government has also announced the guidelines for joint sector participation between major port and minor port, between major port and foreign port and between major port and company. To enable the implementation of joint venture scheme and facilitate equity participation by major ports in any other port including a minor port, the Major Port Trust Act, 1963 has been amended. Since the formulation of the private sector participation guidelines by the Government of India, 24 projects have been identified, which will add a capacity of 60.05 MT at various ports with an investment of Rs. 78.76 billion in the next five years.

7.3.3. The traffic handled by the ports in India was 19.38 MT during 1950-51, which was increased to 33.12 MT in 1960-61, 55.58 MT in 1970-71 and 80.37 MT during 1980-81. But in the next decade, i.e., in 1990-91, it has witnessed the traffic volume of 151.67 MT and further increased to a record level of 281.13 MT traffic during 2000-01. Out of the total traffic handled at major ports, petroleum, oil and lubricants (POL) maintains the largest share of 43 per cent, iron ore 21 per cent, coal 13 per cent and fertiliser 5 per cent. Out of the total traffic of 369 MT during 2000-01, 76 per cent was handled by the major ports and 24 per cent by the minor ports. Ports like Kandla, Visakhapatnam, Chennai and Mumbai together handled around 57 per cent of the total traffic of all major ports.

7.3.4. The average output per ship berth-day at all major ports in India depicts an increasing quantity of 5167 tonnes during 1998-99 against 4912 tonnes in 1997-98. Even though the output per ship berth-day of liquid bulk exhibits a marginal fall from 12772 tonnes in 1997-98 to 11619 tonnes in 1998-99 in terms of volume of output, it still remained in the second position after the dry bulk (mechanical). The output of dry bulks (mech.) was increased to 13346 tonnes in 1998-99 from 12275 tonnes in 1997-98. Among the ports Mormugao port has the highest output per ship berth day, of 10446 tonnes and 11076 tonnes during 1997-98 and 1998-99 followed by Kandla and New Mangalore having output of 8778 tonnes and 7507 tonnes in 1998-99 respectively. Due to increase in number of ships entering into the port and also the increasing efficiency of the berths with the use of mechanised instruments, there has been higher output per ship berth-day at all major ports of the country.

7.3.5. The average berth occupancy reveals fluctuating trend at the Indian ports during the nineties. Kandla port has the highest percentage of berth occupancy of 93.1 per cent in 1998-99 followed by Tuticorin 85.2 per cent and Chennai 81.2 per cent. Calcutta port has the least berth occupancy of 48.4 per cent during 1998-99. The reasons of fluctuating trend are attributed to problems encountered by individual ports, like labour unrest, breakdown of machinery, natural calamities, cyclones, higher tonnage tariffs and non-availability of mechanised berths.

7.3.6. The average turn-around time at almost all major ports have came down significantly to 5.7 days during 1998-99 as against 6.3 days during 1997-98. But this is far behind the international norms. For example, the average turn-around time for the ports at Singapore was only 6 to 8 hours. The analysis reveals that during 1998-99, Kandla port had the longest turn-around time of 8.3 days whereas Cochin port had the least turn-around time of 3.4 days. The breakdown and dry bulk (Conv.) vessels have the highest turn-around time of 10.5 days and 9.2 days during 1997-98 and 10.5 days and 9.3 days during 1998-99 respectively, whereas the container vessels and liquid bulk vessels have the least turn-around time of 3.4 days and 4.1 days respectively during 1998-99. The decline in the turn-around time is due to addition of more number of mechanised berths and efficient labour management at all major ports.

7.3.7. Average pre-berthing time has also declined significantly during the last four years from 1996-97 to 1999-2000. The average pre-berthing time of all major ports was 3.6 days in 1996-97 which was reduced more than half to 1.5 days in 1999-2000. The container type vessels have the least pre-berthing time of 1.3 days whereas break bulk have the longest pre-berthing time of 3.4 days in 1997-98 which was lowered to 2.7 days in 1998-99. During 1999-2000 the Kandla port has the longest pre-berthing time of 3.04 days, whereas J.L.Nehru port has the least pre-berthing time of 0.64 day. Capacity addition into the ports by expansion and mechanisation of berths and operation of new minor ports caused for declining trend in pre-berthing time at the Indian major ports.

7.3.8. The average non-working time at major ports has also declined considerably during 1999-2000. From the analysis it is clear that out of 12 major ports, 6 have less than one day average non-working time at their berths. These are Paradeep, Vizag, Cochin, Mormugao, Kandla and J.L.Nehru port. The rest 6 ports are also in just above average of a day but less than 2 days. Calcutta port has the highest average non-working time of 1.88 days and JNPT has the least average non-working time of 0.13 day in the corresponding year. The analysis further describes that, the fertiliser berths have the longest and liquid bulk berths have the least non-working time at major ports during 1999-2000.

7.3.9. The traffic handled by minor and intermediate ports have increased in absolute terms from 8.37 MT in 1986-87 to 87.9 MT in 2000-01. In terms of percentage, it rose from 8 per cent in 1994-95 to 17 per cent in 1999-2000 and 24 per cent in 2000-01. The post-reform period average traffic was 50.62 MT per annum which is significantly higher than 14.30 MT of the pre-reform period average. In the post-reform period, the different State Governments showed interests in developing their minor ports including creation of new ports through private participation.

7.3.10. The capacity utilisation at Indian major ports was satisfactory during the Five Year Plans. With the increase in aggregate port capacity from 20 MT in First Five Year Plan to 377 MT in the Ninth Five Year Plan, the traffic handled at major ports also increased from 23 MT to 424 MT during the corresponding period. Out of the nine plans the port capacity were utilised above 100 per cent during 3 plans and above 90 per cent during the rest 5 plan periods. The overall capacity utilisation of major ports was 105 per cent during 1999-2000 with 271.92 MT of traffic handled against a capacity of 258.05 MT. As per the norms fixed by GOI, normally the berth occupancy should be 75 per cent. Handling of traffic beyond the normal capacity of berths at Indian ports indicates the absence of adequate matching facilities. The ports with above 100 per cent capacity utilisation during 1999-2000 were Chennai (135 per cent), Visakhapatnam (128 per cent), Calcutta (124 per cent), Kandla (119 per cent) and Paradeep (106 per cent) and the rest have above 70 per cent of capacity utilisation.

7.3.11. The structural re-organisation of major port trusts is made to provide the necessary independence of authority and decision making to coagulate investment, execute projects and manage operations with professional expertise through corporatisation of major ports. A beginning in this direction has been made by declaring Ennore port as a company. It has also been decided to corporatise JNPT and Haldia port. It is expected that corporatisation would facilitate speedier decision making, more autonomy and better accountability leading to efficiency and commercial functioning. The new setup of major ports functioning as company would create conducive environment for allowing the ports to operate on commercial lines.

7.3.12. The on-going economic reforms in the country envisage the downsizing of existing surplus manpower in the port sector to increase the efficiency and enhance productivity of the ports. As a sequel to this, the Indian ports viz. Mumbai, New Mangalore, Tuticorin, Paradeep and Calcutta port trusts have rolled back the age of retirement from 60 to 58 years. The Mumbai Port Trust has also reduced its workforce from 30,000 to 23,000 with an expenditure of Rs.450 crore by announcing a special VRS in January 2001 and it has the plan of further reducing the workforce to 10,000.

7.4. State of Infrastruture Including Port in Orissa

7.4.1. Economic backwardness of Orissa is indicated by symptoms like excessive dependence on agriculture leading to high incidence of rural unemployment, low industrial productivity, low level of infrastructure development and high percentage of population living below poverty line. Absence of necessary infrastructure has been the main factor for the low level of industrial and other developmental activities in Orissa. At the initial stage of economic liberalisation in 1991, Orissa ranked among the top three States in the country in attracting foreign direct investment (FDI). The total investment proposed to be made in Orissa stood at over Rs.One lakh crore. But, most of these projects have fizzled out at the very drawing board stage because of slow progress in getting land and various statutory clearances and mostly the poor infrastructural facilities. Orissa is lagging far behind other advanced States in the country in terms of many infrastructural indicators. The villages connected with all-weather roads was 40 per cent in Orissa as against 48 per cent at all India level. Similarly railway route length per one lakh of population was 6.21 kms whereas it was 6.56 kms at all India level. Percentage of villages electrified in Orissa till 1999 was 73.43 as against national figure at 84.4 per cent. Per capita government expenditure on education, art and culture till 1998-99 was Rs. 354.40 against Rs. 456.10 at all India level. Further, the per capita government expenditure on medical, public health and family welfare in 1998-99 was Rs. 76.20, whereas it was Rs. 110.80 at all India level. Various socio-economic infrastructural facilities should be developed in the State both by the government and allowing private players for the overall development of the State in coming years.

7.4.2. The port infrastructure in Orissa is also in a deplorable situation. Being a coastal State Orissa has only one major port at Paradeep. There are two minor ports Gopalpur and Dhamara working as the fair-weather ports. Agreements are being signed between private investors to develop these ports as all-weather ports and subsequently mega ports with concessional approach. The inland water transport facilities have not been fully utilised to meet the growing demands of the people. At present 20 mechanised launches and 5 country boats are running on 8 different water routes.

7.5. History, Growth and Achievement of Paradeep Port, Policy Guidelines of the Government, Opportunities and Challenges

7.5.1. Paradeep one of the deep water major ports of India situated in the State of Orissa. In 1948, the Port (Technical) Committee formed by Government of India recommended to investigate the feasibility of establishing a sheltered deep sea port on the east coast between Vizag and Calcutta. After the independence, port of Dhaka was separated from the maritime map of India and to compensate such loss, it was required for another port in the east coast. Central Water and Power Commission (CWPC) was requested by Government of Orissa to explore the possibility of commissioning a port in the Mahanadi river delta. CWPC recommended for a port at Paradeep on Mahanadi river in the year 1950. In 1958, the Government of India, declared Paradeep as a minor port and subsequently in 1966, the port was declared as the first major port in the east coast, commissioned in independent India.

7.5.2. Now, there are 13 berths to handle the cargoes up to the capacity of 37 MT. The port has all the modern mechanised facilities and 80 per cent of the jobs are mechanised. The mechanisation process got a boost following the commissioning of Rs. 900 crore mechanised coal handling plant on September 11, 2000 with assistance from Asian Development Bank. The Indian ports association has projected a traffic of 34 MT, 64 MT and 82 MT to be handled by the port by the years 2002, 2007 and 2012 respectively. M/s RITES, in their study "Perspective Plan for Indian Port Sector-Vision 2020", have also projected a capacity requirement of 37.68 MT, 64.18 MT and 103.44 MT for the port by the years 2001-02, 2006-07 and 2019-20 respectively. The port has handled a record traffic of 199.00 lakh tonnes during 2000-01 as against 136.36 lakh tonnes in 1999-

2000. The port has also handled a record number of 915 vessels during the year of 2000-01 as against 741 vessels in the previous year. In terms of export and import cargo, the port also surpassed all the old records and established new records in this direction. During the year 2000-01, the port handled export cargo of 130.52 lakh tonnes and import cargo of 68.48 lakh tonnes as against 88.60 lakh tonnes and 47.76 lakh tonnes in 1999-2000.

7.5.3. Paradeep port plays a significant role in strengthening the infrastructure for development of various industries around the port area. The Paradeep port has an extensive and rich hinterland of about 1,00,000 sq.kms. The hinterland of Paradeep includes the country's largest iron and manganese ore reserves in Keonjhar and Sundargarh districts, the largest chromite and nickel deposit of Cuttack and Dhenkanal districts and huge coal reserve at Talcher. Paradeep is in the offing to enter into the industrial activity and will become instrumental in ushering in an era of economic prosperity for the State of Orissa. A port-based fertiliser plant Paradeep Phosphates Ltd. (PPL) has been commissioned since 1985 to produce 1.5 MT of D.A.P. per annum. In addition, Oswal Chemical and Fertilisers Ltd. has been setup as a fertiliser complex in 1999 to manufacture 2 MT of phosphatic fertiliser per annum. The work for 9 MT capacity Paradeep Refinery by Indian Oil Corporation (IOCL) with an investment of Rs.8000 crore is in progress. The Central Government has declared to establish a Special Economic Zone (SEZ) near Paradeep. The steps like the privatisation and corporatisation of ports, mechanisation and automation of port related activities etc. are considered moves in right direction of reform for enhancing its productivity and profitability. This would hopefully enable Paradeep port to become an active participant in the growth process of the country in general and the poorest State, Orissa in particular.

7.6. Operational Analysis of Paradeep Port

7.6.1. The operational analysis of the port has been done on the various performance indicators during the period 1986-87 to 2000-01. The analysis reveals that though the port has started its operation from 1966, its share of traffic handling was meagre till 1976. Only 25 lakh Metric Tonnes of traffic were handled at the port by 1985. With the establishment of fertiliser industries at Paradeep in 1985 and the onset of New Economic Policy (NEP) from Mid-1991, the traffic rose at the port during the decade of nineties. But the actual reform for infrastructure in general and port infrastructure in particular started after the submission of the Rakesh Mohan Committee Report on infrastructure in 1996.Besides portraying the trends of performance during the whole study period the analysis also encompasses a comparative study of performance during the pre-reform and post-reform period.

7.6.2. The total traffic handled at the port during the study period was increased from 48.52 lakh tonnes in 1986-87 to 199.00 lakh tonnes in 2000-01. The average traffic handled in the pre-reform period was 73.74 lakh tonnes per annum, which has been doubled to 143.05 lakh tonnes per annum in the post-reform period as against the average traffic of 96.85 lakh tonnes per year during the total study period. The overseas traffic also grew from 41.93 lakh tonnes in 1986-87 to 65.73 lakh tonnes in 2000-01. The average of the overseas traffic in the post-reform period registered a growth of 65.73 lakh tonnes per annum as against 49.15 lakh tonnes per annum in the pre-reform period. Similarly the coastal traffic at the port was also increased from 6.59 lakh tonnes in 1986-87 to 100.92 lakh tonnes in 2000-01. The post-reform period average growth of coastal traffic registered a spectacular growth of more than 3 times to 77.32 lakh tonnes per annum from 24.59 lakh tonnes per annum in the pre-reform period. One of the important findings of the study is that during the study period, the port has handled more export traffic as compared to import traffic. The import traffic increased from 20.01 lakh tonnes in 1986-87 to 68.48 lakh tonnes in 2000-01. At the same time the export traffic increased from 28.51 lakh tonnes to 130.52 lakh tonnes. During 2000-01, out of the total traffic handled at the port, 65 per cent is export traffic and the rest 35 per cent is import traffic, thus making the port an export surplus port. The liberalised economic policy of Government of India, implementation of India Infrastructure Report and addition of new mechanised berths to the port resulted in increase of overall traffic during the post-reform period.

7.6.3. The share of the port in handling traffic as compared to major ports of India increased from 3.90 per cent in 1986-87 to 7.07 per cent in 2000-01. The average share of traffic at Paradeep port in the pre-reform period was 4.55 per cent per annum which was increased to 5.57 per cent per annum in the post-reform period. The number of ships sailed at the port increased from 270 in 1986-87 to 886 in 2000-01. The average number of ships sailed at the port was 320 during the pre-reform period which became more than doubled to 695 numbers in the post-reform period.

7.6.4. The overall berth-day output of the port also registered significant growth during the study period. During 1988-89 the berth-day output was 4332 tonnes which was nearly doubled to 8503 tonnes in 2000-01. The average berth-day output during the pre-reform period was 4,915.25 tonnes which rose to 7,055.6 tonnes in the post-reform period. The berth-day output of iron-ore was the highest of 18,593 tonnes at the port followed by coal (9082 tonnes) and fertilisers (7854 tonnes). Since Orissa contains the highest amount of iron ore in the country and Paradeep port is the sole outlet for export of iron ore from the State, the port thus, handles and gives the highest output per berth-day. Due to addition of new coal berth and increasing demand for coal both in terms of export and import, the output of coal berths had increased. The establishment of two fertiliser plants at the port also keeps the berths busy at the port.

7.6.5. The labour productivity of all commodities had increased at the port during the study period. The overall labour productivity was 727.2 tonnes per hook shift per annum in the post-reform period which was significantly higher than 409 tonnes per hook shift per annum in the pre-reform period. The labour productivity of thermal coal was the highest of 918 tonnes per hook shift in 2000-01 followed by coking coal 865 tonnes per hook shift and chrome ore of 771 tonnes per hook shift. Peaceful working environment due to sound labour-management relation has resulted in raising the overall labour productivity at the port.

7.6.6. The average ship turn-around time (ASTA) at Indian ports are much higher than the ports of other developed countries which should have been less to make the port more efficient and productive. The average ship turn-around time of the port got reduced from 8.25 days in 1986-87 to 3.89 days in 1999-2000 and increased marginally to 4.16 days in 2000-01. The ASTA in the pre-reform period was 6.79 days per annum which declined significantly to 4.44 days per annum in the post-reform period against 6.01 days during the whole period. The ASTA at the ports of Singapore are only 6 to 8 hours. Efficient utilisation of port capacity, developed storage facility, well equipped rail and road connectivity and overall port-management are contributory factors for reducing the ASTA in the post-reform period.

7.6.7. Though the berth occupancy has increased at the port in absolute figures from 1361 days in 1986-87 to 2257 days in 2000-01, in percentage terms it varies between 51 days and 86 days during the study period. In the post-reform period, the average percentage of occupancy declined marginally to 64.9 per cent per annum from 67.2 per cent per annum in the pre-reform period. Though the number of berths are added to the port in the post-reform period and the number of ships also increased, but, not to that extent to occupy the berth. Thus, the percentage of occupancy declined marginally in this period.

7.6.8. The study reveals that pre-berthing delays were due to various reasons like non-availability of berths, non-availability of tugs and crafts, non-availability of pilot crew, strikes, night navigation, draft restriction, weather constraints, etc. Due to increase in the number of ships sailing at the port, the pre-berthing time has increased in the post-reform period. In case of non-availability of berth the average hours per annum in the pre-reform period of 9012.5 hours has reduced significantly to 5947.48 hours per annum in the post-reform period.

7.6.9. Both the number of Indian ships and foreign ships have increased during the study period. In 2000-01, out of the total 915 vessels called at the port, 470 were Indian ships and the rest 445 were foreign ships against 97 and 188 ships in 1986-87 respectively. Similarly, the traffic carried by Indian ships during the whole study period was 57.41 per cent per annum and foreign ships 42.58 per cent per annum. In the post-reform period the number of both the Indian ships and foreign ships had increased because of the establishment of new minor ports by the coastal states and two new fertiliser plants at Paradeep, for which there was import of raw materials from the foreign countries and increase in the export of fertiliser from the region. Further, establishment of more thermal units in Orissa during the post-reform period, has swelled the demand for thermal coal which were imported from Australia. This obviously enhanced demand for more number of ships to handle rising traffic.

7.6.10. The study also portrays that major share of traffic was handled through railways compared to other modes of transport like road and pipeline at Paradeep port. The inward rail traffi,c i.e., for export purpose, accounted for 85 per cent of total rail traffic in 2000-01, in order to export more quantities of ores, coal etc., for attaining economies of scale in ports operation. The share of outward rail traffic was 14.50 per cent during the corresponding period because of inadequate railway connectivity to different part of the state and import of less quantity of goods. Thus, for outward traffic rail mode will be costlier as compared to other modes.

7.6.11. The analysis of flag-wise distribution of cargo depicts that, the port had dealt with 47 of countries each in 1995-96 and 1996-97 as against 26 countries in 1986-87. On an average, the port had dealt with 32 number of countries in the pre-reform period which was increased to 37 numbers in the post-reform period. Increasing demand of this mode of transport from cost point of view and the development of new minor ports by the different State Governments caused the growth of fleet and diversification of trade with different countries.

7.6.12. The operating surplus of the port increased inspite of rise in operating expenditures and operating incomes as well during the study period. The operating surplus reached the level of Rs 111.19 crore in 2000-01 as against Rs 9.73 crore in 1986-87. Despite increase in operating expenses, the rising trends of operating incomes and operating surpluses indicate satisfactory performance of the port during the study period and more particularly in the post-reform period. The numbers of accidents both in port and non-port area have been reduced significantly during the post-reform period. The trend of decline in the number of accidents, provisions of insurance for accident compensation and provision of medical facilities have direct bearing on the morale and efficiency of workers in the port.

7.6.13. Class-wise staff strength at the port reveals the picture of downsizing of the existing surplus labour force. The port authorities have reduced the class- III and class-IV low salaried class employees. However, the authorities have increased the employment of class-I and class-II officers, the high salaried class people in the port which has nullified to some extent the beneficial effects of downsizing at lower levels. Use of more mechanised equipment and consequently employment of technically trained manpower have reduced the need for more class-III and class-IV employees in the port. Reduction of class-III and class-IV employees on the one hand and increase in productivity of the port on the other speaks about the favourable impact of downsizing of surplus employees on operational efficiency and productivity of the port.

7.7. Testing of Hypotheses

Hypothesis-I

Traffic handled at Paradeep port has increased over the years. The increasing trend is more pronounced in the post-reform period compared to pre-reform period

7.7.1. The total traffic (overseas and coastal) handled at the port during 1986-87 was 48.52 lakh tonnes which was increased significantly to 199.00 lakh tonnes in 2000-01. The proportion of traffic handled by Paradeep port to all major ports also rose from 3.90 per cent in 1986-87 to 7.07 per cent in 2000-01. The average annual growth of total traffic handled during the period was 96.85 lakh tonnes. In the pre-reform period, the average growth was 73.74 lakh tonnes per annum, which had registered nearly two fold rise to 143.05 lakh tonnes per annum in the post-reform period. The total overseas traffic (unloaded and loaded) handled at the port depicts a fluctuating trend in both pre-and post-reform period. The average overseas traffic handled in the pre-reform period was 49.15 lakh tonnes per annum which was increased to 65.73 lakh tonnes per annum in the post-reform period as against 54.67 lakh tonnes per annum during the whole study period. Similarly the coastal traffic also witnessed an increasing trend during the study period. The average coastal traffic in the pre-reform period was 24.59 lakh tonnes per annum which increased more than three times to 77.32 lakh tonnes per annum during the post-reform period.

The overall growth of traffic handled at the port was due to the liberalised export import (EXIM) policy and more particularly the implementation of the recommendations of the Rakesh Mohan Committee Report on infrastructure. Besides this, seven new berths including a mechanised coal handling plant were commissioned at the port to handle more traffic which ultimately reduced the average ship turn-around time and pre-berthing time at the port and increased the traffic handling capacity. Hence the findings of the study prove the hypothesis of rising trends of traffic handled at the port during the study period.

Hypothesis-II

Both overseas and coastal traffic at the port have increased in the post-reform period, but the increase in coastal traffic is significantly higher in the post-reform period than the rise in traffic in the pre-reform period

7.7.2. The overseas traffic handled at the port increased from 41.93 lakh tonnes in 1986-87 to 98.08 lakh tonnes in 2000-01. On an average the overseas traffic handled per annum was 54.67 lakh tonnes during the whole study period, which was 49.15 lakh tonnes in the pre-reform period and increased significantly to 65.73 lakh tonnes per annum in the post-reform period. The coastal traffic handled at the port also contributed considerably in total traffic handling. The coastal traffic handled at the port increased from 6.59 lakh tonnes in 1986-87 to 100.92 lakh tonnes in 2000-01. On an average the port handled coastal traffic of 42.17 lakh tonnes per annum during the study period. During the post-reform period, the coastal traffic at the port increased from 60.29 lakh tonnes in 1996-97 to 100.92 lakh tonnes in 2000-01, i.e., 77.32 lakh tonnes per annum which is more than three times of traffic handled at the port in the pre-reform period of 24.59 lakh tonnes per annum. Of the total 100.92 lakh tonnes of coastal traffic handled at the port during 2000-01, 92.59 lakh tonnes were loaded traffic, i.e., for export purpose and the rest 8.33 lakh tonnes were unloaded traffic, i.e., import traffic. The reasons of increase in coastal trade at the port during the post-reform period can be attributed to the development of minor ports by different State Governments with private sector participation and the increasing efficiency of the port with additional berth facilities. Further, increase in export of coking coal for the thermal plants of Tamil Nadu caused for more coastal traffic at the port. Hence, the hypothesis of increase in both overseas and coastal traffic in the post-reform period as compared to pre-reform period is proved.

Hypothesis-III

The average ship turn-around time has declined in the study period and more particularly in the post-reform period resulting in higher operational efficiency and productivity of the port

7.7.3. The overall ship turn-around time at the port was 8.25 days in 1986-87 which declined significantly to 4.16 days in 2000-01. The average ship turn-around time in the pre-reform period was 6.79 days which was reduced to 4.44 days in the post-reform period as against 6.01 days during the whole study period. During 1999-2000, the place of Paradeep port was third after Cochin and New Mangalore among the 12 major ports in terms of lowest turn-around time. The turn-around time for commodities like coking coal, thermal coal and chrome ore, charge chrome, ferro-manganese, etc. have reduced in the post-reform period in comparison to pre-reform period whereas the turn-around time for iron-ore and fertiliser raw materials have increased in the post-reform period as compared to pre-reform period. The average turn-around time for coking coal in the pre-reform period was 7.95 days which was reduced to 4.40 days in the post-reform period as against 6.77 days during the whole period. Similarly, the average turn-around time for thermal coal also declined to 3.79 days in the post-reform period as against 6.68 days in the pre-reform period. The average turn-around time for chrome ore, charge chrome etc. was also reduced from 7.57 days in the pre-reform period to 5.05 days in the post-reform period. On the other hand the average turn-around time for iron-ore increased marginally from 4.28 days in the pre-reform period to 4.43 days in the post-reform period. Fertiliser raw materials also reveals a higher turn-around time of 5.66 days in the post-reform period as against 3.09 days in the pre-reform period. The efficient utilisation of port capacity, mechanised handling facility, developed storage facility, well equipped rail and road connectivity and overall port-management are the contributory factors for reducing the average turn-around time at the port during the post-reform period. Hence the hypothesis of decline in ship turn-around time and more particularly in the post-reform period is proved.

Hypothesis-IV

The berth-day outputs of different commodities at the port have risen during the study period. But the rise is more significant in the post-reform period than the rise in pre-reform period

7.7.4. Since Orissa possesses the highest amount of iron-ore in the country and Paradeep port is the sole outlet for export of iron-ore from the State, the port of Paradeep handles and gives the highest output per berth-day of iron-ores. The average berth-day output of iron ore was 16,226.7 tonnes in the pre-reform period, which was increased to 16,939 tonnes in the post-reform period. Similarly the berth-day output of hard coke and chrome ore also increased marginally to 2,855.6 tonnes and 2821 tonnes in the post-reform period as against 2035.5 tonnes and 2237.9 tonnes in the pre-reform period respectively. The berth-day output of coal and limestone increased significantly in the post-reform period as compared to pre-reform period. The average output of coal was 5,243.3 tonnes per annum in the pre-reform period which was increased to 8,814 tonnes per annum in the post-reform period as against 6,433.5 tonnes per annum during the whole period. The average berth-day output of limestone also increased from 4,808.9 tonnes per annum in the pre-reform period to 6,476.2 tonnes per annum in the post-reform period. The overall berth-day output of all commodities increased with 5,738.4 tonnes per annum during the whole study period, whereas the corresponding figures in the post-reform period was 7,055.6 tonnes as against 4,915.25 tonnes per annum in the pre-reform period. Use of mechanised cargo handling equipment by the port and increased demand for the commodities in the coastal and overseas market caused the increasing berth-day output at the port. Hence the said hypothesis is proved.

Hypothesis-V

The port of Paradeep has witnessed higher labour productivity during the study period, but tl e rise is more visible in the post-reform period reflecting the positive impact of on-going infrastructure reform on the port

7.7.5. The overall labour productivity of Paradeep port in 1986-87 was 233 tonnes per hook shift, which rose significantly to 800 tonnes per hook shift in 2000-01. The average labour productivity at the port during the pre-reform period was 409 tonnes per hook shift per annum which was increased significantly to 727.2 tonnes per hook shift per annum in the post-reform period. Similarly commodity-wise, coking coal depicts the productivity of 865 tonnes per hook shift in 2000-01, which was significantly higher than 465 tonnes in 1987-88. The average productivity of coking coal in the pre-reform period was 550.55 tonnes per hook shift which increased to 805.8 tonnes per hook shift in the post-reform period. The productivity of thermal coal had increased from 358 tonnes per hook shift to 918 tonnes per hook shift in 2000-01. The average productivity in the pre-reform period was 455.11 tonnes per hook shift which also rose to 799.2 tonnes per hook shift in the post-reform period. Hard coke and limestone also exhibit the higher average productivity of 447.4 tonnes per hook shift and 667.8 tonnes per hook shift in the post-reform period as against 319.66 tonnes and 452.77 tonnes per hook shift in the pre-reform period respectively. Similarly, the chrome ore, charge chrome, ferro chrome, ferro manganese etc and fertiliser raw materials also reveal the increasing trend during the study period. The peaceful working environment due to sound labour-management relation has resulted in raising the overall labour productivity. More significantly, in the post-reform period the pro-labour policy of the government, the use of machines with advanced technology and safety measures provided by the port are the plausible reasons for the growth of productivity of all commodities.Thus the hypothesis of higher labour productivity of the port during the study period, more so in post-reform period is found to be on the basis of the findings of the study.

Hypothesis-VI

Paradeep port handles more export traffic as compared to import traffic

7.7.6. The total (overseas and coastal) export traffic handled at the port during 1986-87 was 28.51 lakh tonnes, i.e., 59 per cent of total traffic which was increased to 130.52 lakh tonnes (65.58 per cent of total traffic) in 2000-01. Though the overseas export traffic was not significant as compared to overseas import traffic, but in coastal trade the export traffic is considerably higher, i.e., 92 per cent of total coastal trade. The average export traffic in overseas trade was near about same, i.e., 21 lakh tonnes per annum in both pre-and post-reform period. But the coastal export traffic was increased from 6.56 lakh tonnes in 1986-87 to 92.59 lakh tonnes in 2000-01 registering a growth of 40.57 lakh tonnes per annum during the study period. The post-reform period export traffic of coastal trade stood at 72.97 lakh tonnes per annum as against 24.37 lakh tonnes per annum in the pre-reform period. The liberalised export-import policy of the Government of India and implementation of recommendations of the Rakesh Mohan Committee Report on infrastructure had brought about more export trade at all ports in general and Paradeep port in particular. In addition, during the post-reform period, the development of minor ports by the respective State Governments with private participation and the increasing efficiency of the port with additional berth facilities enhanced the export trade at Paradeep port. In view of this, Paradeep has emerged as an export surplus port in the region and hence the hypothesis is proved.

Hypothesis-VII

Number of ships sailed at the port increased significantly during the nineties and more particularly in the post-reform period

7.7.7. With the increase in trade, the number of ships sailed at the port had increased during the study period. In 1986-87, there were 270 number of ships sailed at the port which were increased significantly to 523 numbers in 1995-96 and further increased to 886 numbers in 2000-01. The average number of ships sailed at the port per annum during the whole study period was 445. In the post-reform period, the average number of ships sailed per annum was 695 as against 320 numbers per annum in the pre-reform period. On the other hand the total number of vessels called at the port also increased to 915 in 2000-01 of which 470 were Indian vessels and the rest 445 were foreign vessels. The natural advantage of the port is that it can dredge upto 40 metres for accommodation of vessels without obstruction and delay because no rock surface is there till 40 metres. At present, the port has 14 metres depth. Provision of additional facilities at the berth, rising import of fertiliser raw materials and export of fertiliser by the two fertiliser plants situated near Paradeep enhanced the demand for more number of ships at the port. Hence the hypothesis that rising number of ships sailed at the port during the nineties and particularly in the post-reform era is substantiated.

Hypothesis-VIII

Operating surplus of the port increased during the nineties

7.7.8. With increase in operating expenditure and operating income, the operating surplus of the port increased significantly during the study period. In 1986-87, the operating surplus was Rs. 9.73 crores which was increased to Rs. 73.41 crores in 1997-98 and further increased to Rs.111.19 crores in 2000-01. The average growth of operating surplus during the whole period was Rs.46.15 crores per annum. In the pre-reform period the average surplus per annum was Rs. 31.56 crores which further rose to Rs. 75.32 crores per annum in the post-reform period. The average operating expenditure of the port was Rs. 73.23 crores per annum during the whole study period. In the post-reform period the average expenditure per annum was Rs.118.02 crores as against Rs.50.84 crores in the pre-reform period. Similarly the operating income of the port during the pre-reform period was Rs.82.41 crores which increased to Rs.191.75 crores in the post-reform period as against Rs. 118.85 crores during the total study period. Despite increase in operating expenses, the rising trends of operating incomes and operating surplus indicate satisfactory performance of the port during the study period. Due to increase in operations at the port during the nineties and particularly in the post-reform period contributed significantly to operating incomes and surplus of the port. Hence the said hypothesis is found to be true and valid.

Hypothesis-IX

The railways have major share of both export and import traffic by way of transportation for the port during the study period

7.7.9. From the analysis, it is crystal clear that the rail mode of transport has emerged as the most significant mode among the total modes of transport for handling cargo. The quantity of export traffic received by rail mode was increased from 21.71 lakh tonnes in 1986-87 (which is 76 per cent of the total export traffic), to 103.27 lakh tonnes in 2000-01 (80 per cent of total export traffic). The share of rail mode of transport in total export cargo received remained near about same of 80 per cent during the whole study period. The rest 20 per cent of export cargo were received by other modes of transport. The port exports mainly the mineral resources such as iron-ore, chrome ore, charge chrome, thermal coal, etc. which need to be exported in huge quantities for attaining economies of scale in operation. So the rail mode is economical, cheaper and quicker for this purpose. On the other hand for import cargo despatched by different modes, rail mode occupies near about 50 per cent of total traffic. On an average the share of rail mode in total import traffic was 46 per cent per annum. The port has its own railway section operating within the ports areas. But for handling of inward and outward traffic at the port, the port depends upon the South Eastern Railway authorities for transportation of goods traffic. Hence the hypothesis that the railways handle the lion's share of total traffic is valid and thus proved.

Hypothesis-X

The number of accidents at the port has been reduced and more so in the post-reform period

7.7.10. The accidents occurred at the port can be classified into two types, such as fatal and non-fatal. So far as fatal accident is concerned, 20 such cases were reported in port area and 23 cases in the non-port area during the study period. The non-fatal accidents in the port area were higher than the non-port area. There were 307 accidents of non-fatal nature occurred in the port area, which was on an average 21 accidents in a year.

In the post-reform period, non-fatal accidents were slightly higher, i.e., 24 cases per year. In the non port-area, there were only 27 accidents occurred out of which 26 were in the pre-reform period and one in the post-reform period. The study also reveals that the number of accidents in port area both fatal and non-fatal are higher, i.e., 327 than the non-port area accidents which were 40 only. Similarly, in the port area accidents per year in the post-reform period were 26 as against 22 in the pre-reform period. This is due to more number of ships handled by the port during the post-reform period than in the pre-reform period. As the port authorities are taking adequate measures, the number of accidents has been reduced significantly. In case of accidents in non-port area the number of cases had fallen drastically to only two in the post-reform period as against 48 numbers in the pre-reform period. The port has started a free medical advice centre in medical campus to examine and prescribe required medicines to the patients. Eye camps were organised by the Paradeep Branch of Lion's Club with the help of medical and paramedical staff of Paradeep Port Trust Hospital on suitable occasions. Employees, cargo handling workers and auxiliary workers were provided with necessary financial assistance to meet medical expenses in the event of acute financial hardship. In the context of welfare measure, proper care was taken for the dependents of employees who died in service. Janata Personal Accident Insurance Policy has been introduced at this port for covering accidents of port employees. On the basis of findings of the study one can reasonably substantiate the hypothesis of less number of accidents occuring at the port during the study period.

Hypothesis-XI

As a sequel to on-going infrastructure reform in the country, the downsizing of employees at the port has enhanced its operational efficiency and productivity

7.7.11. There are mainly four categories of employees working at Paradeep port such as Class I, II, III and IV. The number of Class I staff which is high salaried in nature were reduced to 86 in 2000-01 as against 94 numbers in 1996-97. Similarly, the Class II staff position also reduced from 218 in 1996-97 to 213 in 2000-01. But in case of Class III and Class IV, the average figures of the employees were reduced in the post-reform period to 1378 and 1016 persons from 1593 and 1167 persons per annum in the pre-reform period respectively. In absolute terms the figures of Class-III employees reduced significantly from 1700 persons in 1986-87 to 1366 in 2000-01. Similarly, the number of Class-IV employees also reduced considerably from 1239 in 1986-87 to 1063 in 2000-01. The total staff strength figures exhibits an increasing trend till 1994-95 and then declined for two years, but it rose again in 1997-98 to 4227 persons the all time highest during the study period. From 1997-98 onwards till 2000-01, there has been marginal reduction and reached 4116 persons in 2000-01. In this era of economic reforms there is an urgent need for rightsizing the overmanned organisation. Use of more mechanised equipment and consequently employment of technically trained manpower have reduced the need for more Class-III and Class-IV employees in the port. In view of this during the post-reform period, the productivity of the port has increased significantly as compared to pre-reform period. Hence the hypothesis of downsizing surplus workforce and consequent enhancement of operational efficiency and productivity is found valid.

7.8. Conclusions

7.8.1. India, being a major maritime nation, is critically dependent on its national port system to ensure sustainable economic growth through expanding exports and timely availability of essential imports. At present, India's port system comprises 12 major ports and 160 minor ports and handles about 90 per cent in volume and 75 per cent in value of India's foreign trade. Until the end of the 20th century, there were severe capacity constraints in the ports and ships had to wait for berths whereas elsewhere berths wait for ships. However, in tandem with policy of on-going economic reforms, investments by private sector are now allowed in Indian ports. Now with the creation of some 60 million tonne capacity through private investments, the assessed capacity of major ports is 291 million tonnes against which cargo handled in 2000-01 was 281 million tonnes. According to the Tenth Plan projection made by the Ministry of Shipping, the capacity of ports is expected to be 470 million tonnes by 2007 against a cargo handling requirement of 415 million tonnes.

7.8.2. The foregoing analysis reveals that inspite of immense potential, Indian ports so far have been able to exploit only 12.5 per cent of its 6000 kms long coastline. Though operational efficiency of major ports has improved over years when judged in terms of parameters like average pre-berthing time, average ship turn-around time, ship berth-day output, etc., but failed to compare favourably with competing ports in the neighbourhood. The reasons like poor utilisation of equipment, over staffing, cumbersome documentary procedures, such as customs clearance, inadequate port access facilities, lack of inter-port and intra-port competition, inability of existing ports to handle new categories of cargo, etc. are attributed to less than satisfactory performance of Indian ports. These problems need to be redressed in right perspectives so that our ports become cost effective, efficient and globally competitive.

7.8.3. Started as a mono-commodity port to export iron ore, in 1966 the port of Paradeep today operates as a multi-commodity port with 13 berths dealing with fertiliser raw material, POL, iron ore, and general cargo. Night navigation was started in the year 1998. Paradeep port's main advantage lies in its nearness to deep sea. Offering a depth of 13 metres with a channel less than a kilometre long from roads, the port is considered to be one of the deepest inner harbour ports in the country. The cargo handling in Paradeep port has grown significantly during the study period, i.e., 48.52 lakh tonnes in 1986-87 to 199.00 lakh tonnes in 2000-01 which is highest in port's history. It is also highest among all the major ports of India, thus taking the port from its previous 9th position amongst the major ports to 6th position in terms of volume of cargo. The commissioning of Nilachal Ispat Nigam Ltd. and the decision of the government for early completion of Oil Refinery of Indian Oil Corporation Ltd. would give fillip to cargo turnover at the port thereby enabling the port to fulfil the Indian Ports Association (IPA's) projected cargo turnover target of 640 lakh tonnes by the year 2007. The study reveals that the share of Paradeep has increased from 3.90 per cent in 1986-87 to 7.07 per cent in 2000-01 of the total traffic handled by all major ports in the country. The other parameters of performance like berth-day output, labour productivity, ship turn-around time, berth occupancy, pre-berthing delay, operating surplus etc., of the port have shown improvement during the study period. More strikingly, the higher operational efficiencies in the post-reform period over pre-reform period indicate the favourable impacts of infrastructure reform on Paradeep port. The opportunities of transport infrastructure coupled with rich hinterland of 1 lakh sq.kms have made the port an active participant in the economic development of the country as well as of the poorest State

Orissa. The decision of the Central Government to setup a Special Economic Zone (SEZ) at Paradeep would definitely give further fillip to industrial and other business activities in the region.

7.8.4. Despite the fact that Paradeep port and all major ports of India have shown resilence of growth and diversification during the study period, still they have a long way to go to catch up with the performance standards of foreign ports. The infrastructural reforms based on the recommendations of Rakesh Mohan Committee, implemented way back in 1996, have started yielding results in the country. The privatisation of Jawaharlal Nehru Port Trust (JNPT), Mumbai India's premier container port and Tuticorin are cases in point. The drive to corporatise the existing ports is a move in right direction in ensuring operational flexibility and efficiency. As a sequel to reforms, the implementation of VRS and rolling back of retirement age to 58 have helped to bring down the number of workers to increase labour productivity. Though actions have been initiated, the pace of reform in port sector is slow as is evidenced from the fact that so far only 2 major ports (Nava Seva and Tuticorin) and 2 minor ports (Mundra and Pipavav) have been privatised. Except Ennore port, which has been set up initially as a company, no other port has been corporatised yet. Fast and discernible improvements in infrastructural facilities provided by Indian ports brook no delay because absence of adequate infrastructure would crumble the entire edifice of economic development of the country. Hence, port reform must be coherent and carry with it a sense of urgency. Unless this happens, India's trade would fail to cope with increasing competition in international markets with high transport and transaction cost.

7.9. Limitations of the Study

7.9.1. The analysis of this research endeavour is based on the secondary data collected from the Basic Port Statistics of India published by Ministry of Surface Transport, Government of India, Annual Administration Reports of Paradeep Port Trust, The Economic Survey of India, Ministry of Finance, GOI, Indian Ports Association and National Institute of Port Management. Data were collected from different sources according to the need of the study and accessibility to the sources of data. Consequently, they are bound to show some variations even for the same bank for the same port. Inspite of their limitations, secondary data constitute the major data source for the study mainly due to scarcity of time and resources which are otherwise essential for collection of primary data. The average figures calculated in the study have been based on the principles and techniques of arithmetic mean which have their own limitations. Coverage of all individual ports by specific indicators for the whole study period could not be worked out due to non-availability of data. This constitutes another limitation of the study. However, the data used in the study have been analysed and interpreted keeping in view the above said limitations for making objective assessment and arriving at meaningful conclusions.

7.10. Practical Utility of the Study

7.10.1. The present study is primarily a fact finding research work pertaining to the basic operations of Paradeep port for the period from 1986-87 to 2000-01. The study also contains the performance of major ports of India and the challenges it faces. The performance analysis of the Paradeep port has been made on a comparative basis between pre-and post-reform period. The study also seeks to bring into focus the strengths and weaknesses of the Indian ports in general and Paradeep port in particular in contrast with the ports of Asian region and other developed countries. The study, thus would help to know the improvement in the performance of the Indian ports and more particularly the Paradeep port brought about by the economic reform started in early nineties and infrastructure sector reform from mid-nineties. In addition to this, the study will help in reviewing the policy measures adopted by the government after 1996, keeping in view the progress of the transport infrastructure sector reform in general and port infrastructure in particular in the country. The study too will be of immense help to the private investors who intend to invest in this sector. Further, the study would also serve useful purpose as a reference document to financial institutions, the port authorities, the researchers and others concerned with the development of infrastructure in general and port infrastructure in particular.

7.11. Scope for Further Research

7.11.1. There are certain aspects of port infrastructure that came up in course of the study which provide scope for further research on the subject. An intensive comparative study can be undertaken between the ports situated in the east coast, e.g., comparative study between Paradeep port and Visakhapatnam port. Similarly, study for the ports of west coast also can be undertaken. If the present study which is based entirely on the secondary data, is supplemented by the primary data, it will provide more accurate and better insight into the performance, opportunities and challenges facing the the port sector in the country. Against such backdrop, the present study provides the scope for further research in the area.

Annexure – I
Topography of Major Ports

Port	Location		Entrance Channel			Turning Circle		
	Latitude	*Longitude*	*Distance of anchor from Harbour entrance (km)*	*Minimum Depth (Mtrs.)*	*Minimum Width (Mtrs.)*	*No.*	*Diameter (in mtrs)*	*Type of Dock/Port*
Kandla	23°01′N	70°13′E	25	4.6 (Below chart datum)	200	No	Turning Circle	Estuary Port
Vadinar	22°30′ 34″ N	69°42′04″ E	8.0	23.5	1500	-	-	Off-shore oil terminal (Single Buoy Mooring)
Mumbai	18°54′N	72°49′E	9.6	10.9	366	1	366	Natural Harbour and Impounded Wet Docks

(Contd...)

(Contd. Annexure-1)

Port	Location		Entrance Channel			Turning Circle		
	Latitude	Longitude	Distance of anchor from Harbour entrance (km)	Minimum Depth (Mtrs.)	Minimum Width (Mtrs.)	No.	Diameter (in mtrs)	Type of Dock/Port
J.L.Nehru	18°56.43′ N*	72°56.24′ E*	17.0	11.0	350	1	600	Natural Harbour Protected by a break-water. (At the mouth of River Zuari)
Mormugao	15°25′N	73°48′E	4.5	13.0	250	1	480	All weather tidal port.
New Mangalore	12°55′N	74°48′E	7.5	15.4	245	1	570	Artificial lagoon port with open berth.
Cochin	9°58′N	76°14′E	10.5	11.7	200	3	120-250	Artificial Lagoon Port

(Contd...)

(Contd. Annexure-1)

Port	*Location*		*Entrance Channel*			*Turning Circle*		
	Latitude	Longitude	Distance of anchor from Harbour entrance (km)	Minimum Depth (Mtrs.)	Minimum Width (Mtrs.)	No.	Diameter (in mtrs)	Type of Dock/Port
Tuticorin	8°47'M	78°12'E	2.4	10.8	152	1	488	Artificial Harbour
Chennai	13°06'N	80°18'E	6.7	IH 18.6 OH 19.2	244	1	548	Artificial Harbour with Wet Docks
Visakhapatnam-Inner Harbour	17°41'N	83°18'	2.2	10.7	97.54	1	366	Natural Harbour
-Outer Harbour			0.4	17.5	200	1	610	
Paradeep	20°15'N	86°40'E	2.0	12.8	160	1	520	Wet Dock
Calcutta	22°32' 53''N	88°18' 05''E	233	2.9	100	2	183/250	Riverine with impounded wet docks and river side jetties.
Haldia	22°2'N	80°6'E	115	6.7	467	1	549	Impounded dock with riverine oil jetties.

Source : Government of India, *Basic Port Statistics of India*, Ministry of Surface Transport, New Delhi, 1990-2000, p. 57.

Annexure – II

Definitions of Terms Used

Berth Occupancy	The time for which a berth is occupied (by ships).
Berth-Day	A day of occupation of a berth (quay or mooring) by a ship.
Cranage	The hire charges for providing a port crane for cargo handling.
Dead Weight Tonnage (DWT)	It is the number of tons of (2240 pounds) stores, fuel and cargo that a ship can transport. This presents the actual carrying capacity of a ship.
Draft	The depth necessary to submerge a ship to their road line.
Export	Loaded overseas traffic.
Gross Registered Tonnage (GRT)	It applies to vessels and not to cargo. It is the weight of the volume occupied by the closed-in-spaces of a ship taking 100 cubic feet of such closed-in-spaces as equivalent to one vessels ton. It thus refers to the cubic capacity of the vessels.
Idle Time	Non-working time of a ship (without loading or unloading of cargo) at berth.
Import	Unloaded overseas traffic

Net Registered Tonnage (NRT)
It refers to the earning space capacity of a ship available for the storage of cargo and accommodation of passengers. It is obtained by deducting from GRT the cubic capacity space (taking 100 cubic feet = 1 ton) occupied by stores, fuel, machinery, crew etc. which does not represent the earning capacity of the ship.

Output per Berth Day Total tonnage handled distributed over the total number of berth days.

Pilotage A port charge for guiding a ship in or out of a harbour through channels, passages or other waters by an authorised pilot.

Port Dues A levy of port authority on a ship.

Pre-berthing Detention The time for which a ship waits before getting entry into a berth.

Roll-on/Roll-off Vessels It is frequently called a vehicle ferry. It is designed for the conveyance of road vehicles and private cars. At each terminal port, a tramp of link span is provided enabling the vehicles to drive on or off the vessels, thereby eliminating cranage and cargo handling (and also pilferage) and permitting a quick turn round of the ships.

Ship-Day A day spent in harbour by a ship.

Traffic A scalar with only magnitude but no direction such as the total of exports and imports or loaded and unloaded cargo.

Traffic flows A vector with magnitude and direction such as passengers embarked/disembarked or cargo exports/imports.

Turn-Round Time Total time spent by a ship since its entry till its departure.

Wharfage A port charge on the ships for all cargo conveyed on over or through a wharf/berth.

Source : Government of India, Ministry of Surface Transport, Transport Research Wing, New Delhi.

Bibliography

Books

Abdul Kalam, A.P.J. & Rajan, Y.S., *India-2020 : A Vision for the New Millennium,* Penguin Books India Ltd., New Delhi, 1998.

Agrawal, A.N., *Indian Economy : Problems of Development and Planning,* Wishwa Prakashan, , 27th Revised Edition, New Delhi, 2001.

Batten, D.F. and Karlsson, C. (ed.), *Infrastructure and Complexity of Economic Development,* Springer, New York.

Bhattacharya, K.P., *Affordable Housing and Infrastructure in India,* Reliance Publishing House, New Delhi, 1998.

Brockman, R.A.C. and Williams, A. (ed.), *Urban Infrastructure Finance,* Asian Development Bank, Manila, 1996.

Dagli, V. (ed.), *Infrastructure for the Indian Economy,* Vora, Mumbai, 1970.

Datt, R. and Sundaram, K.P.M., *Indian Economy,* S. Chand & Company Ltd., 43rd Revised Edition, New Delhi, 2001.

Deb, S. (ed.), *The India Infrastructure Report : Policy Imperatives for Growth and Welfare,* Vol. II, The Main Report, National Council for Applied Economic Research, New Delhi, 1996.

Deb, S. (ed.), *The Indian Infrastructure Report : Policy Imperatives for Growth and Welfare,* Vol. I, Executive Summary, Government of India, New Delhi, 1996.

Dhar, P.K., *Indian Economy - Its Growing Dimensions,* Kalyani Publishers, New Delhi, 8th Revised Edition, 2000.

Dhingra, I.C., *The Indian Economy – Environment and Policy,* Sultan Chand and Sons, 14th Revised Edition, New Delhi, 2000.

Estache, Antonio, *Decentralising Infrastructure : Advantages and Limitations* (Edited Volume) World Bank Discussion Papers No. 290, World Bank, Washington D.C., 1995.

Farrell, S., *Financing European Transport Infrastructure : Policies and Practices in Western Europe,* Macmillan, Hampshiure 1999.

Ganesh, G., *Privatisation in India,* Mittal Publications, New Delhi, 2001.

Gulyani, S., *Innovating with Infrastructure : The Automobile Industry in India,* Palgrave, New York, 2001.

Indian Ports Association (IPA), *Major Ports of India : A Profile 2000-01,* New Delhi.

Irwin, T. (Ed.), *Dealing with Public Risk in Private Infrastructure,* World Bank, Washington, D.C. 1997.

Kapila, R. & Kapila, U. (ed.), *India's Economy in the 21st Century,* Published by Academic Foundation, New Delhi, 2001.

Kapila, Uma., *Indian Economy since Independence,* Academic Foundation, New Delhi, New Revised Edition, 2001-2002.

Kessides, Christine, *Institutional Options for the Provision of Infrastructure,* World Bank Discussion Papers No. 212, World Bank, Washington, D.C., 1993.

Kohli, H., Mody, A. and Walton, M. (ed.), *Choices for Efficient Private Provision of Infrastructure in East Asia,* World Bank, Washington D.C., 1997.

Kumar, A. (Ed.), *Mobilising Domestic Capital Markets for Infrastructure Financing : International Experience and Lessons for China,* World Bank Discussion Paper No. 377, World Bank, Washington, D.C., 1997.

Lalitha, N., *Commercialising Road Projects : Lessons for India,* Gujarat Institute of Development Research, Ahmedabad, 1998.

Lekhi, R.K., *The Economics of Development and Planning,* Kalyani Publishers, 2001 Edition.

Mathur, B.L., *Economic Policy and Development,* RBSA Publishers, Jaipur, 1st Edition, 2000.

Mitra, A., *State Infrastructure and Productivity Performance in Indian Manufacturing,* Organisation of Economic Cooperation and Development (OECD), Paris, 1998.

Mody, A. (ed.), *Infrastructure Delivery : Private Initiative and the Public Good,* World Bank, Washington, D.C., 1997.

Mody, A. (ed.), *Infrastructure Strategies in East Asia,* World Bank, Washington, D.C., 1997.

Mungerkar, B.L., Nachane, D.M., and Monohar Rao, M.J., (ed) *Indian Economy in the New Millennium,* Himalaya Publishing House, Ist Edition - 2001.

Panigrahi, K.C., *History of Orissa.*, Kitab Mahal, Cuttack, 1981.

Parikh, K.S. and Ramanathan, R., *Reprint Reforms in Infrastructure with Special Reference to Indian Railways : An Analysis,* Indira Gandhi Institute of Development Research, Mumbai, 1998.

Peschel, Karin, *Infrastructure and the Space-Economy – Essays in Honour of Rolf Funck,* Springer Verlag, Berlin, 1990.

Port Handbook and Guide ; Exim India Limited, 1998.

Port of Paradeep, A Brochure Published by Paradeep Port Trust in August 1999.

Port of Paradeep, A Special Volume Published in Shipping and Marine Industries Journal, Vol. 24, Mumbai, May 2001.

Ports of India, The Economic Times, 1999.

Quinet, E. and Vickerman, R.(ed.), *The Econometrics of Major Transport Infrastructure,* Macmillan, 1997.

Raghuram, G., Jain, R. et. al. (ed.), *Infrastructure Developing and Financing Towards a Public-Private Partnership,* Macmillan India Ltd., 1999.

Ray, A., *Maritime India : Ports and Shipping,* Munshiram Manoharlal Publishers Pvt. Ltd., New Delhi, 1993.

Ray, B.C., *Orissa under the Mughals,* Chapter - IX, Shipping and Maritime Activities.

Ray, S.K., *Transport Planning for Developing Countries,* Prentice-Hall of India, New Delhi (1995).

Rosengren, S. and Jordan, J.S.(ed.), *Building an Infrastructure for Financial Stability,* Federal Reserve Bank of Boston, Boston, 2000.

Sahoo, S., *Role of Infrastructure in Economic Development : The Indian Case,* An Unpublished Ph.D. Thesis Submitted to Department of Humanities and Social Sciences IIT, Kanpur, July 1998.

Sen, R.K., and Chatterjee, B. (ed), *Indian Economy: Agenda for the 21st Century,* (Essays in Honour of Prof. P.R. Brahmananda) Deep and Deep Publications Pvt. Ltd., New Delhi, 2002.

Singh, R., *Infrastructure of Tourism in India,* Kanishka Publishers, New Delhi, 1996.

Smith, G.R., *Getting Connected : Private Participation in Infrastructure in the Middle East and North Africa,* World Bank, Washington D.C. 1997.

Sriraman, S. (ed.), *Transportation System Analysis and Policy Studies,* The Department of Economics, University of Mumbai as part of its Platinum Jubilee Celebrations, 1996.

Vaidyanathan, A., *Water Resource Management : Institutions and Irrigation Development in India,* Oxford University Press, 1999.

Varma, Ram K., *Development Infrastructure for Rural Economy,* Printwell, Jaipur, 1996.

Wanmali, S., *Rural Services Rural Infrastructure and Regional Development in India,* International Food Policy Research Institute, Washington, D.C., 1995.

Wanmali, Sudhir and Ramasamy, C., *Developing Rural Infrastructure : Studies From North Arcot*, Tamil Nadu, India, Macmillan, New Delhi, (1995)

Wanmali, Sudhir, *Rural Infrastructure the Settlement System and Development of the Regional Economy in Southern India,* International Food Policy Research Institute, Washington, 1992.

Winstron, Clifford, *Efficient Transportation Infrastructure Policy,* Brooking Institution, Washington, 1993.

World Bank, *Financing Private Infrastructure : Lessons of Experience,* Washington, D.C., 1996.

World Bank, *The Private Sector in the Infrastructure Strategy, Regulation and Risk,* International Forum for Utility Regulation, Washington, D.C. 1997.

Yadav, Subah Singh, Gurjar, Ram Kumar, *Infrastructure to Rural Development,* Pointer Publishers, Jaipur, 1993.

Articles

Adam, T., "Port-related Logistics - Need for Innovative System", *The Hindu Survey of Indian Industry* 2001, p.119.

Akkina, K.R., "Convergence and the Role of Infrastructure and Power Shortages on Economic Growth Across States in India", *Indian Economic Journal* 47(2), Oct.-Dec., 1999, pp. 42-53.

Anand, M. & Jayaram, A., "The Highway Men – A Special Cover Story on National Highway Projects", *Business World,* Vol. 22, Issue 17, New Delhi, September 23, 2002, p. 28.

Anil, M.K., "Ports Must Anchor on Low Costs Efficiency", *The Hindu Business Line,* Vol. 9, No. 174, Visakhapatnam, June 24, 2002, p. 6.

Apte, K.G., "Productivity at Jawaharlal Nehru Port", *Paper Presented at the National Conference on Infrastructure Project Management,* Organised by the National Institute for Industrial Engineering, Mumbai, 2000.

Arun Kumar, A.V. and Upendranadh, C., "Infrastructure Development in India : An Alternative Approach to Measurement", *Productivity,* Oct-Dec.1993, 34(3), pp. 455-457.

Bagchi, S., "Infrastructure Financing in India - Alternatives and Associated Problems", *The Hindu Business Line*, Vol. 9, No. 333, Visakhapatnam, December 3, 2002, p. 8.

Balaramulu, Ch., "Infrastructure and Development in India – Macro and Micro Analysis", *Indian Journal of Public Administration* 46(4), October-December 2000, pp. 601-616.

Bhat, T.R., "Port Privatisation : Running into Rough Weather ?", *The Hindu Business Line,* Vol. 9, No. 146, Visakhapatnam, May 27, 2002, p. 6.

Bhatikar, A.P., "Privatisation of Indian Ports", *Indian Shipping,* Vol.47, No.7, Mumbai, 1995.

Binswanger, H.P.,Khandker, S.R. & Rosenzweg, M.R., "How Infrastructure and Financial Institutions Affect Agricultural Output and Investment in India", *Journal of Development Economics,* August 1993, 41(2), pp. 337-366.

Bongirwar, A.L., "Major Ports – Prospects and Challenges", A Publication of *Indian Ports Association,* June 2001, Mumbai.

Bose, K., " Port Privatisation : Unlocking Value", *The Hindu Business Line,* Vol. 9, No. 118, Visakhapatnam, April 29, 2002, p. 6.

Bose, S.K., "Cargo Handling of Major Ports in India : A Case Study", *Economic and Political Weekly,* Vol. XXXVI, No. 34, Mumbai, August 25, 2001.

Das Gupta, T., "The Infrastructure Sector", *Yojana,* Vol.43, No. 1, January 1999, p. 43.

Dattatreyulu, M., "Establishment of Free Port in India", *Indian Shipping,* Vol. 46, No. 1, Mumbai, 1994.

Dayal, R., "The Pusillanimity of Port Management", *The Economic Times,* Vol. 35, No. 291, Kolkata, December 25, 1995, p. 4.

De, P & Palit, T.K., "Impact of Performance on Traffic : Evidence from Major Ports of India", *Indian Ports,* Vol. XXXII, No. 3, New Delhi, January 2001, p. 27.

De, Prabir., "A Policy for Ports", *The Economic Times,* Vol. 41, No. 280, Kolkata, December 15, 2001, p. 4.

Desai, V.V., "Infrastructure : Policies and Industry", *The Economic Times,* Kolkata, November 11, 1997.

Dubey, S., "Export Processing Zones : An Evaluation", *Yojana,* Vol. 46, New Delhi, March 2002, pp. 30-31.

"Ensuring SEZs Work", *The Economic Times,* Vol.-40, No.-86, June 2, 2000, Kolkata.

"Export Pessimism – Make SEZs A Competitive Conduct For Export Growth", *The Financial Express,* Vol. XI, No. 44, December 22, 2001, Kolkata.

George, A., "SEZs : Hubs of Economic Activity", *The Hindu Business Line,* Vol. 8, No. 345, Visakhapatnam, December 15, 2001, p.12.

Ghosh, B. and De, P., "Indian Ports and Globalisation – Grounding Economics in Geography", *Economic and Political Weekly,* Vol. XXXVI, No. 34, Mumbai, Aug. 25, 2001.

Gopalakrishna, V.S., "Planning our SEZs Properly", *The Economic Times,* Vol. 40, No. 237, 24 July 2000, p. 8, Kolkata.

Gopalan, S. & Motwani, S.C., "Modernisation of Ports", *Indian Shipping,* Vol. 45, Nos 4 & 5, Mumbai, 1993, p. 23.

Gopalan, S., "Port Development Scenario in India" *Indian Shipping,* Vol. 49, No. 5, Mumbai, 1997.

"Government Announces New Pattern of Financing for IWT", *The Hindu,* Vol. 125, No. 248, Visakhapatnam, October 19, 2002, p. 13.

"Indian Infrastructure", Ports and Shipping Special, Vol. 3, No. 12, New Delhi, July 2001.

Indiresan, P.V., "Vision 2020 – Reducing Poverty by Sharing Infrastructure", *The Hindu Business Line,* Vol. 8, No. 347, Visakhapatnam, December 17, 2001, p. 8.

"Inland Water Transport / Moves to Exploit Potential Shipping Ministry Plans Higher Outlay, Incentive Package", *The Hindu,* Vol. 125, No. 271, Visakhapatnam, November 16, 2002, p. 13.

Jayanth, V., "Roads and Ports – Crying for Attention", *The Hindu Survey of Indian Industry,* 1999, p.158.

Jose, J., "Major Ports of India : Trade, Shipping and Strategy" , *Paper Presented at BCCI Conference,* Mumbai.

Kanthimathinathan, S., "Infrastructure and Economic Development of India" *Third Concept,* Vol. 16, No. 181, New Delhi, March 2002, p. 15.

Kar, P., "Welfare and Infrastructure Services", *The Economic Times,* Vol. 40, No. 234, Kolkata, July 21, 2000.

Kar, P., "Development of Infrastructure Services", *The Economic Times,* Vol. 40, No. 220, Kolkata, July 7, 2000.

Kar, P., "Reforms and Infrastructure Development", *The Economic Times,* Vol. 40, No. 93, Kolkata, June 9, 2000.

Khander, S.A.,"Productivity In Infrastructure", *Yojana,* Vol. 42, No. 1, January 1998, p.13.

Kulkarni, M.A., "Infrastructure Facilities in Indian Ports – An Overview of Bombay Port", *Indian Shipping,* Vol. 45, Nos 1 & 2, Mumbai, 1993, p. 30.

Kundra, A.K., "SEZs : How Well Will They Perform", *The Hindu* (Business/ Science) August 16, 2001, Visakhapatnam. p. BS - I.

Kurup, N.K., "Corporatisation of Ports – Time-bound Plan Called For", *The Hindu Business Line,* Vol. 7, No. 342, Visakhapatnam, December 11, 2000, p. 4.

Lall, S.V., "Role of Public Infrastructure Investment in Regional Development : Experience of Indian States", *Economic and Political Weekly,* Vol. 34, No. 12, March 20, 1999, pp. 717-725.

Mohapatra, S.K. (Chairman, Paradeep Port Trust), "Nucleus for Development", Eastern Business Review – Focus : Infrastructure, *Business Standard,* Vol. XXVIII, No. 28, Kolkata, April 30, 2002, p. 5.

"Marginal Rise in Major Ports Handling, but Short of Target", *The Hindu Business Line,* Vol. 9, No. 107, Visakhapatnam, April 18, 2002, p. 9.

Modi, B.K., "Private Investment in Infrastructure", *The Economic Times,* Vol. 40, No. 230, Kolkata, 17, July 2000.

Mohammed, S.H. and Rajanala, S., "Need for Focus on Infrastructure Growth", *The Economic Times,* Kolkata, August 17, 2000, p. 13.

Mohapatra, S.K. (Chairman, PPT), "A Big Day for Paradeep Port ; *The New Indian Express,* Bhubaneswar, September 11, 2001, p. 5.

Mookerji, N., "Infrastructure Development Need of the Hour", *The New Indian Express,* Bhubaneswar, December 25, 2000, p. 15.

Mukul, Jyoti., " Call for Cost-based Pricing, Simple Tariff Regime for Ports", *The Financial Express,* Janurary 5, 2000, Chennai.

Nalinakhan, K., "Privatisation and its Challenges", *Indian Shipping,* Vol. 45, No. 11 & 12, Mumbai, 1993, p. 17.

Narain, Y., "New Initiatives in Infrastructure Sector", *Yojana,* Vol. 42, No. 1, January 1998, p.5.

Natarajan, K.V., "Port Infrastructure : Luring the Private Sector", *The Hindu Servey of Indian Industry,* 1999, p. 412.

Panda, J.P., "Special Economic Zones - A Chinese Model in India", *Third Concept,* Vol. 16, No. 182, New Delhi, April, pp. 38-41.

Panda, J.P., "Special Economic Zones in India with Special Reference to Paradeep", *Orissa Review,* Vol. LIX, No. 3, Information and Public Relation Department, Government of Orissa, Bhubaneswar, October 2002, p. 60.

Panda, J.P., "Special Economic Zones in India", *Third Concept,* Vol. 16, No. 188P, New Delhi, October 2002, pp. 31 - 33.

Paradeep Port Continues To Sail High", Orissa A State Survey - A Commercial Report Published in *Business Standard,* Vol XXVIII, No. 126, Kolkata, 31 August 2002, p. IV.

Peter, H.J., "India's Growing Conflict Between Trade and Transport", World Policy, Planning and Research Paper No. 1, WPS 346, 1996.

"Ports Urged To Become Solitary Profit Centres", *Business Standard,* Vol.XXVIII, No.68, Kolkata, June 24, 2002, p. 5.

Prabhu, P.P., "SEZs Must Retain Distinct Character", *The Hindu Business Line,* Vol. 9, No.143, Visakhapatnam, May 24, 2002, p. 8.

"Private Sector Role in Port Privatisation Finalised", *Business Standard,* Vol. XXV, No. 173, 24 February 2000, p. 9, Kolkata.

Raghuraman, V., "Some Issues on Infrastructure Development in India", *Productivity* 36(2), July-Sept., 1995, pp. 181-187.

Rajan, A. and Rajan, I., "Urban Growth and Infrastructural Development in India", *Productivity* 36 (2), July-Sept., 1995, pp. 215-227.

Ramakrishnan, R., "Potentials, Problems and Strategies for Port Development in India", *Indian Shipping,* Vol. 50, No. 5, Mumbai, 1998, p. 17.

Ramakrishnan, R., "Privatisation of Port Development – Indian and Foreign Ports", *Indian Shipping,* Vol. 53, Mumbai, September-October 2001, p. 13.

Ramakrishnan, R., "Certain Experiences on Privatisation of Port Development–Foreign Ports and Indian Ports". *Indian Ports,* Vol. XXXIII, No. 2, Indian Ports Association, Mumbai, October 2001, p. 25.

Rao, S.L., "Private Investment in Infrastructure", *The Economic Times,* Vol. 41, No. 13, Kolkata, March 19, 20001, p. 8.

Ravikumar, M., "Policy Changes Called for Infrastructure Growth", *The New Indian Express,* Bhubaneswar, August 6, 2001, p. 13.

Saez, L., "A Comparison of India and China's Foreign Investment Strategy Towards Energy Infrastructure", *Journal of Developing Areas,* Winter 32(2), 1998, pp. 199-220.

Sambandan, V.S., "Transport Mode with Great Promise", *The Hindu* (Business/Science) Visakhapatnam, March 15, 2001, p. BS - I.

Sampath, R., "Port Management - Privatisation Holds the Key", *The Hindu Survey of Indian Industry* 2001.

Sanyal, S., "Paradeep Port Sees Break-even Earlier than Anticipated", *The Hindu Business Line,* Vol. 9, No. 63, Visakhapatnam, March 5, 2002, p. 8.

Sarkar, B., "Privatisation of Ports in India – An Overview", *Indian Shipping,* Vol. 47, No. 6, Mumbai, 1995.

Satish Chandran, T.R., "Infrastructure for India's Development", *Journal of Social and Economic Development* 1(2), July-December 1998, pp. 211-233.

Satya Sundaram, I., "Ports at the Crossroads", *Facts For You,* Vol.-20, No.-6, March 2000, New Delhi, p. 31.

Satya Sundaram, I., "Ports – Productivity Holds the Key" *Facts For You,* Vol. 22, No. 4, New Delhi, January 2002.

Satya Sundaram, I., "Shipping – Search for Smooth Sailing" *Facts For You,* Vol. 22, No. 3, New Delhi, December 2001.

"SEZ Sops Bring Cheer to Tata Steel", *The Hindu Business Line,* Vol. 9, No. 92, Visakhapatnam, April 3, 2002, p. 4.

Shah, Y.S. & Jindal, N.K., "Western Regional Cooperation Infrastructure-Vision 2000", Background Note – Port Sector ; *Indian Merchant's Chamber,* Mumbai, 1997.

Sharma, M., "Infrastructure Development – Shifting Paradigms", *Paper Presented at Indira Gandhi Institute of Development Research (IGIDR),* Mumbai. in the International Symposium in Honour of Prof. K.S.Parikh, July, 2000.

Shridharan, S., "Providing Infrastructure - Needed a Paradigm Shift in Thinking", *Yojana,* Vol. 46, New Delhi, February 2002, pp. 16-19.

Singh, M., "Special Economic Zone Rules by Mid-Nov", *The Statesman,* Vol. XXXVI, No. 255, Kolkata, October 28, 2002, p. 11.

Singh, S.K., "The Public and Private Sector Role in the Provision of Infrastructure Services", *Indian Journal of Transport Management,* Vol. 25, No. 3, Central Institute of Road Transport, March 2001, p. 191.

Sreenivasan, N., " Exim Policy : SEZs, the Key", *The Hindu Business Line,* Vol. 9, No. 88, Visakhapatnam, March 30, 2002, p. 8.

Srinivasan, G., "Towards Better Infrastructural Facilities", *Yojana,* Vol. 42, No. 1, January 1998, p. 9.

Sriraman, S. & Bagchi, A., "Financing Transport Infrastructure and Services in India" *Asian Transport Journal.*

Sriraman, S., "Efficient Utilisation of the Transport Sector in India" *Paper presented to the National Conference on Infrastructure Project Management,* Organised by the National Institute for Industrial Engineering, Mumbai, 2000.

Sriraman, S., "The Two Gateway Ports : Mumbai and Jawaharlal Nehru Ports" *Asian Transport Journal,* 1998.

Sriraman, S., "Two Mega Ports in Mumbai : Past, Present and Future", *RITES Journal,* April, 2001.

Srivastava, P.K., "Future for Indian Ports and Development of Hub Port", *Indian Shipping,* Vol. 52, December 2000, p. 11, Mumbai.

"State – ICICI and Dhamra Impase", *The Hindustan Times,* Vol. LXXVIII, No. 238, New Delhi, September 6, 2002, p. 3.

"Sticking to Port Policies", *The Economic Times,* Kolkata, January 1, 2002, p. 8.

"The Infrastructure Sector : Sound Foundation To Build Upon (Editorial)", *Yojana,* Vol. 42, No. 1, Special Volume on Infrastructure Sector, January 1998.

"To be Competitive, Major Ports Must Become Profit Centres", *The Hindu Business Line,* Vol. 9, No. 119, Visakhapatnam, April 30, 2002, p. 6.

Tripathy, P.C., "Interface Between Infrastructure and Economic Development", *The Orissa Journal of Commerce.* Vol. XXI, No. 1, 1997, p. 10.

Vasudevan, R., "Indian Shipping and Ports", *Indian Shipping,* Vol. 47, No. 1&2, Mumbai, 1995.

Venugopal, K., "Where Infrastructure Wears Work Clothes", *The Hindu Business Line,* Vol. 9, No. 253, Visakhapatnam, September 12, 2002, p. 1.

"Vizag Ports Gearing to Improve Productivity", *The Hindu,* January 6, Chennai, 2000.

Reports

Asian Institute of Transport Development ; *National Infrastructure Report 1998 India,* New Delhi.

Centre for Monitoring Indian Economy (CMIE) ; *Survey of Investment Projects in Infrastructure,* Mumbai, November 2001.

Government of Orissa ; *Economic Survey 1990-91 to 2000-01,* Directorate of Economics and Statistics, Bhubaneswar.

Government of India (1966); *Report of the Committee on Transport Policy and Coordination,* Planning Commission.

Government of India (1980); *Report of the National Transport Policy Committee,* Planning Commission.

Government of India (1988); *Report of the Steering Committee on Transport Planning,* Planning Commission.

Government of India (1996); *Report of the Working Group on Ports for the Ninth Plan,* Ministry of Surface Transport.

Government of India; *Economic Survey 1990-91 to 2001-02,* Ministry of Finance, Economic Division, New Delhi.

Government of India; *Statistical Abstracts of India,* Central Statistical Organisation, Ministry of Planning and Programme Implementation, New Delhi, 1998.

Government of India ; *The India Infrastructure Report : Policy Imperatives for Growth and Welfare,* Vol. II, Submitted to Ministry of Finance, June 22, 1996.

Organisation of Economic Cooperation and Development (OECD); *Investment, productivity and employment,* Paris, 1995.

Organisation of Economic Cooperation and Development (OECD); *Road infrastructure rehabilitation and safety strategies in Central and Eastern Europe,* Paris, 1995.

Organisation of Economic Cooperation and Development (OECD); *Transport infrastructure in Central and Eastern European Countries : Selection Criteria and Funding,* Paris.

Organisation of Economic Cooperation and Development (OECD); *Privatisation of Utilities and Infrastructure : Methods and Constraints,* Paris, 1997.

Organisation of Economic Cooperation and Development (OECD); *Telecommunication infrastructure : The benefits of competition,* Paris, 1995.

Oxford University Press ; *Indian Infrastructure Report 2002,* 3i Network

Oxford University Press ; *Infrastructure Development in Africa, Africa Development Report 1999,* New York.

Oxford University Press; The India Infrastructure Report 2000, *Issues in Regulation and Market Structure,* Edited by Sebastian Morris, New Delhi.

Paradeep Port Trust; *Annual Administration Report 1980-81 to 2000-01.*

Reserve Bank of India; *Report on Currency and Finance*, 2000-01.

The World Bank; *Global Development Finance Report 2000*, Privatisation in Developing Countries – A Global Perspective on Recent Divestitures.

The World Bank; *Private Infrastructure in East Asia - Lessons Learned in the Aftermath of the Crisis*, Technical Paper No. 501, Washington D.C., 2001.

Index

J

K

N

R